NEAL SLAVIN

WHEN TWO OR MORE ARE GATHERED TOGETHER

Memo: June 5, 1973
To: Neal Slavin
From: Neal Slavin

STEREOTYPES AND CLICHÉS: Uniforms, Statue of Liberty, Grand Canyon, Staten Island Ferry, Sabrett frank stands. The words trigger bland mental images. Seeing photographs rearranges that experience.

HOW? Photographs are believable. Photographs emphasize detail and give that detail importance. Photographs document the space between me and my subject. Photographs are memories. They are fantasies of ourselves.

THE RELATIONSHIP OF THE ONE TO THE MANY: Troupes, clubs, societies, and organizations. I am interested in the conflict between individuality and belonging.

PEER GROUPS: How do we look among our peers? There is a preoccupation about who we are and whom we want to associate with. Which group will enhance (sometimes even create) our identities? I want to photograph this search for identity.

VANITY, FRAILTY, AND EGO: I want to photograph who we are trying to be in order to discover who we really are.

MAPS: Group portraits are like maps. We tend to look into the pictures and become fascinated with the thousands of faces within the entire work, much as we read a map and discover the relationship of each town and city to the state and the nation.

COLOR AND INFORMATION: A gold trophy can mean something different from a silver trophy and the distinction cannot be rendered in black and white. In my pictures distinctions will be vital. Color is the solution.

A color photograph calls attention to detail. If photographs are our most believable method of showing reality, then color is an important dimension for heightening realism.

METHOD: Each organization should provide as much information as it can by including in the picture many "things" that will differentiate its particular group.

Polaroid pictures of the space in which the group functions will be an important way to set up the picture. I am also interested in making drawings as a way to pre-visualize my photographs.

The group should always pose itself. I believe that no outsider knows the status and rank of each individual as well as the membership does. I don't want to interfere with that process.

POSSIBLE OUTCOME: When a group presents itself fully to the camera, revealing the totems and markings that make it unique and individual, then that group will simultaneously reveal the innate sensation of belonging.

I envision a work that communicates the desire to belong in America in the mid-1970s and the conflicts caused by that wish. In short, I want to photograph groups—they are the American icon.

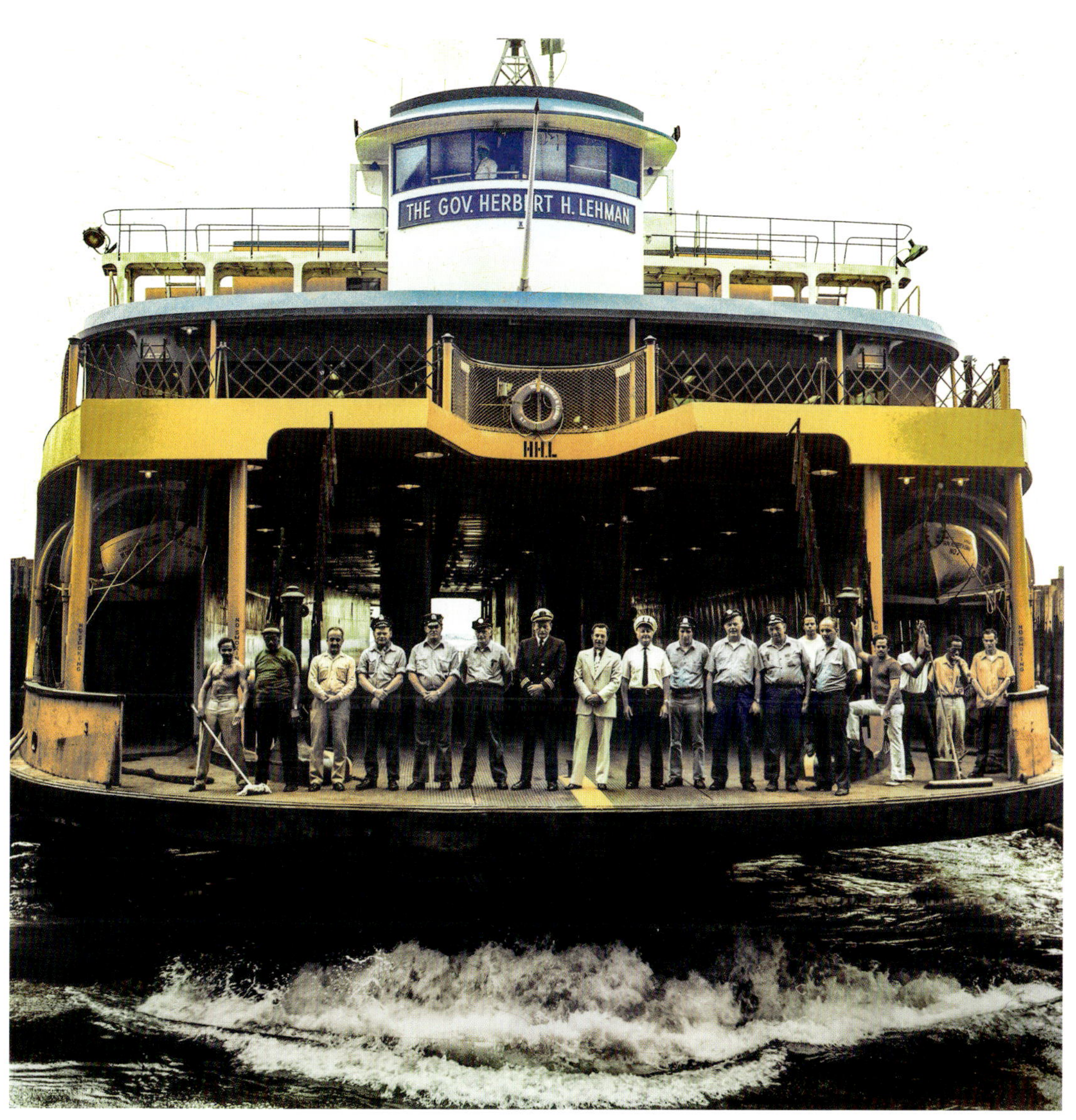

Staten Island Ferry, New York, New York, 1972-75

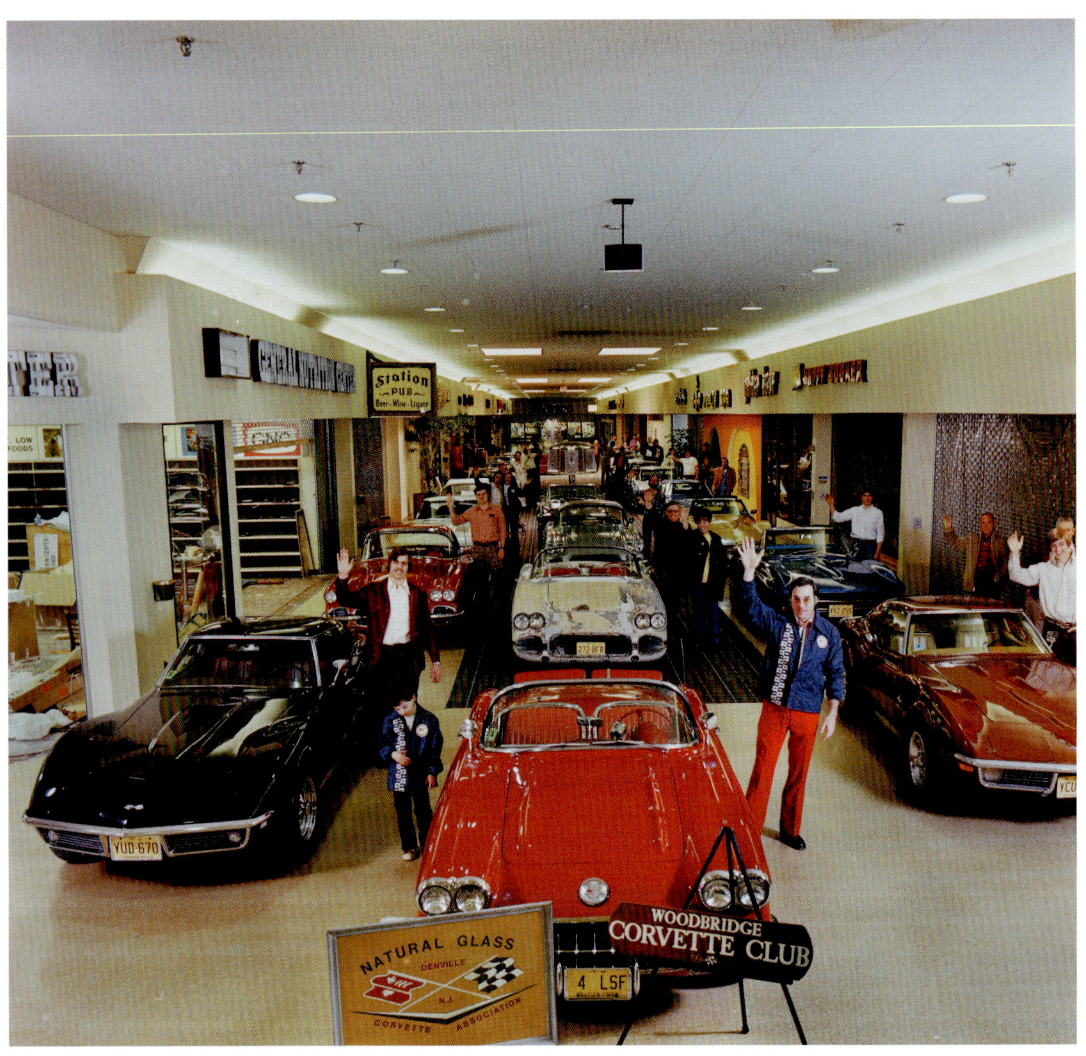

Natural Glass Corvette Association, Denville, New Jersey, 1972-75

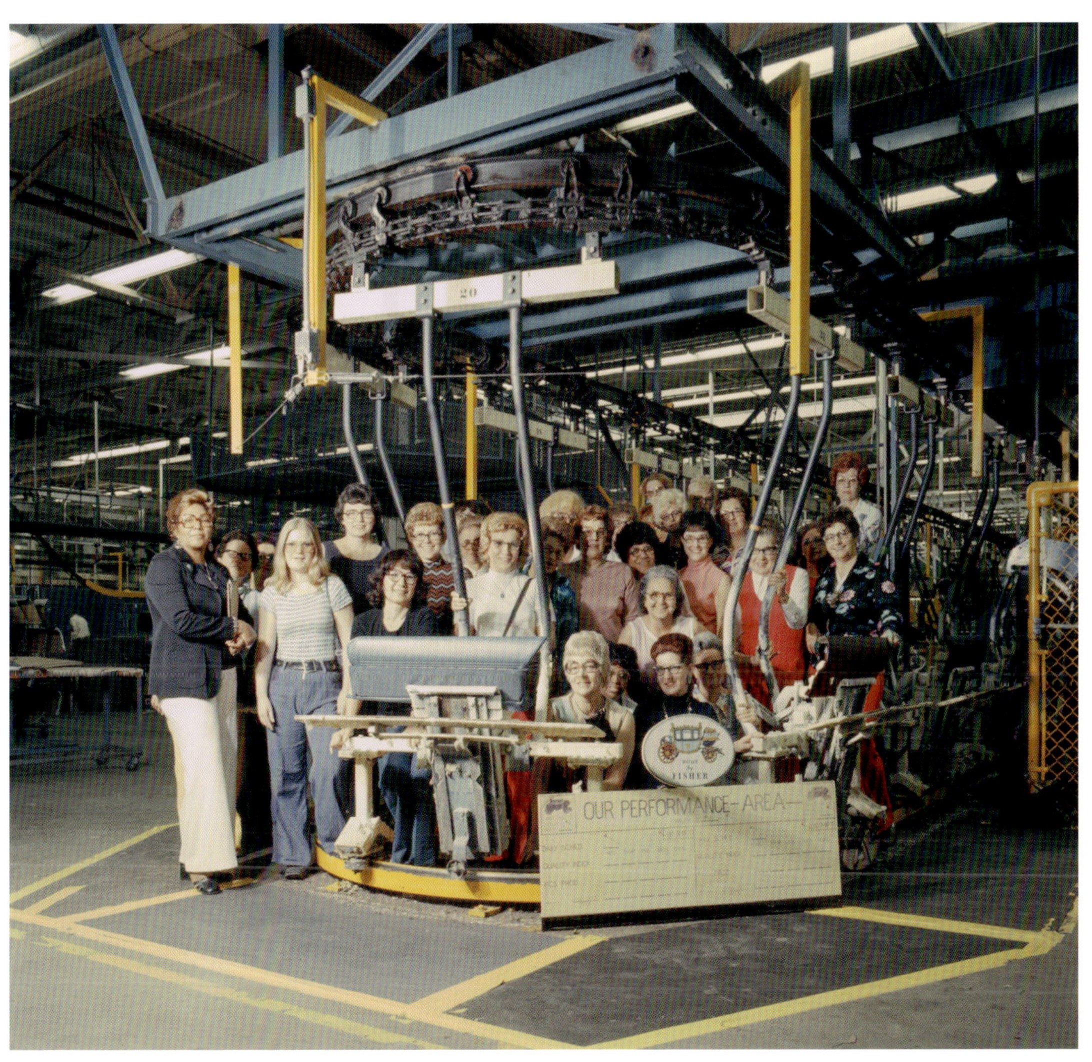

Coalition of Labor Union Women (C.L.U.W.), Detroit, Michigan, 1972-75

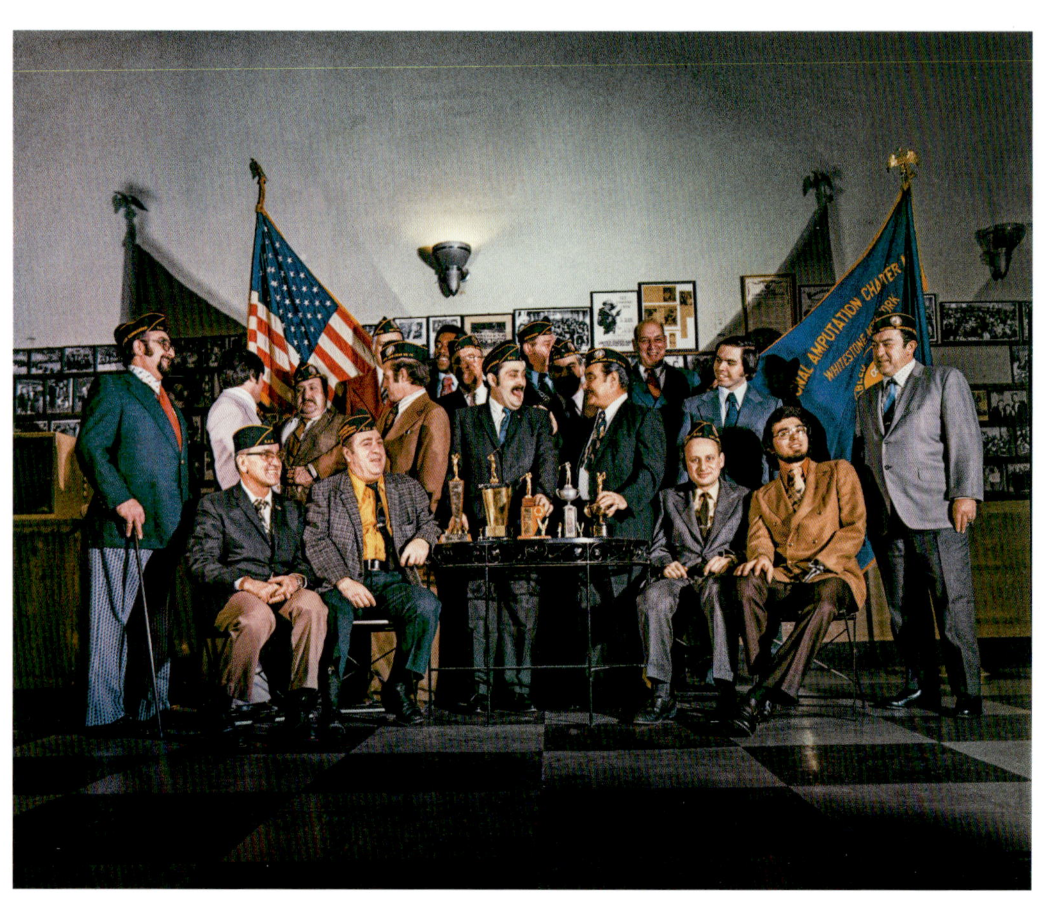

Chapter 76 of the Disabled American Veterans (D.A.V.), Whitestone, New York, 1972-75

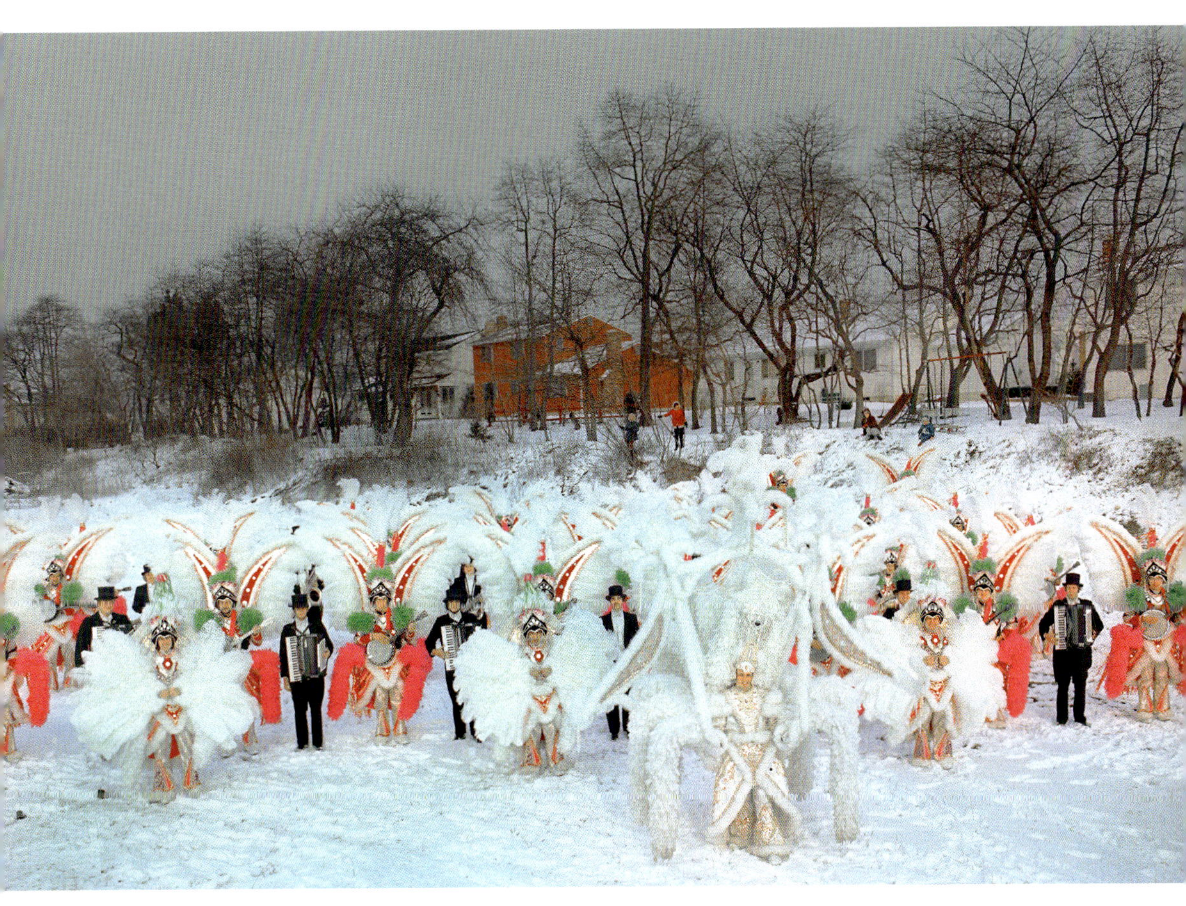

The Harrowgate String Band, Inc., Philadelphia Mummers
and New Year's Shooters Association, Hulmeville, Pennsylvania, 1972-75

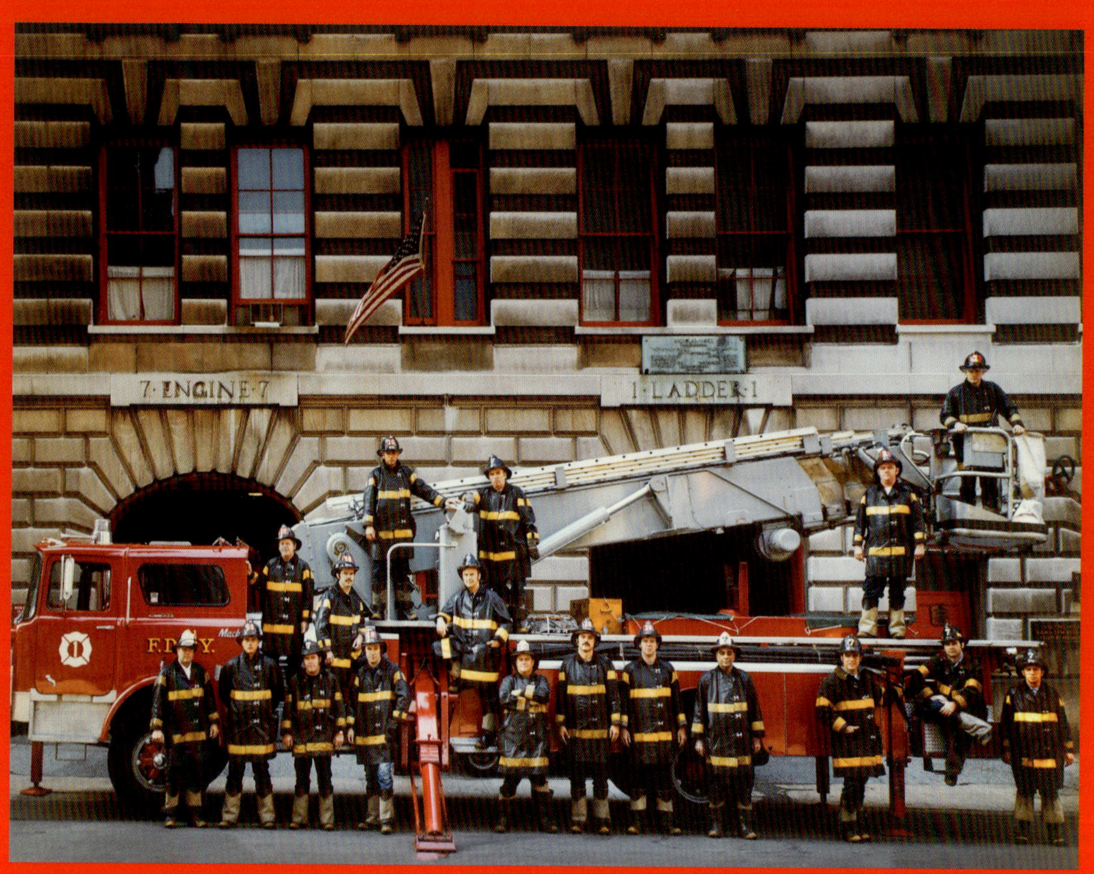

New York City Fire Department (F.D.N.Y.), New York, New York, 1972-75

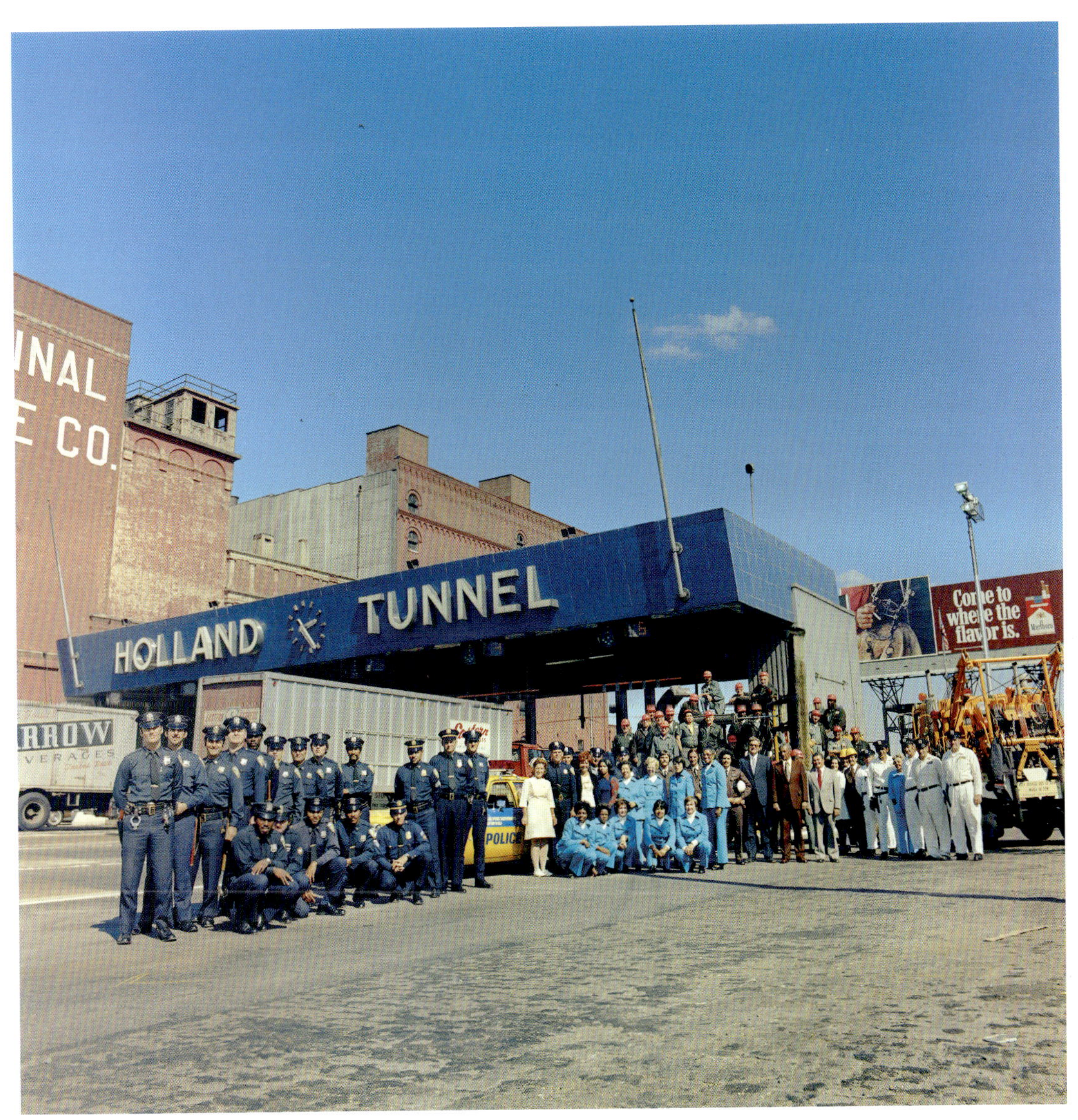

Holland Tunnel, New York, New York, 1972-75

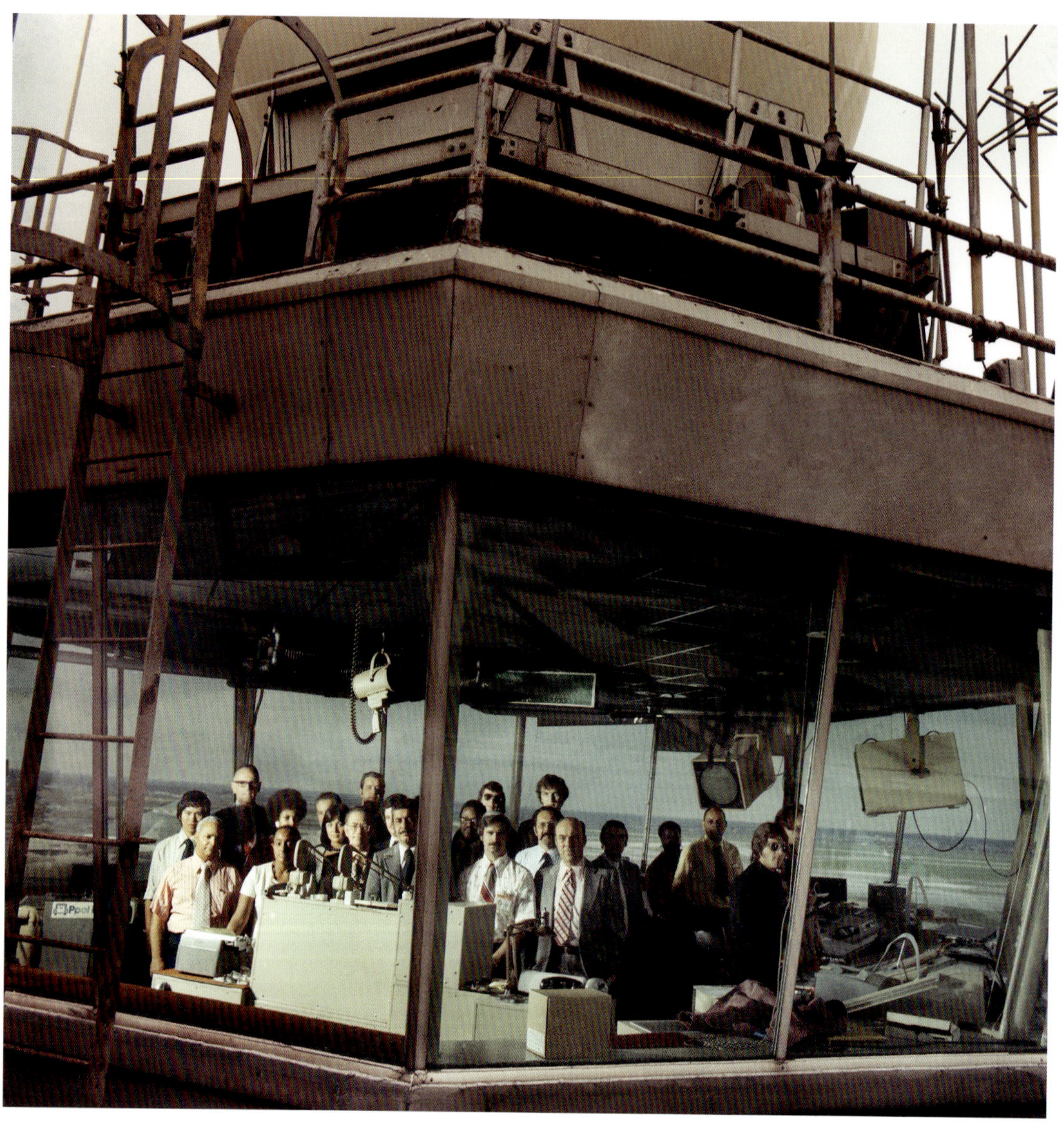

J.F.K. International Airport Control Tower Federal Aviation Administration, Jamaica, New York, 1972-75

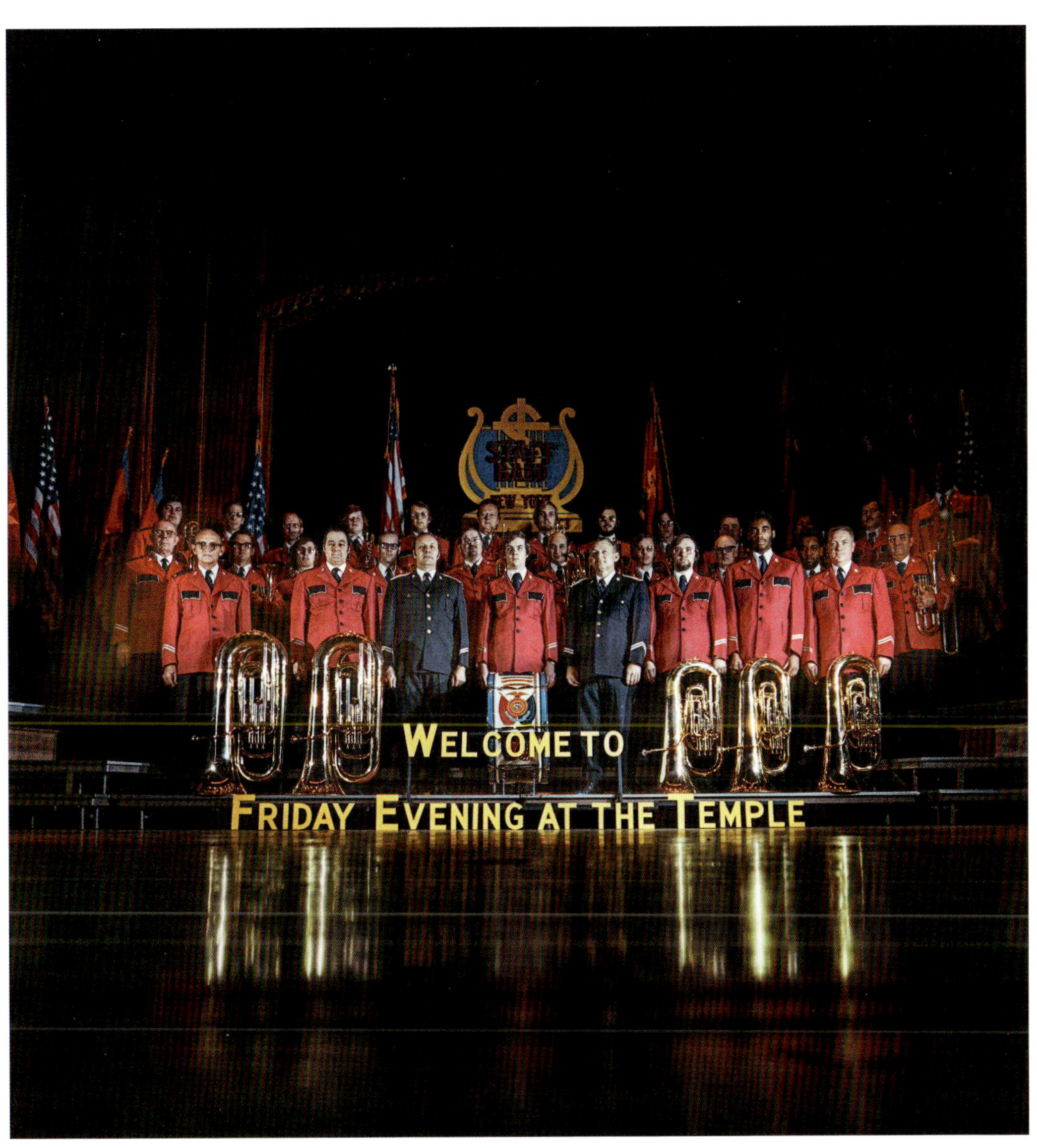

Salvation Army Headquarters Band, New York, New York, 1972-75

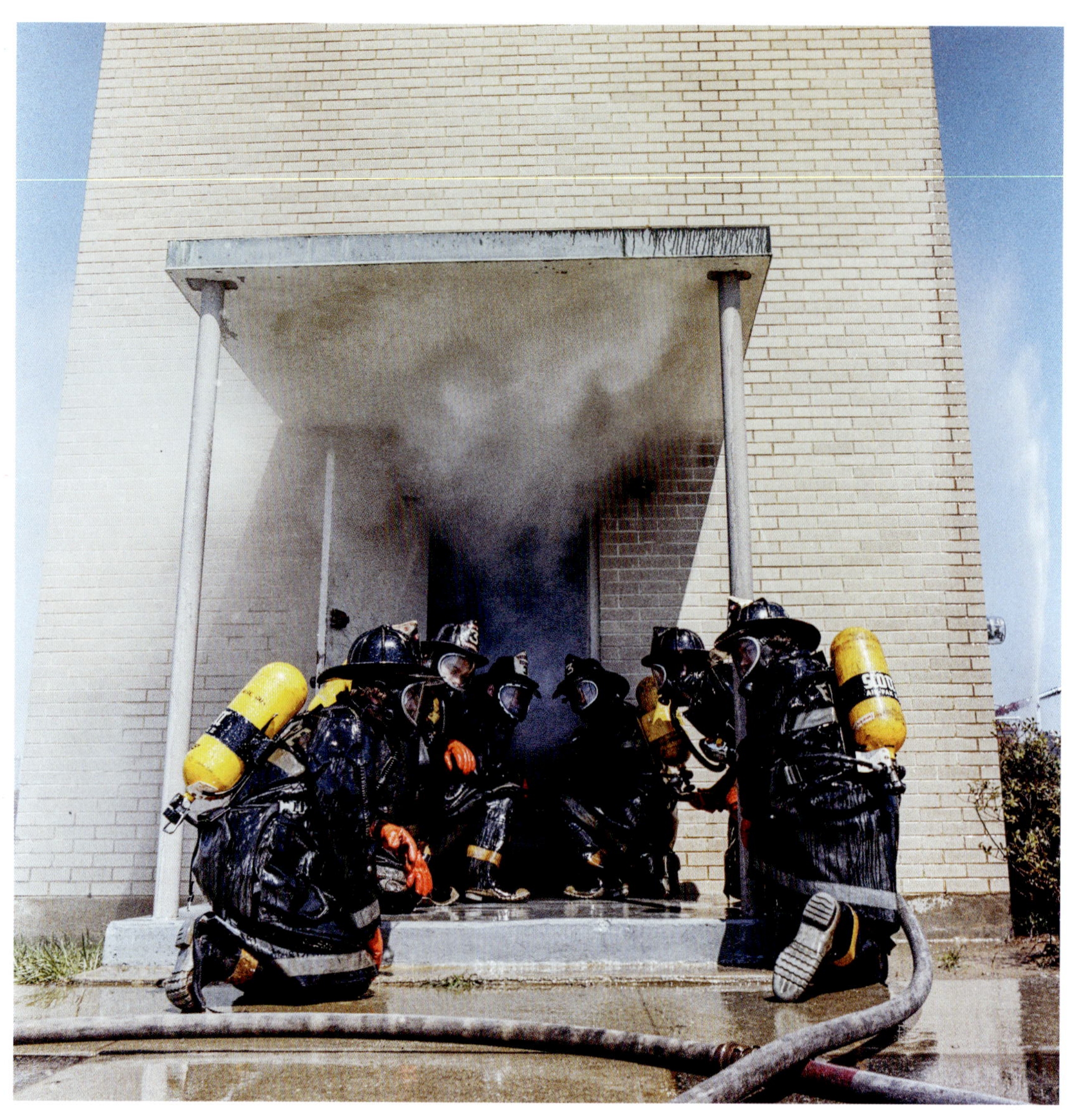

Empire Hose Company #3, Merrick, Long Island, New York, 1972-75

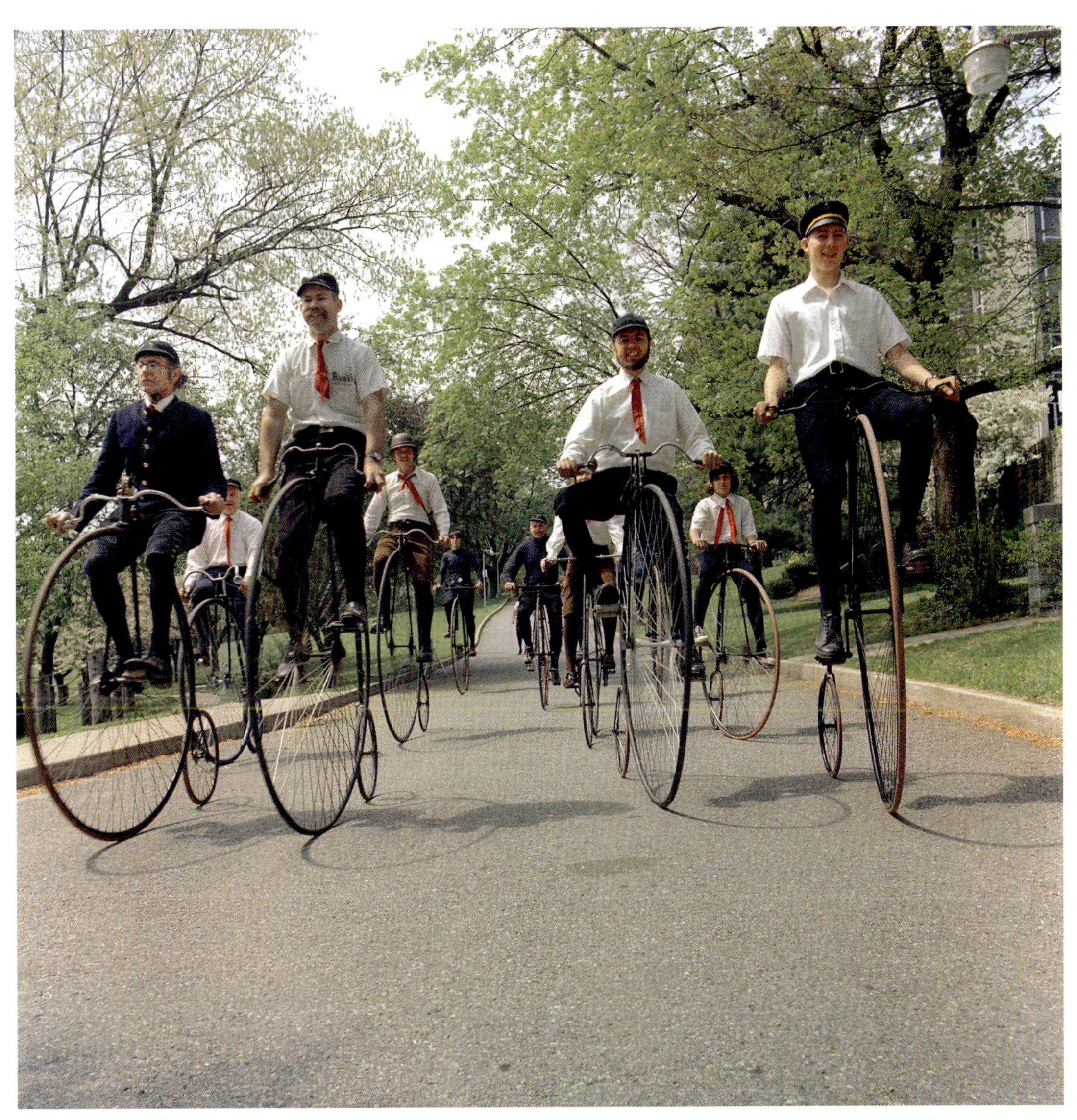

The Wheelmen, Swarthmore, Pennsylvania, 1972-75

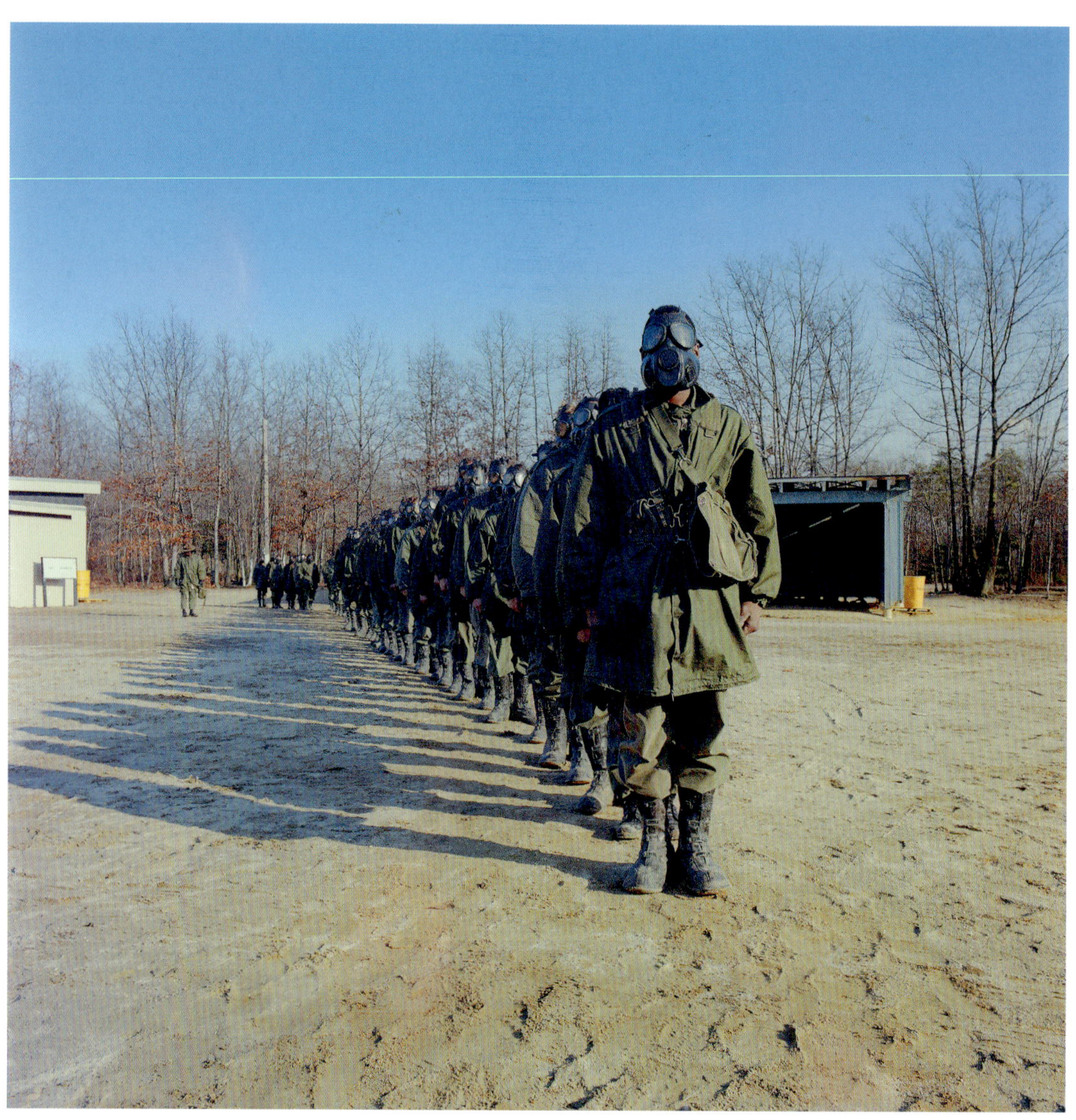

Gas Chamber, Basic Training Company of the Third Basic Combat Training Brigade, Fort Dix, New Jersey, 1972-75

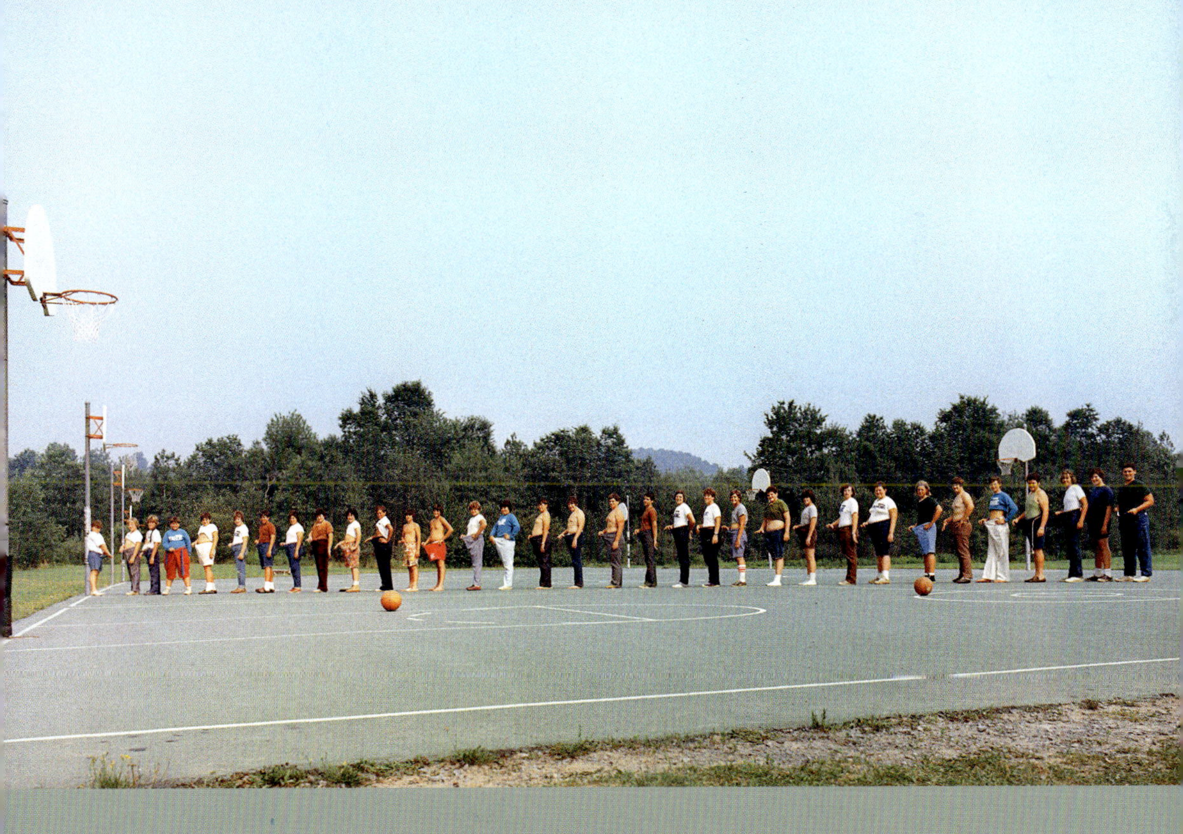

Camp Tahoe, Loch Sheldrake, New York, 1972-75
OVERLEAF
The Star Trek Convention, Star Trek Associates, A Division of Tellurian Enterprises, Inc., Brooklyn, New York, 1972-75

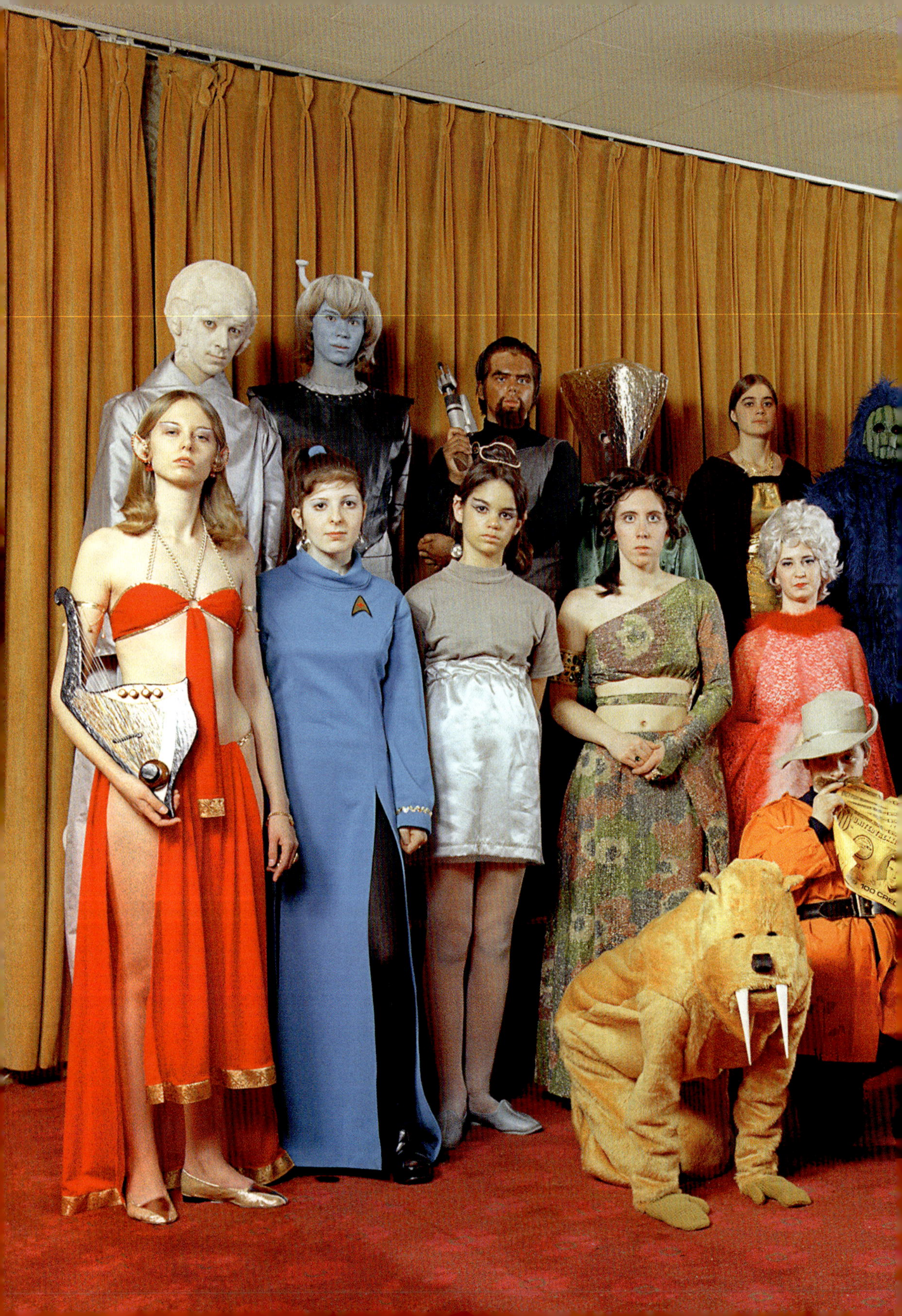

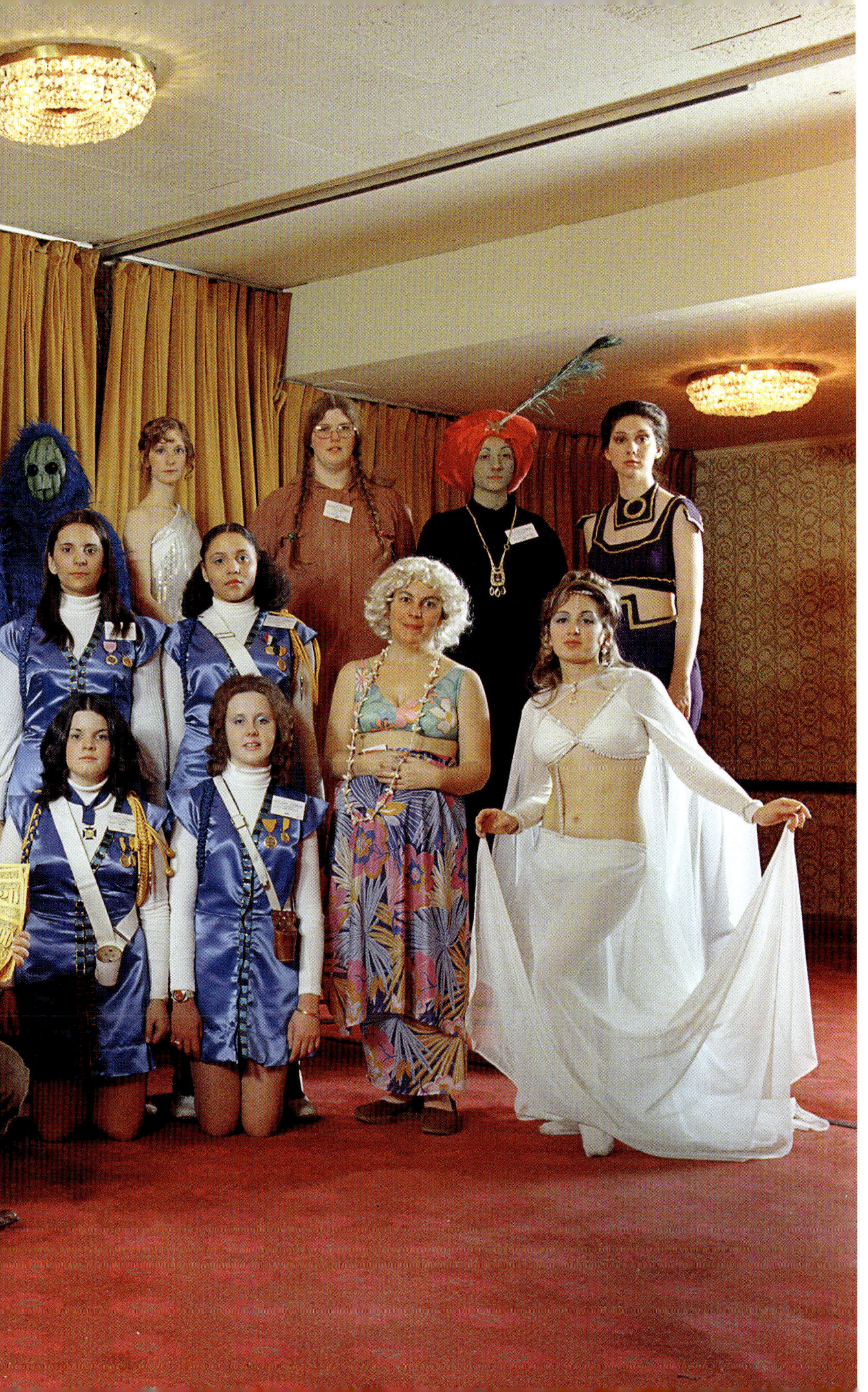

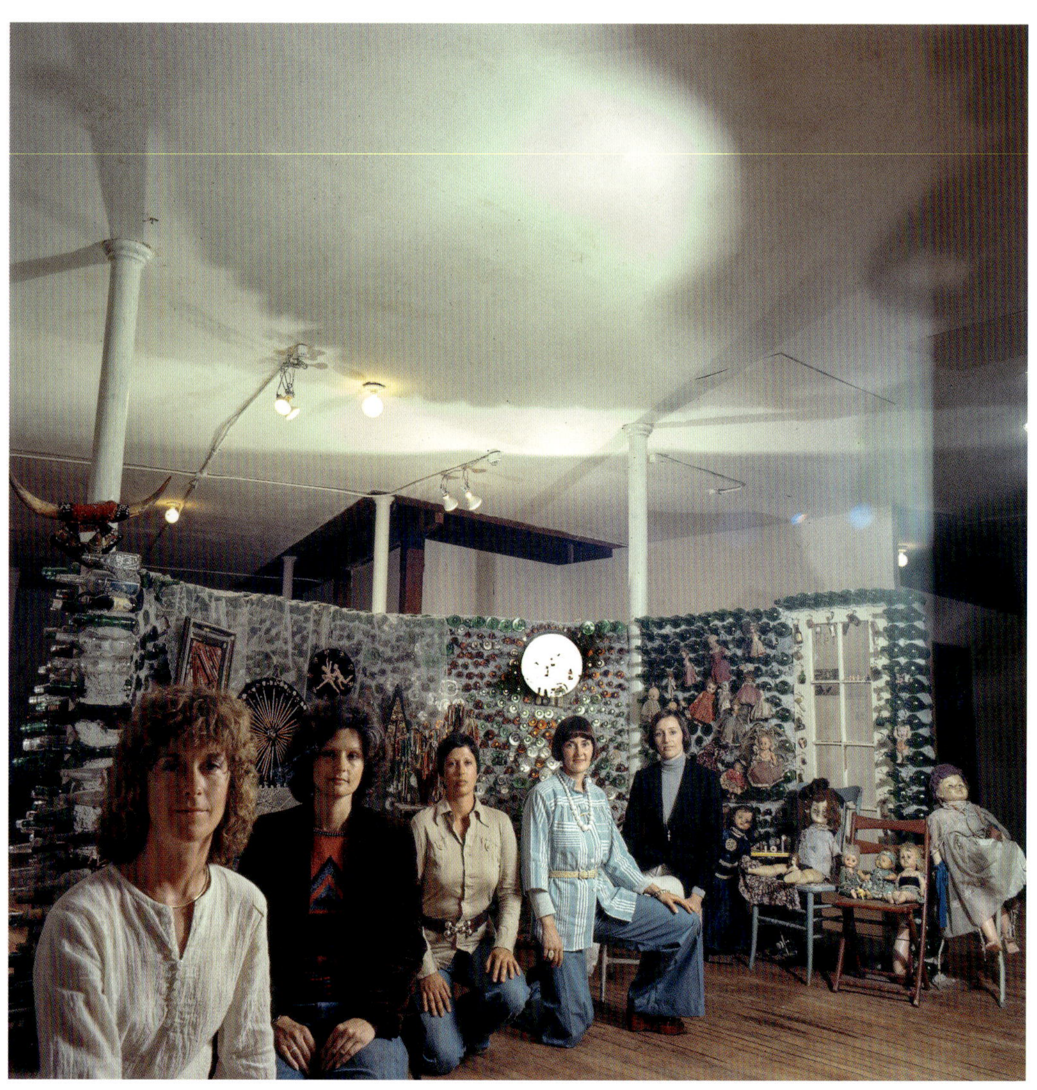

Feminist Studio Workshop Collective of the Woman's Building, Los Angeles, California, 1972-75

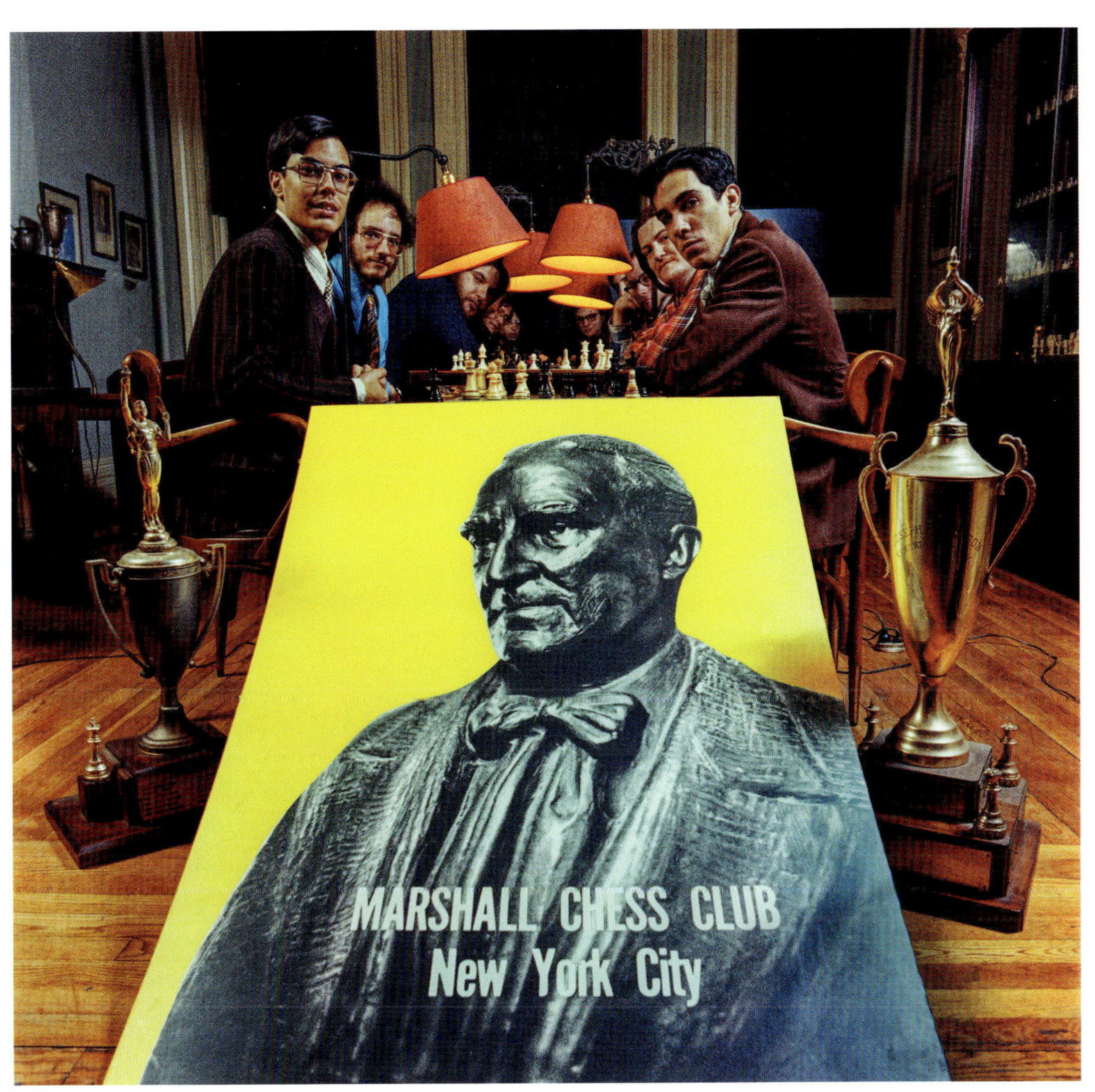

Marshall Chess Club, Inc., New York, New York, 1972-75

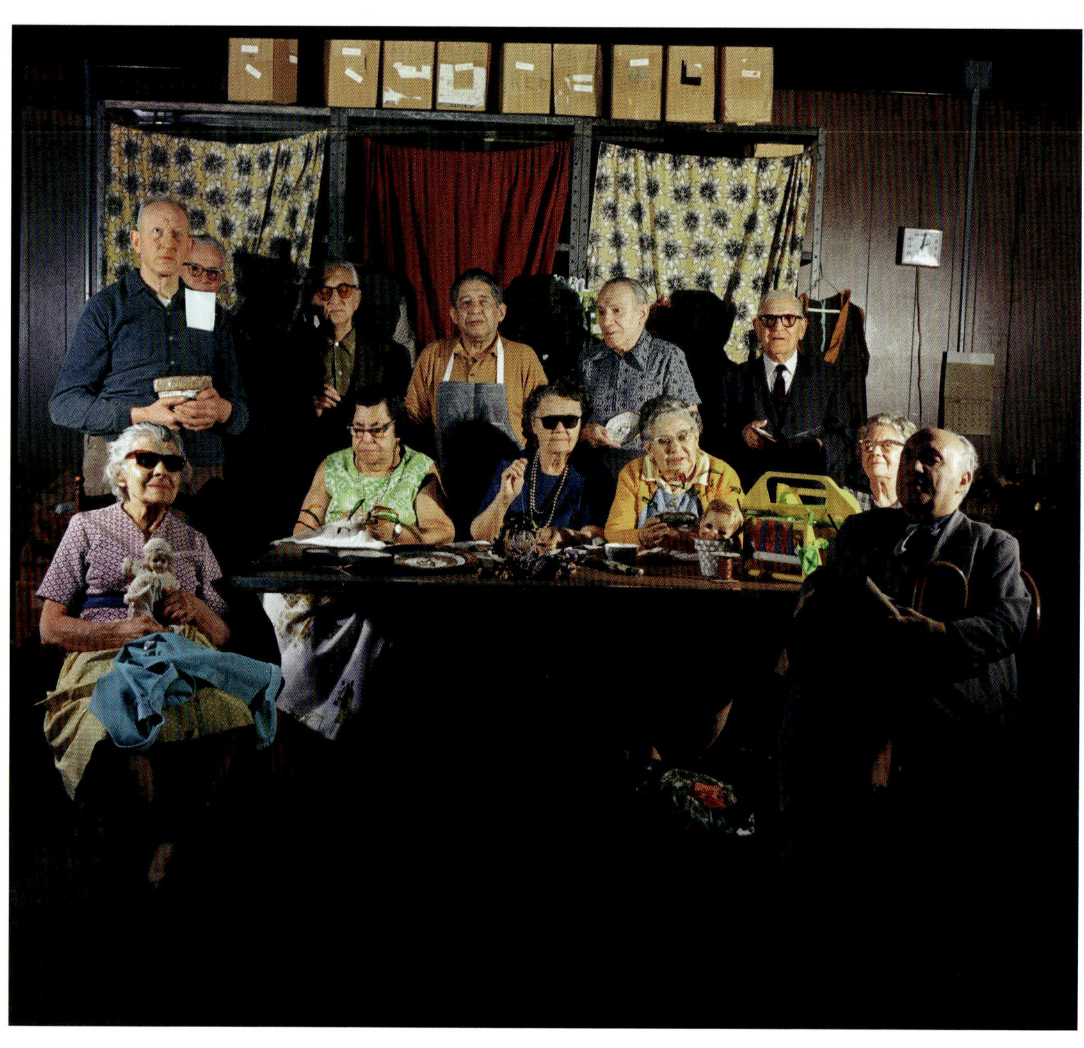

The Associated Blind, Inc., New York, New York, 1972-75

Capitol Wrestling Corporation, Washington, D.C., 1972-75

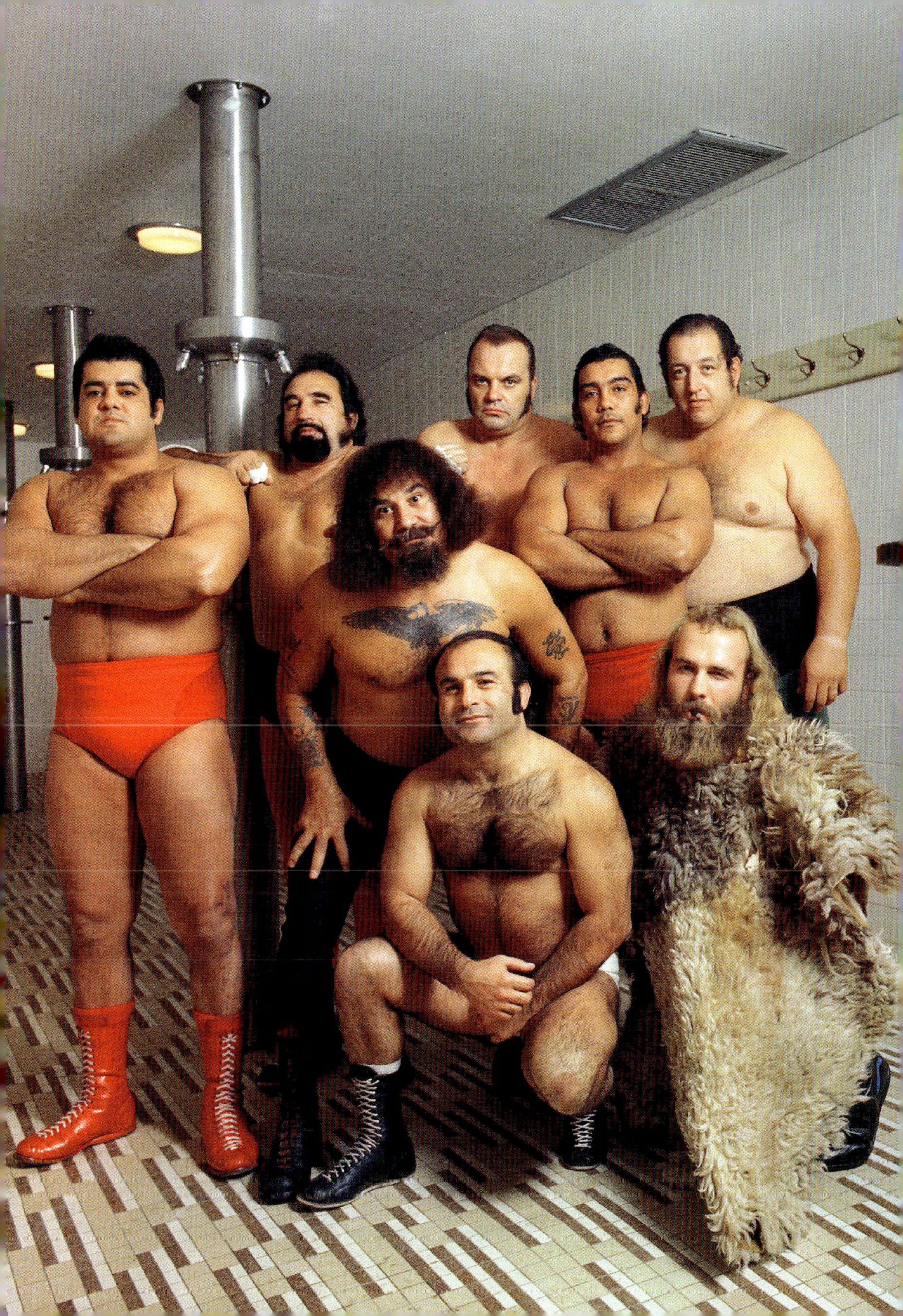

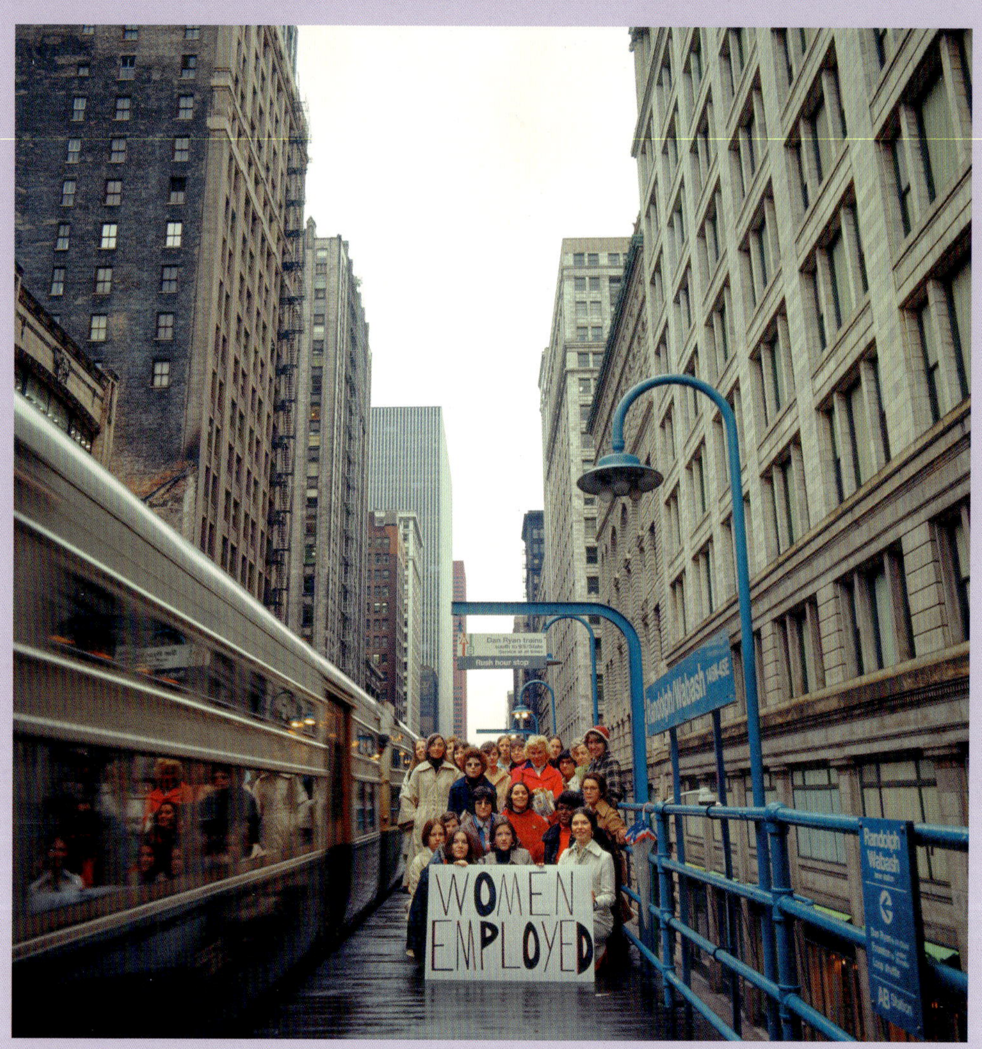

Women Employed (W.E.), Chicago, Illinois, 1972-75

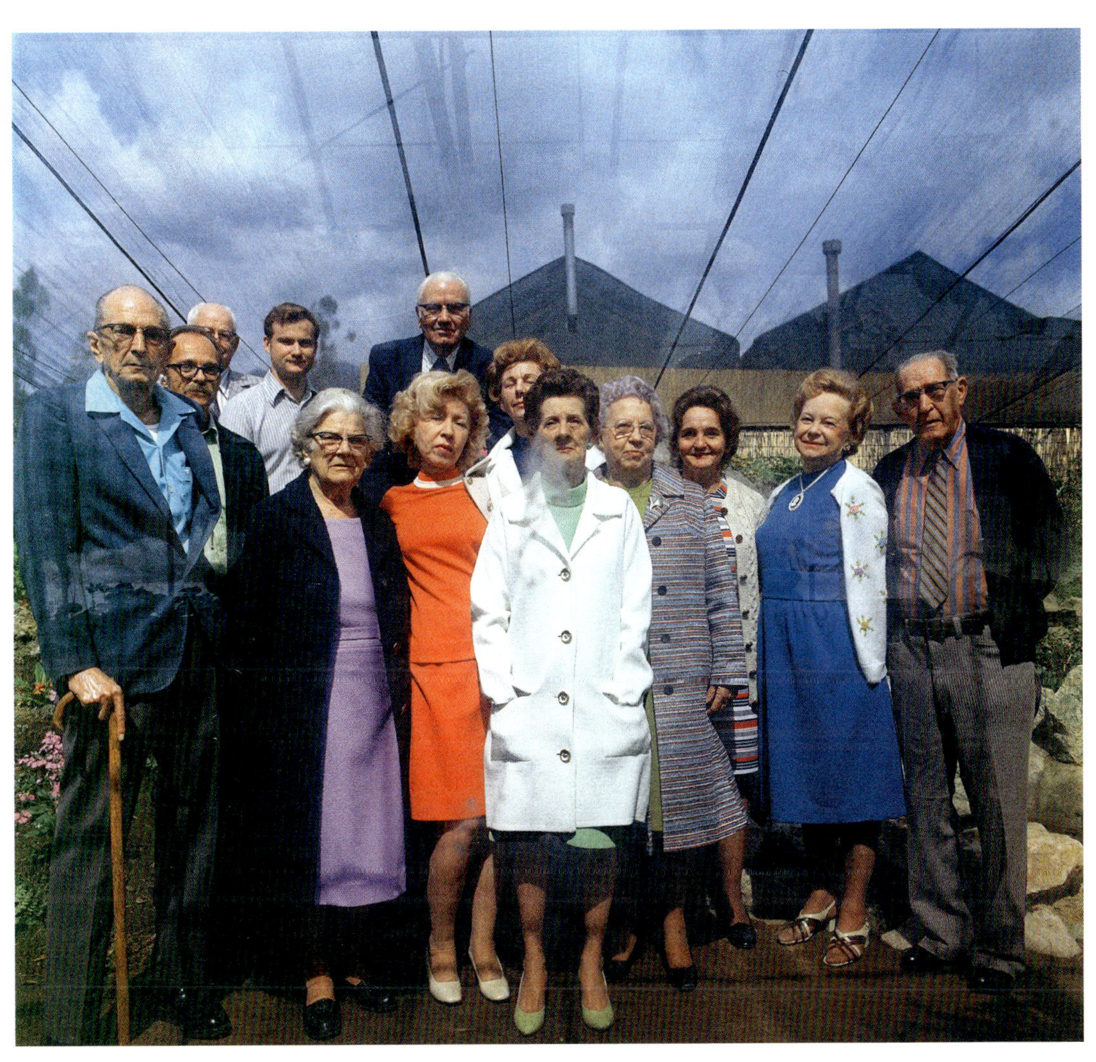

The American Begonia Society, Culver City, California, 1972-75

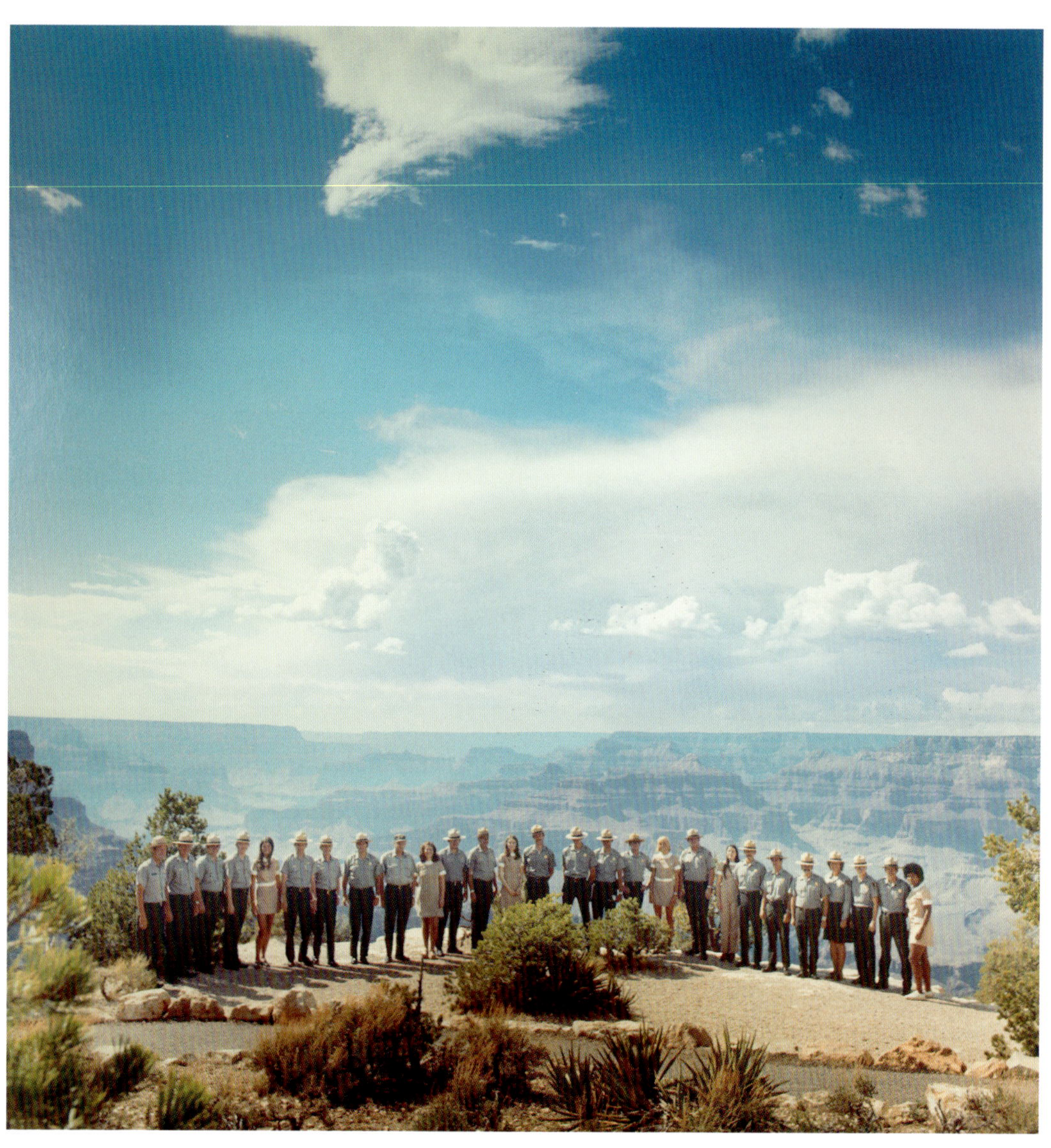

Grand Canyon National Park, National Park Service, Grand Canyon, Arizona, 1972-75

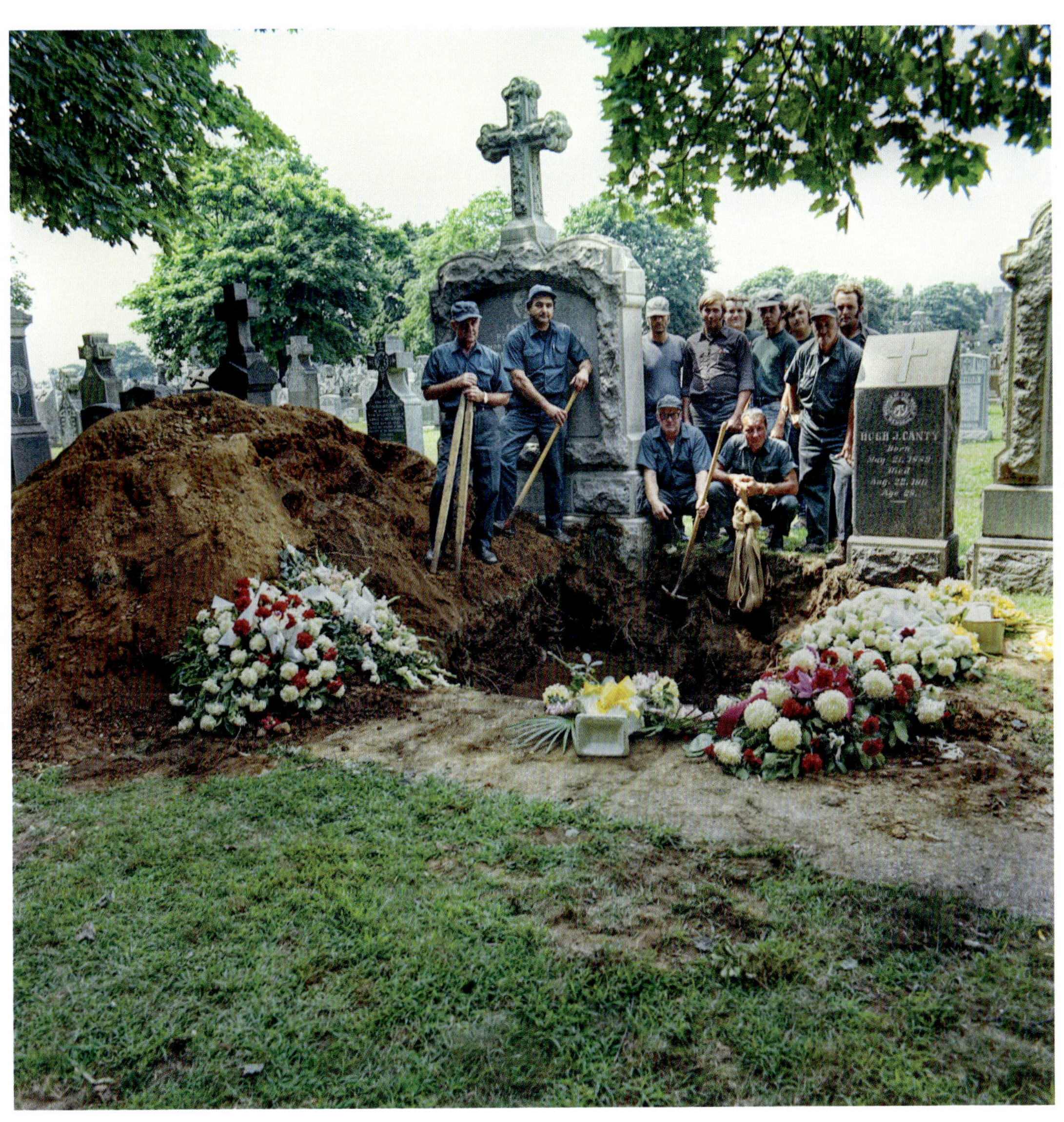

Cemetery Workers and Greens Attendants Union, Local 365 S.E.I.U. A.F.L.-C.I.O., Ridgewood, New York, 1972-75

OVERLEAF

International Twins Association, Muncie, Indiana, 1972-75

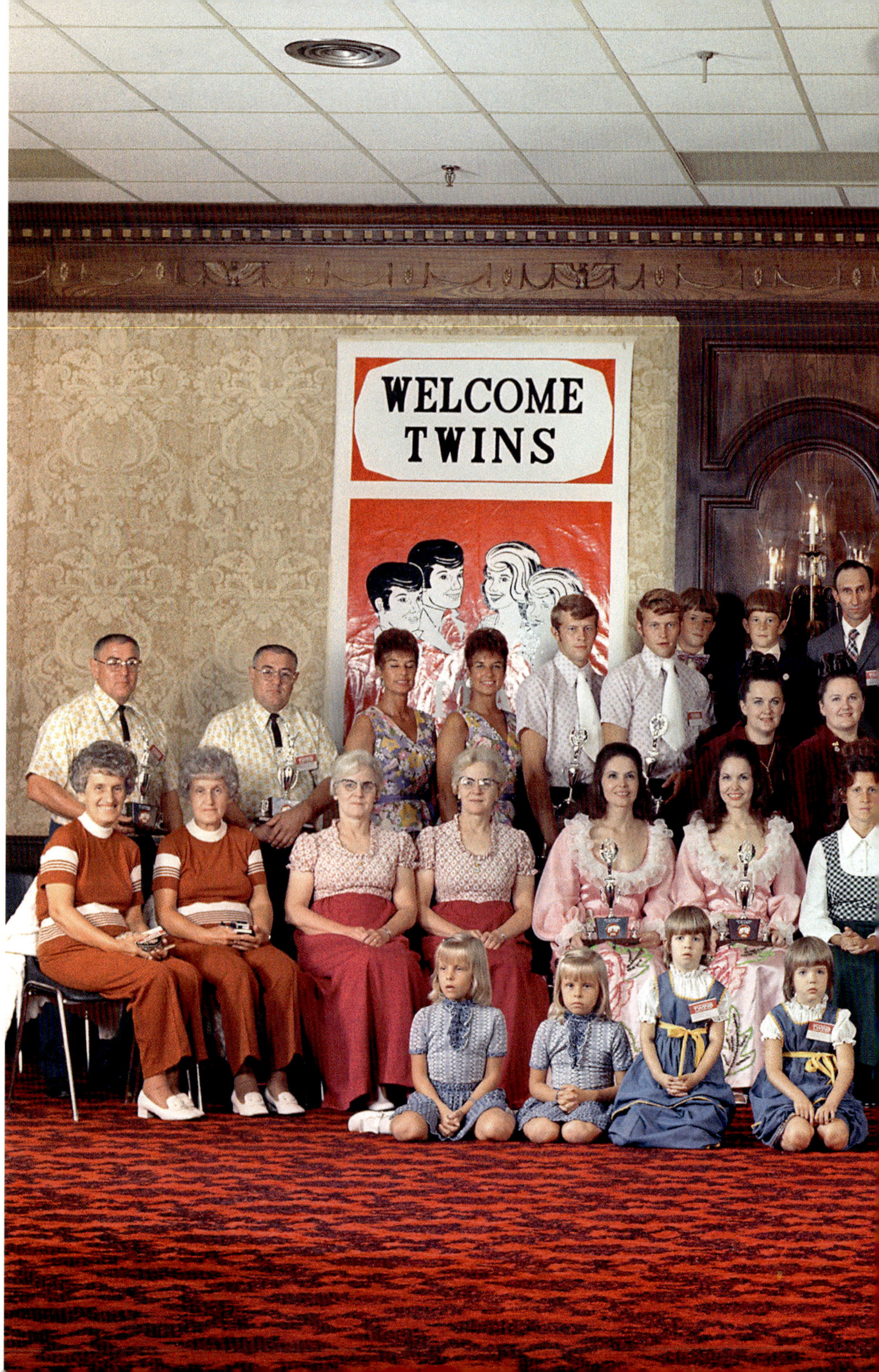
WELCOME
TWINS

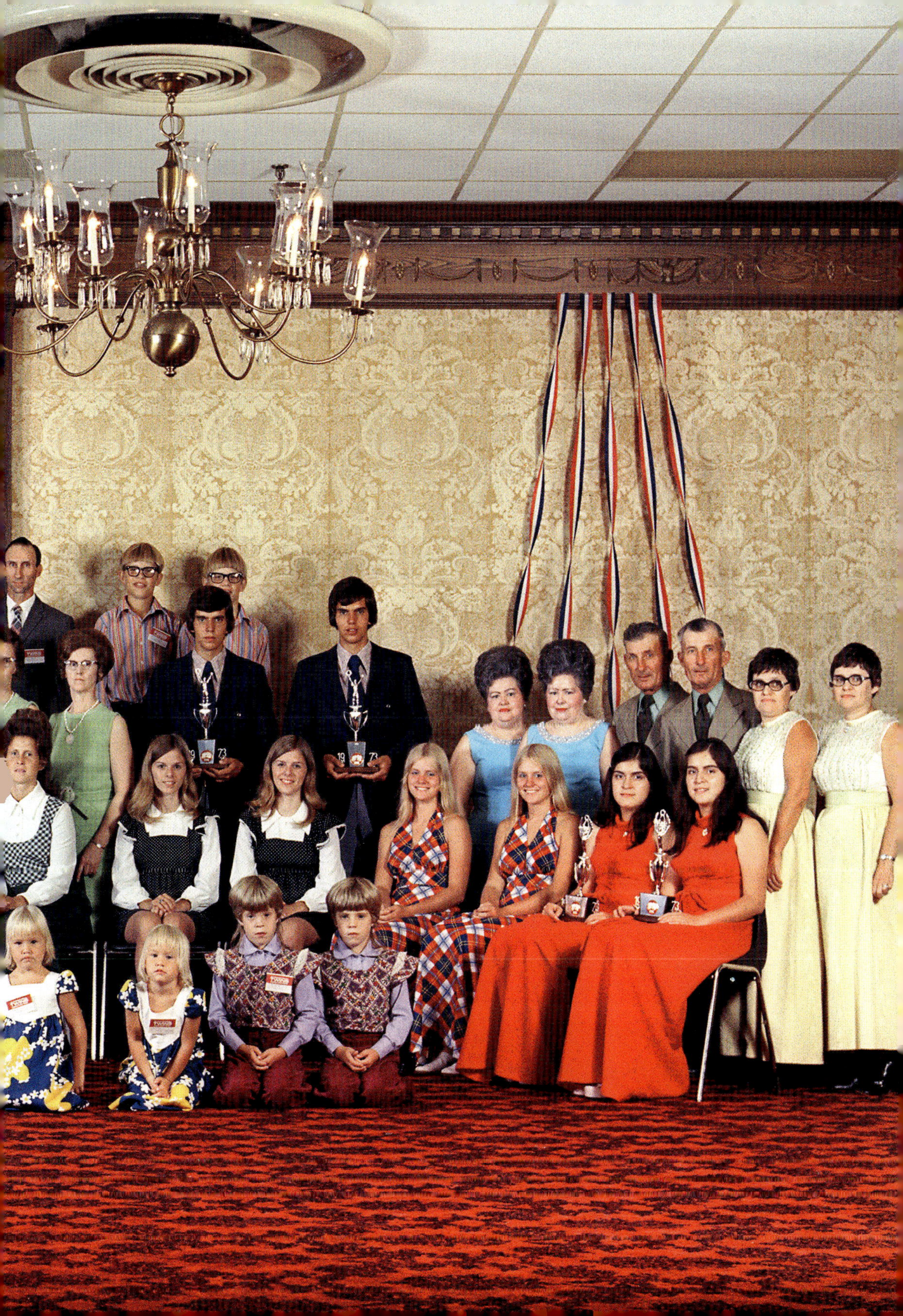

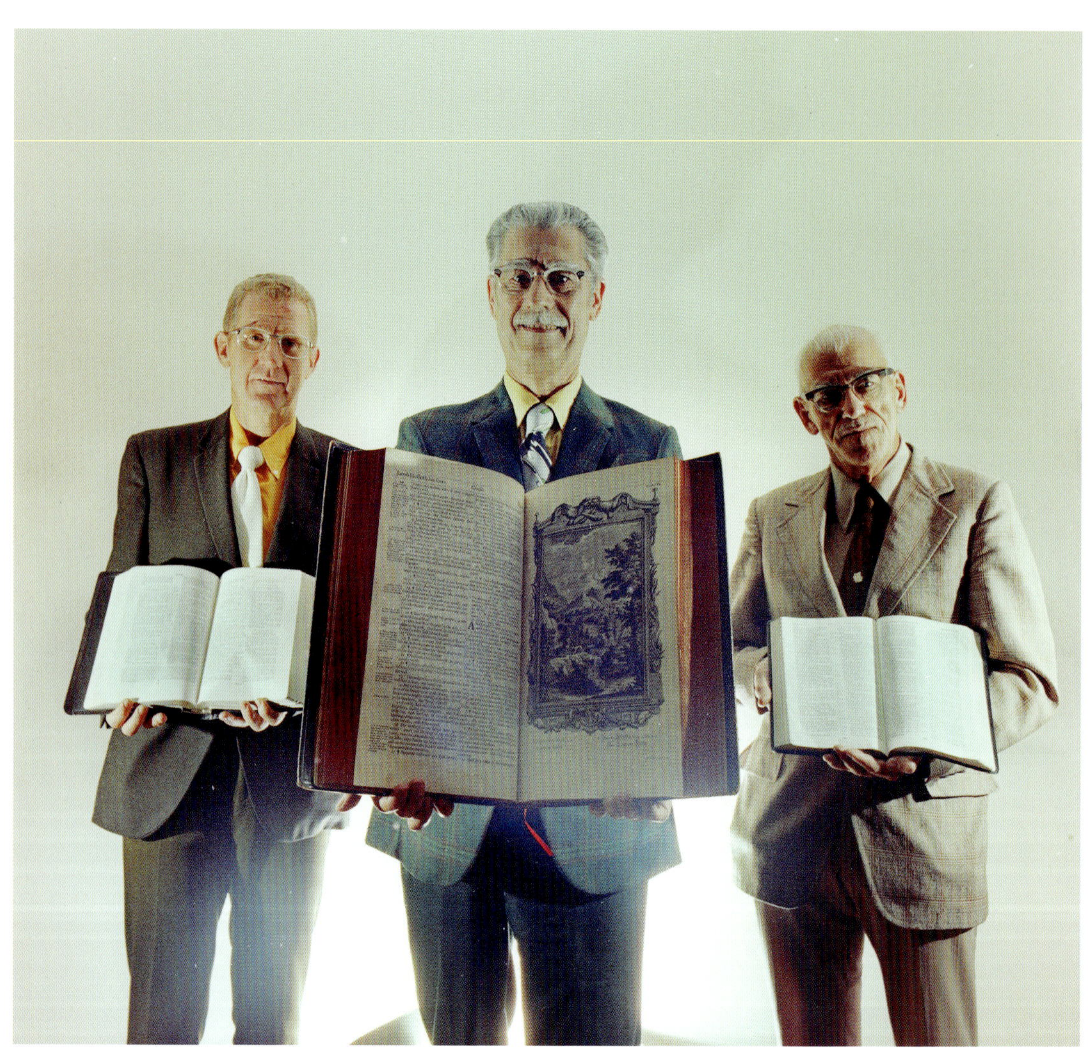

International Society of Bible Collectors, El Cajon, California, 1972-75

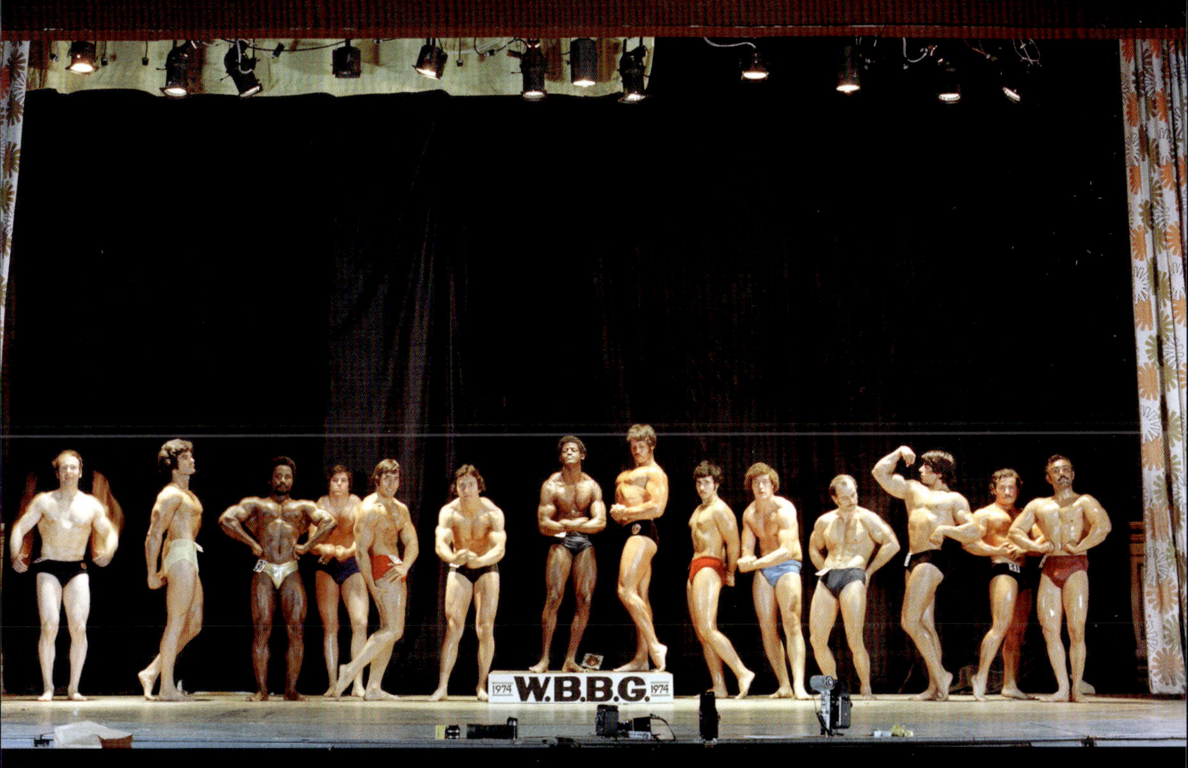

World Body Building Guild (W.B.B.G.), Brooklyn, New York, 1972-75

OVERLEAF

Lloyd Rod and Gun Club, Highland, New York, 1972-75

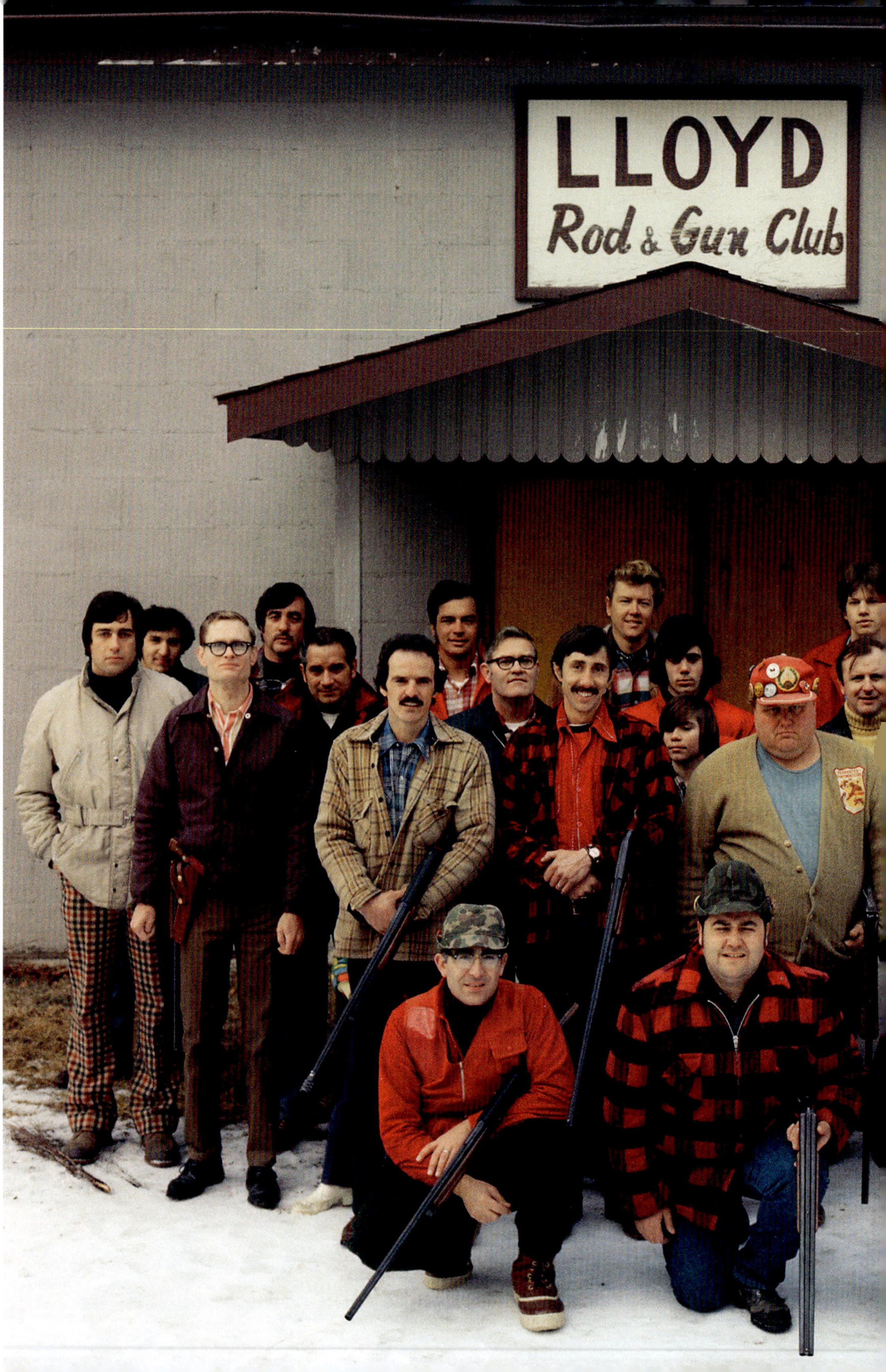

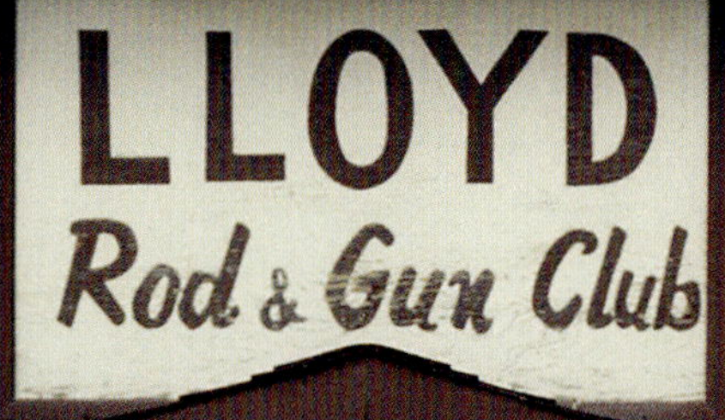

LLOYD
Rod & Gun Club

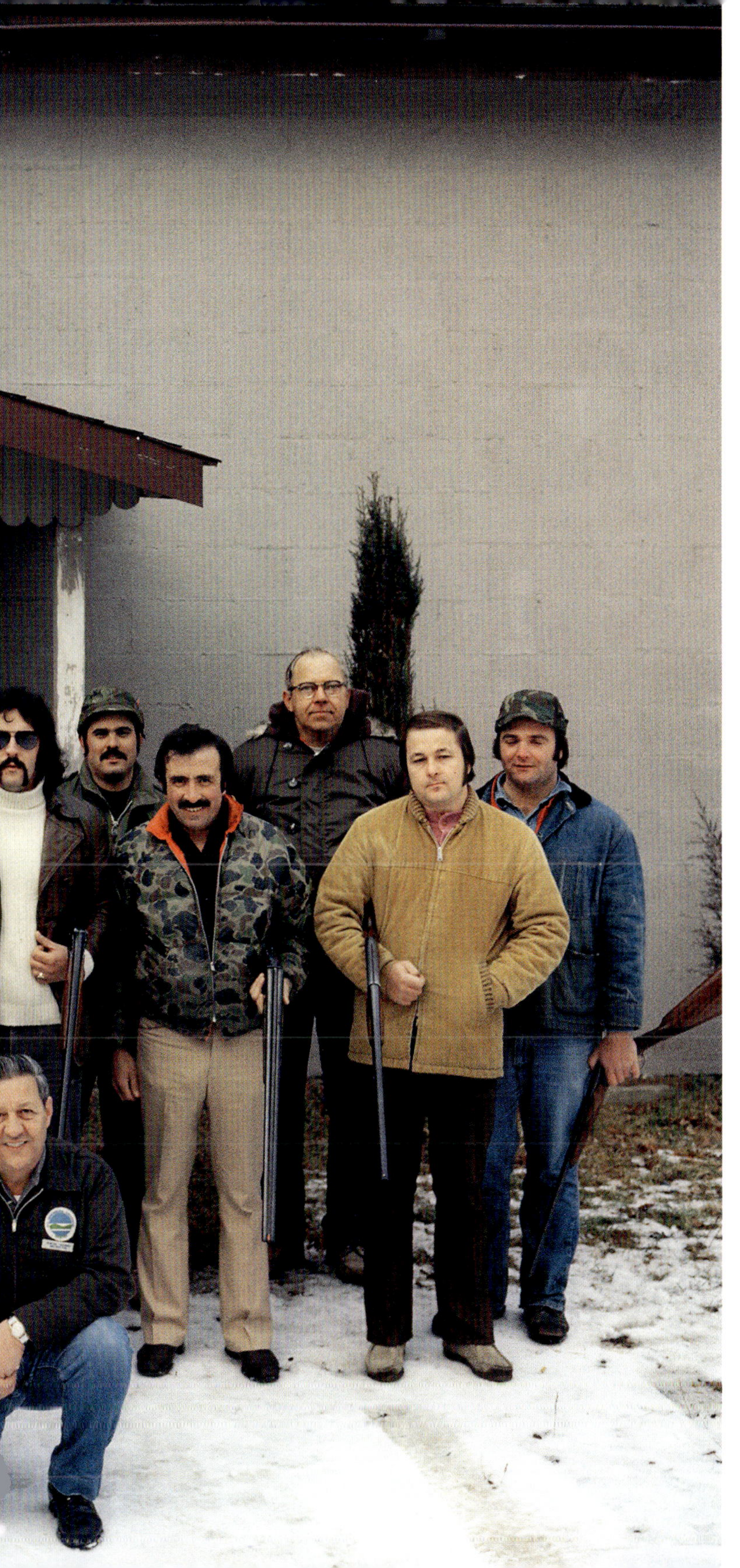

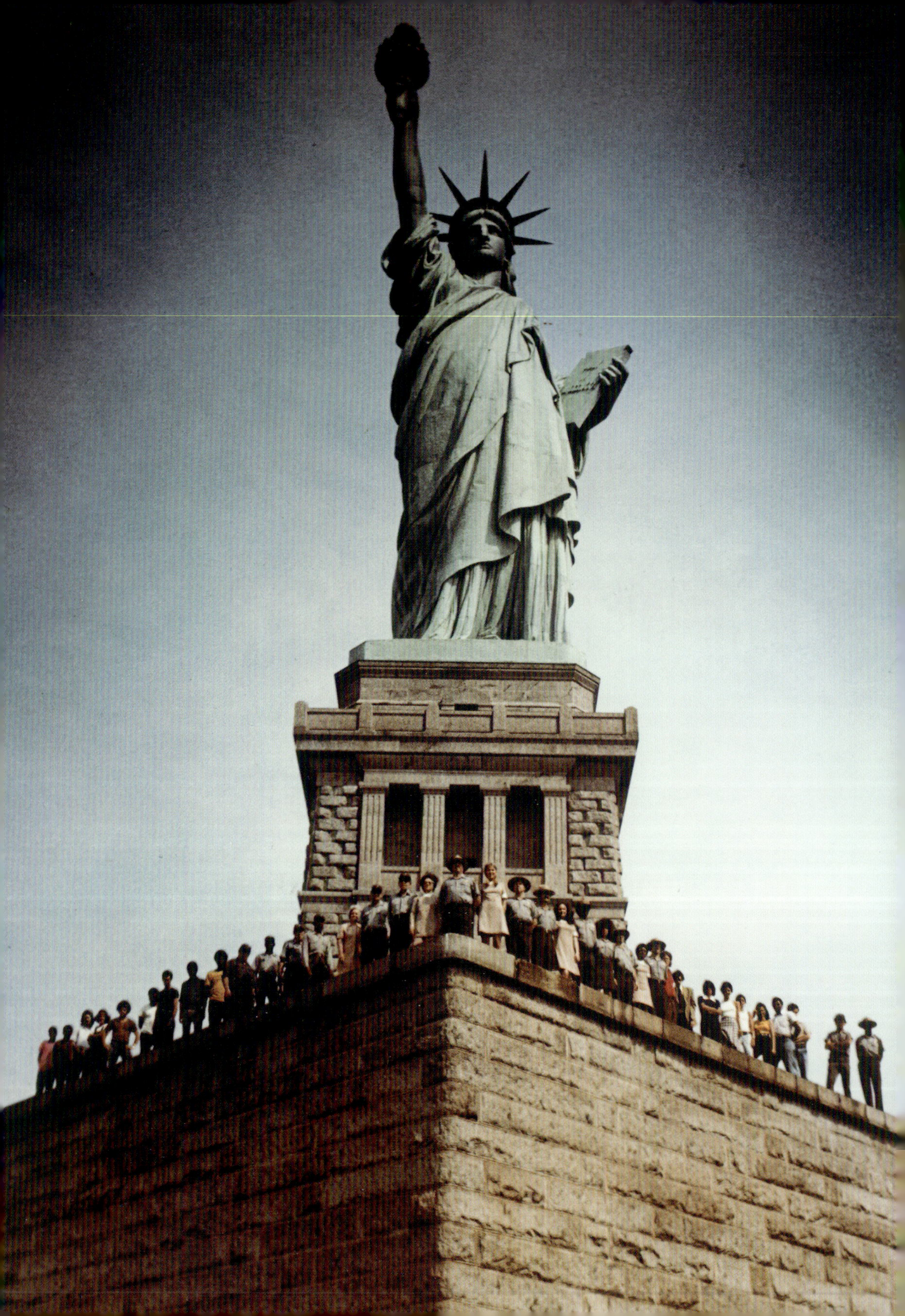

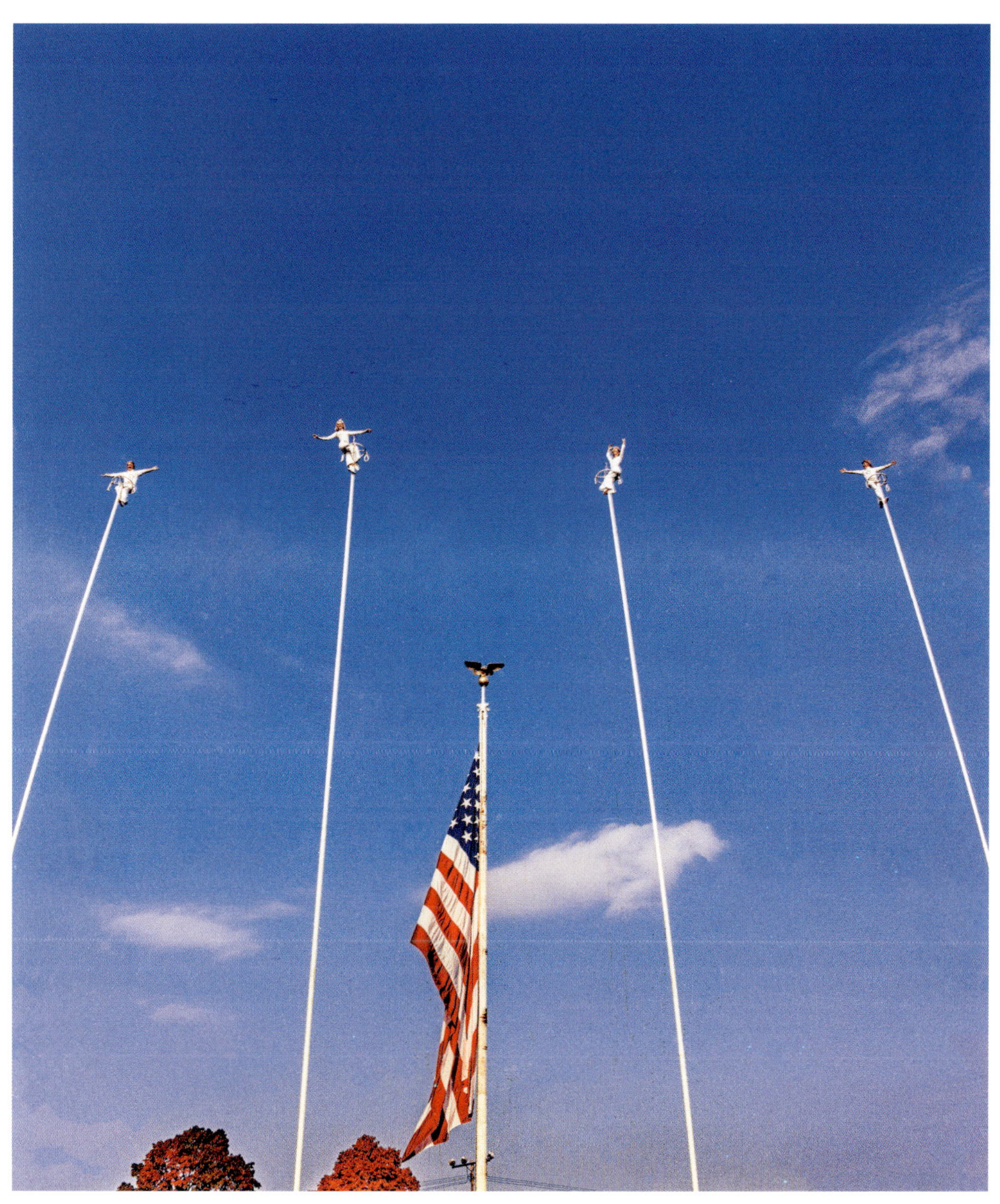

Nerveless Nocks, Churchville, Pennsylvania, 1972-75

Statue of Liberty, Liberty Island, New York, 1972-75

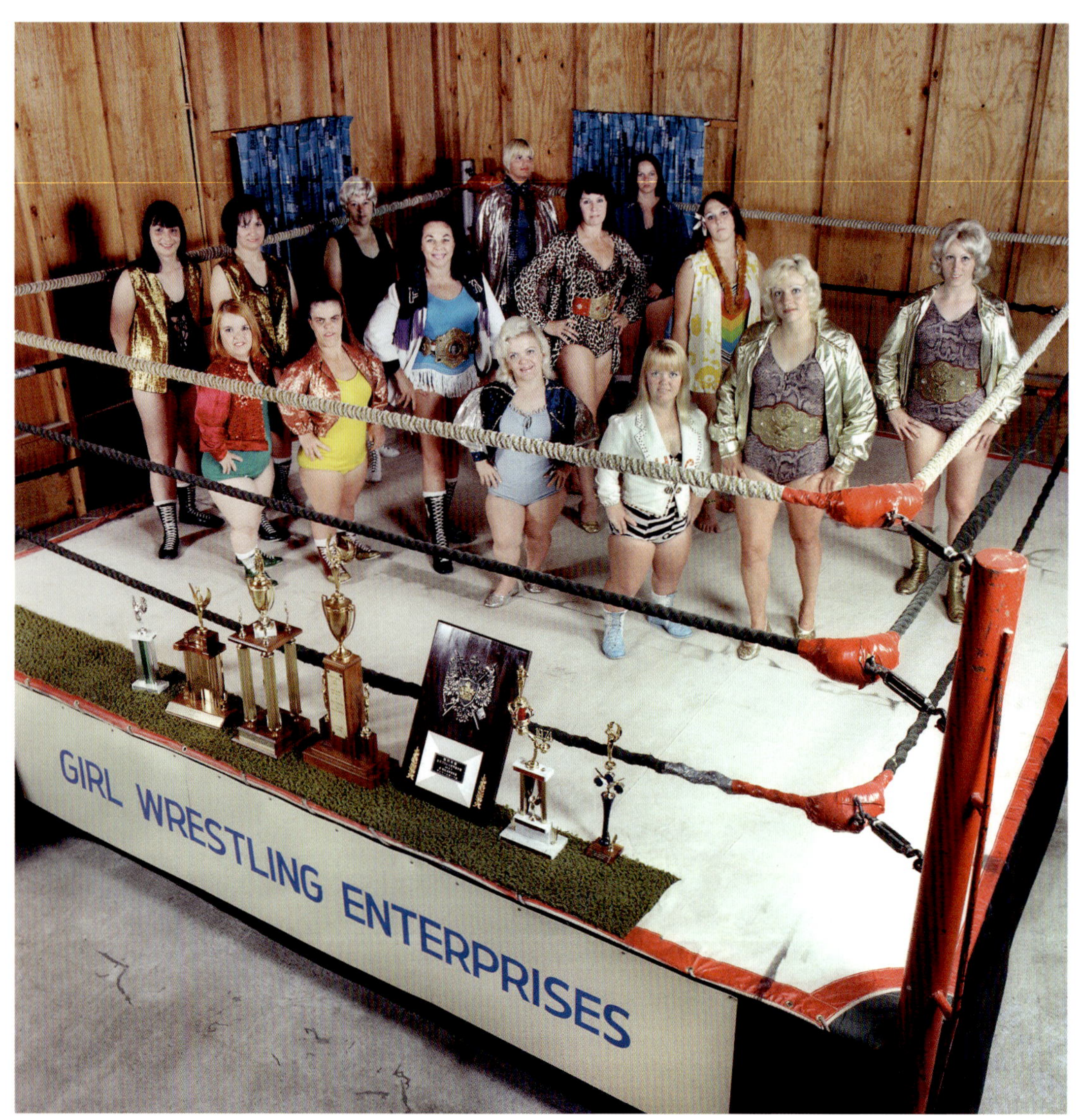

Girl Wrestling Enterprises, Columbia, South Carolina, 1972-75

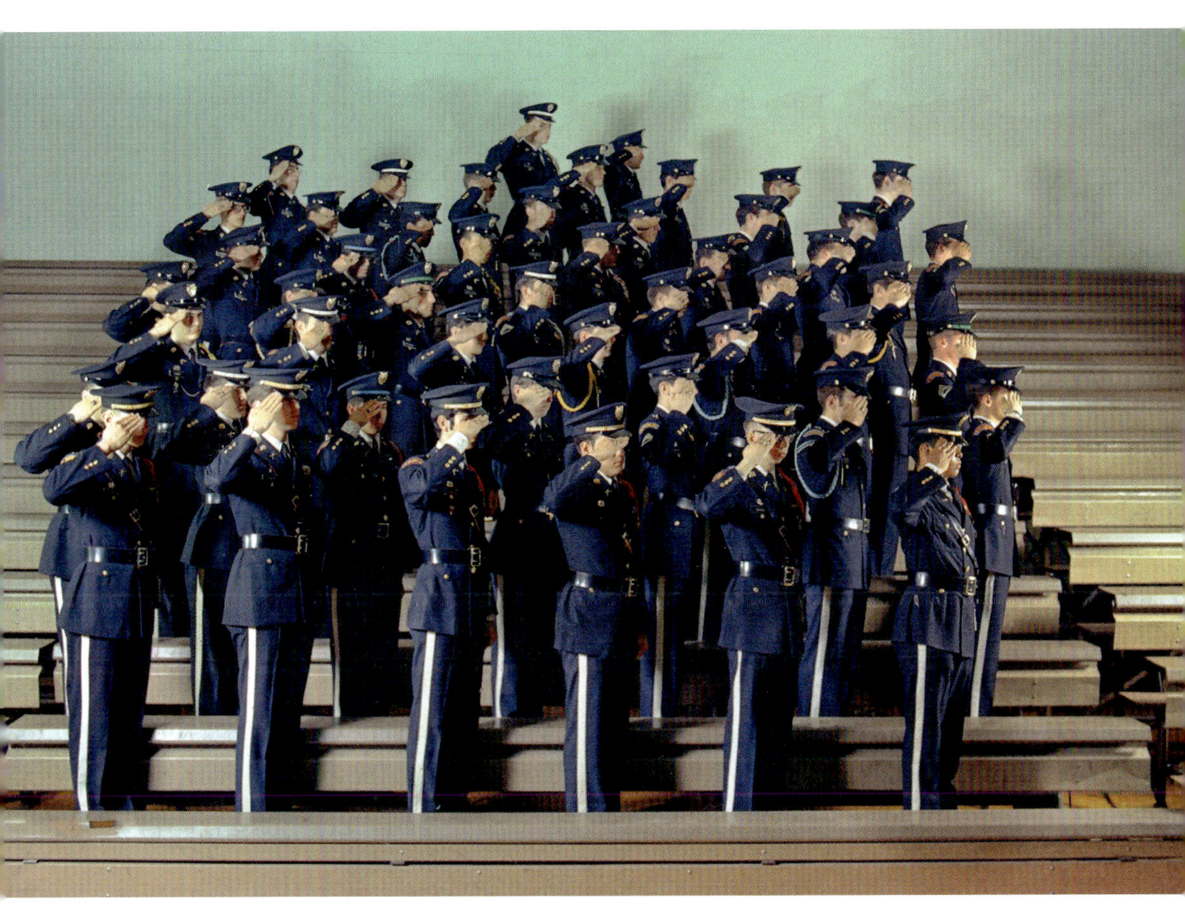

Xavier High School, United States Army Junior R.O.T.C., New York, New York, 1972-75

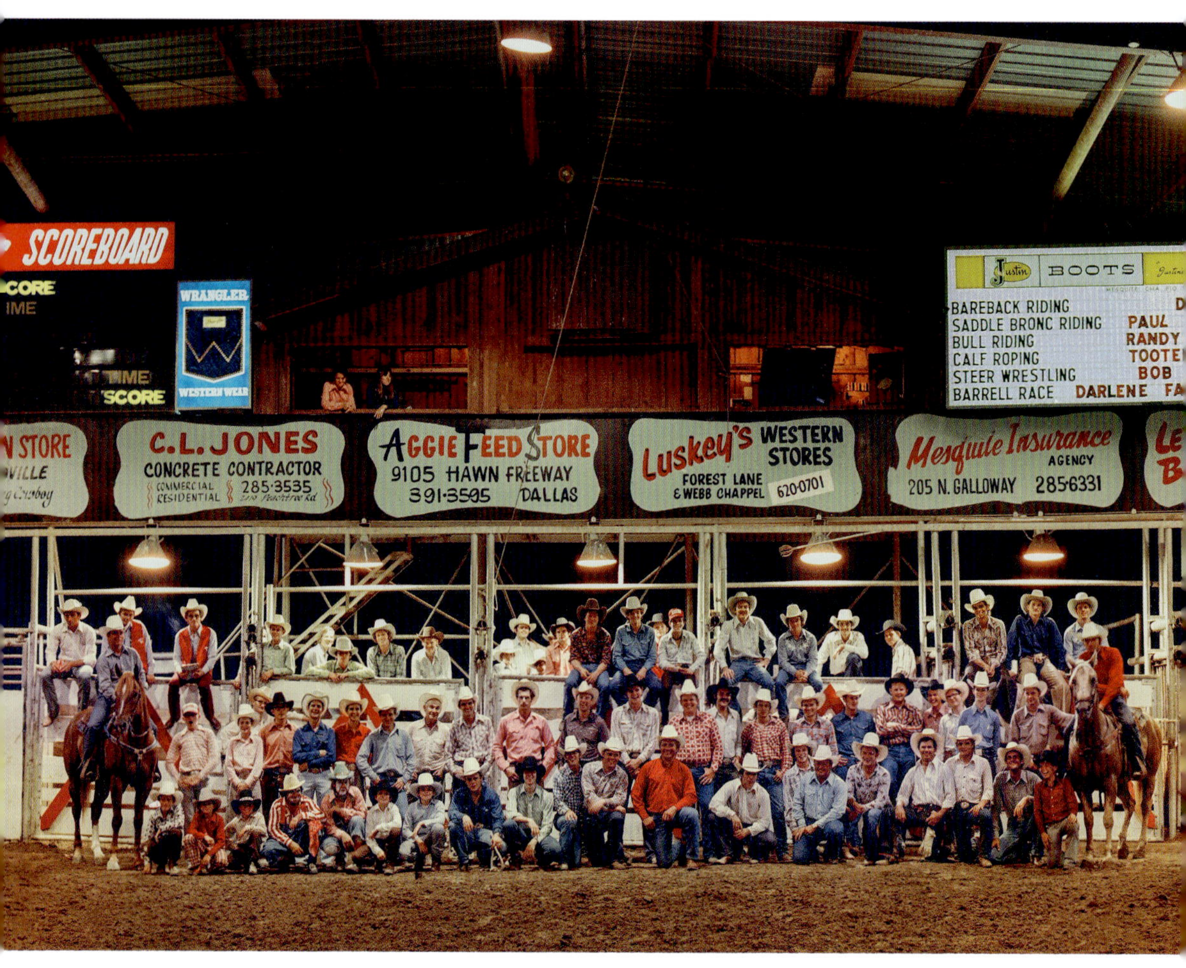

Mesquite Rodeo Corporation, Mesquite, Texas, 1972-75

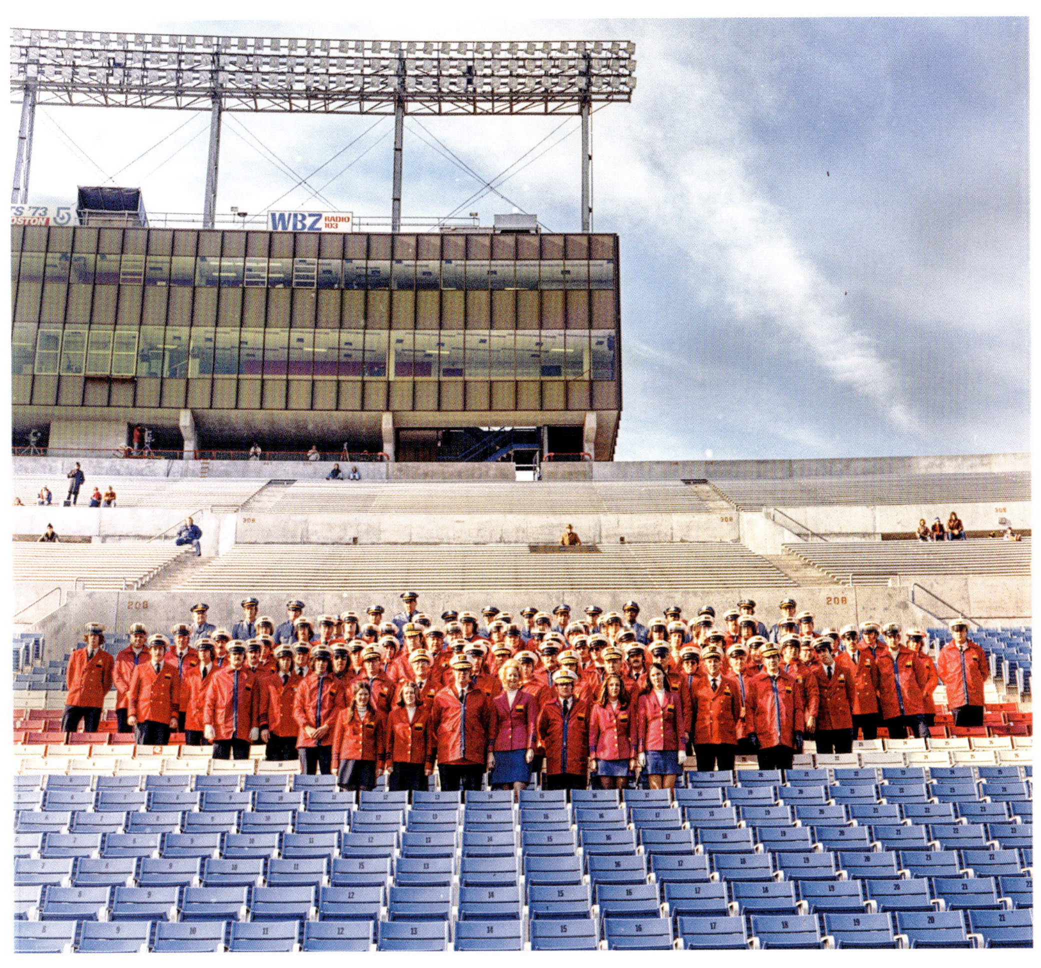

Burns International Security Services, Inc., Briarcliff Manor, New York, 1972-75

OVERLEAF

Miss U.S.A. Pageant Miss Universe, Inc., New York, New York, 1972-75

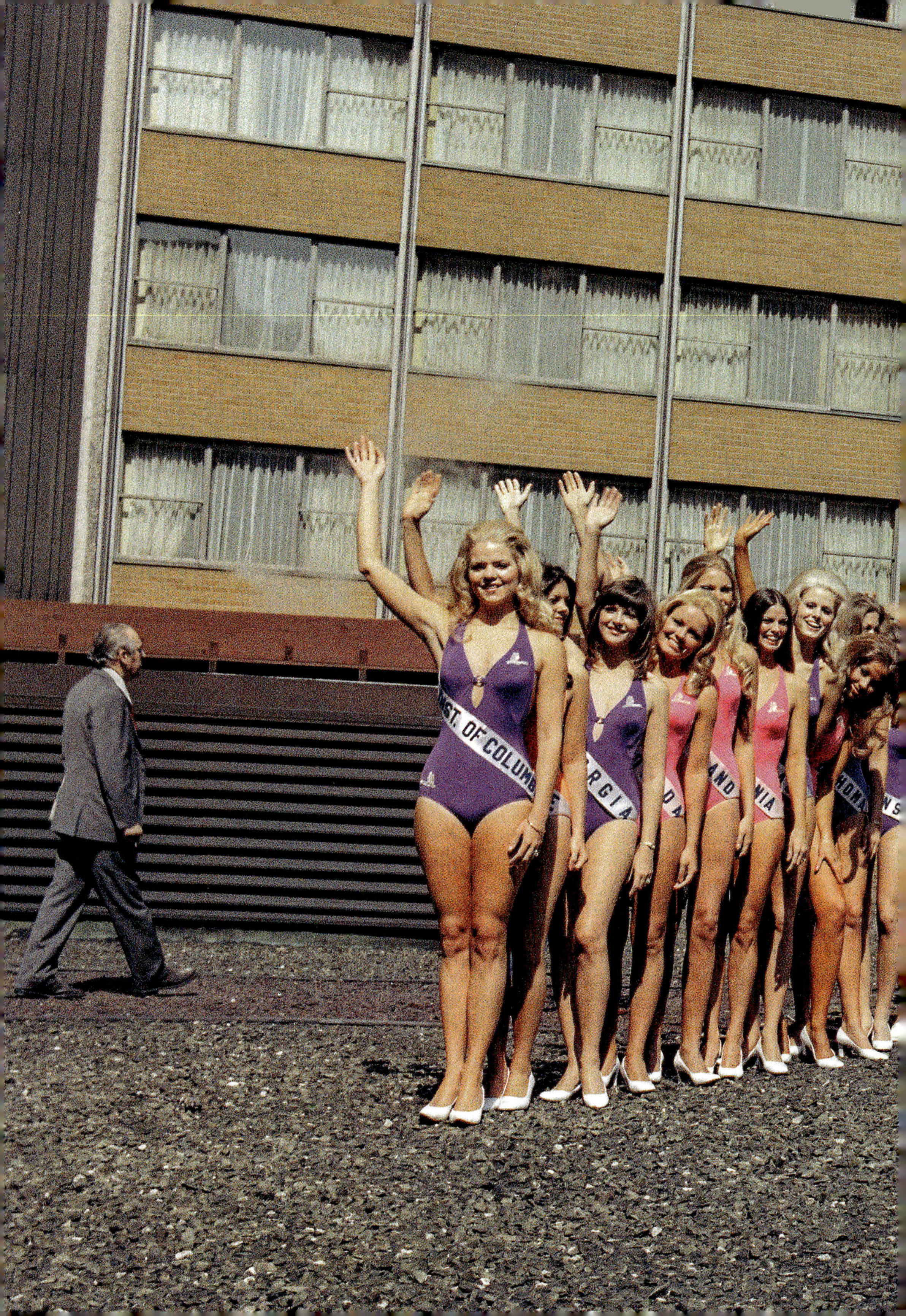

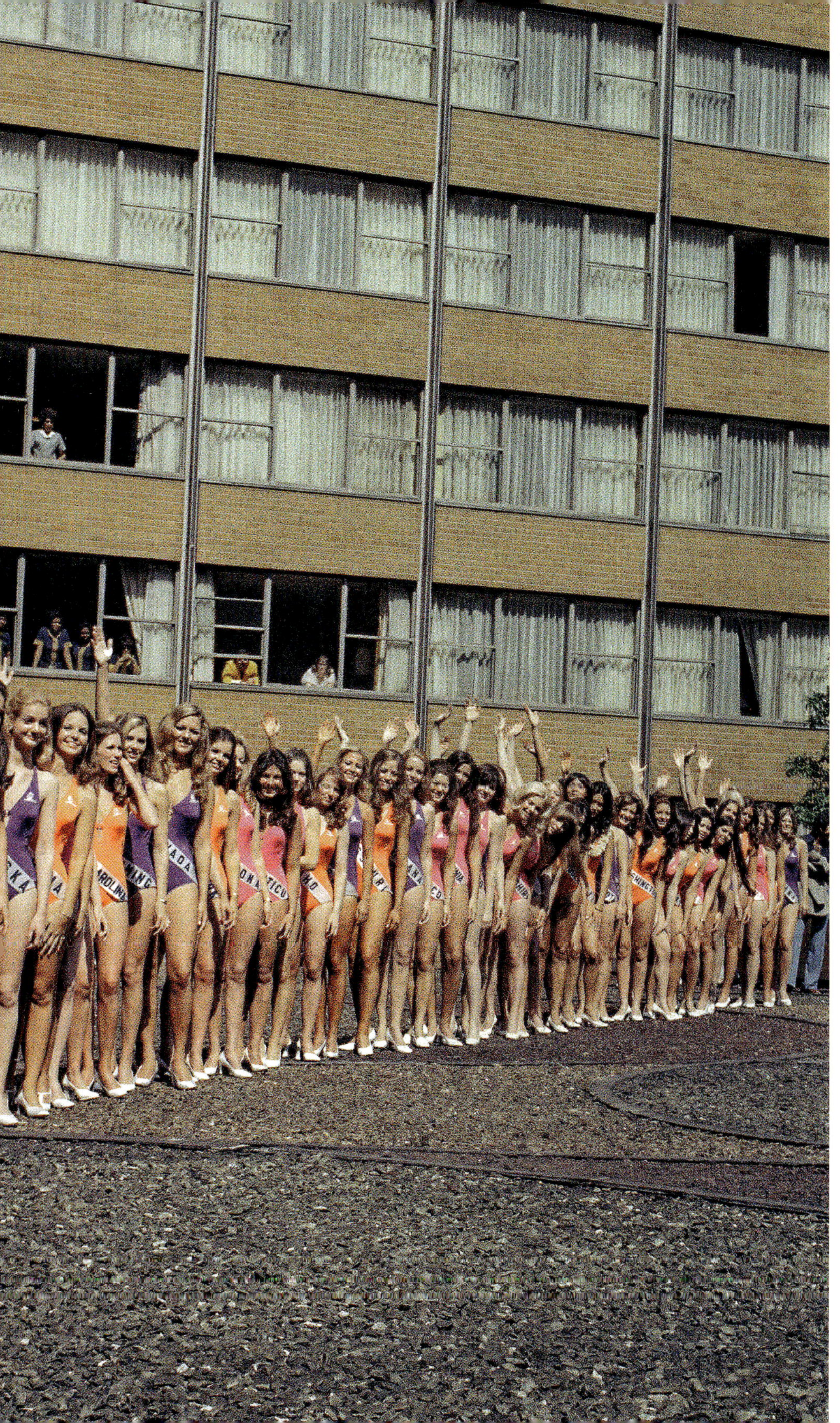

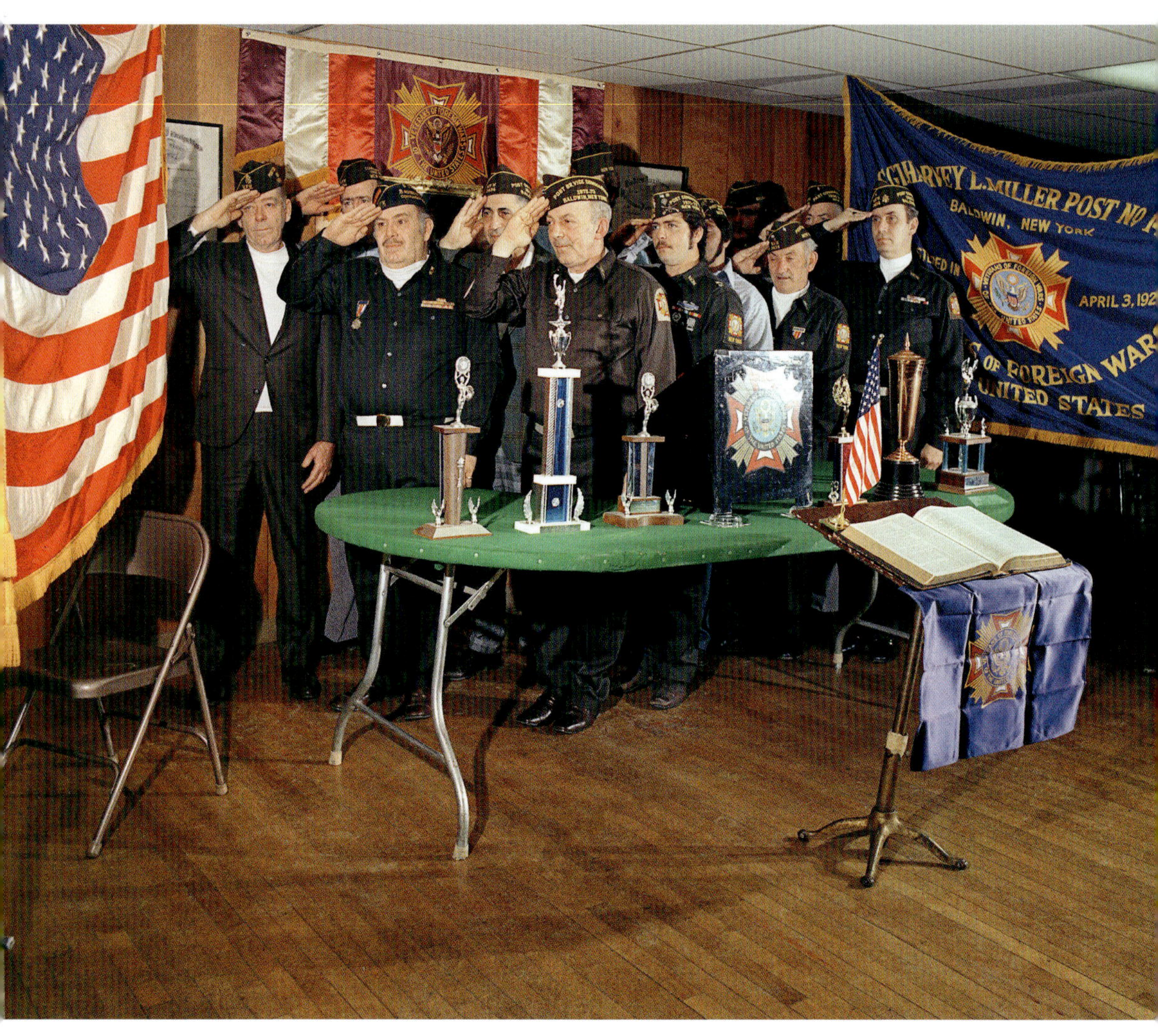

Sgt. Harvey I. Miller Post 1434, Veterans of Foreign Wars (V.F.W.), Baldwin, New York, 1972-75

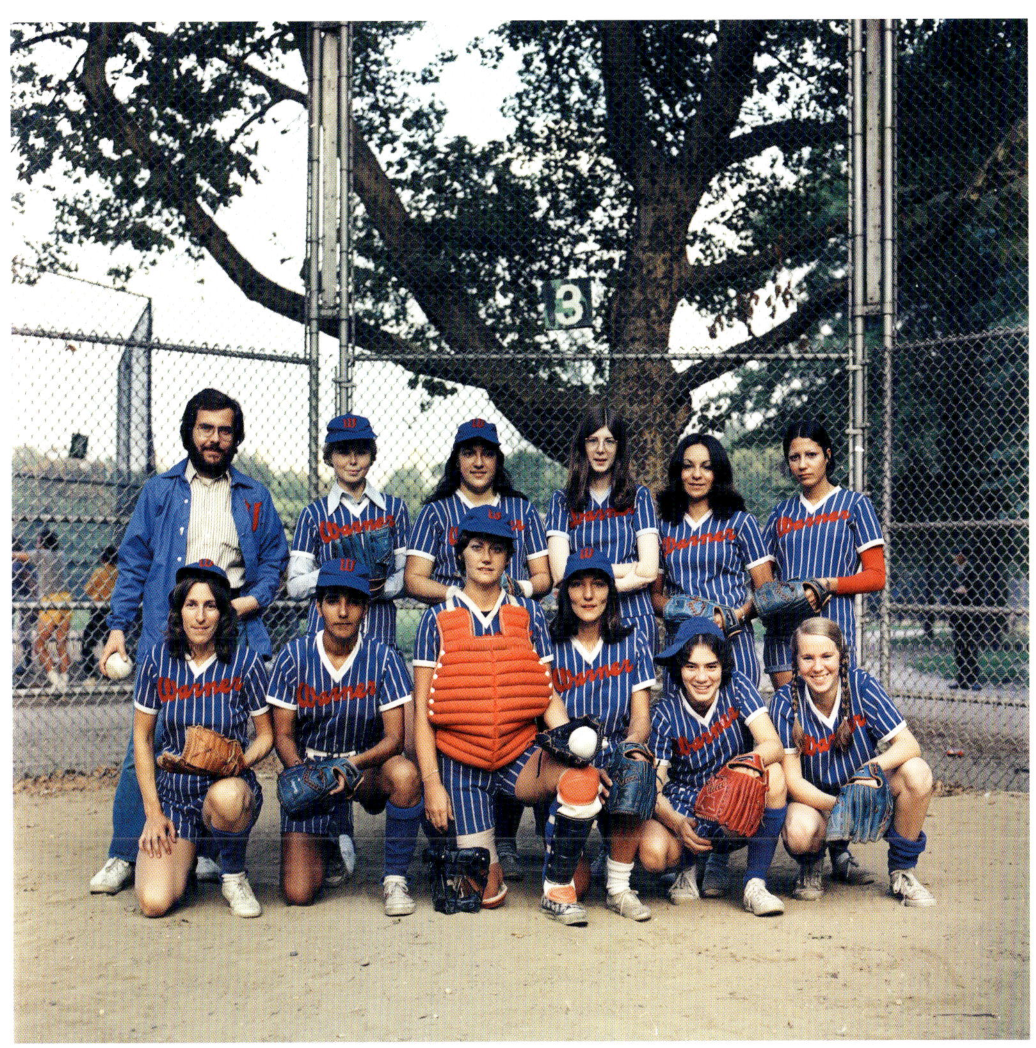

Women's Intramural Softball Team of Warner Communications, Inc., New York, New York, 1972-75

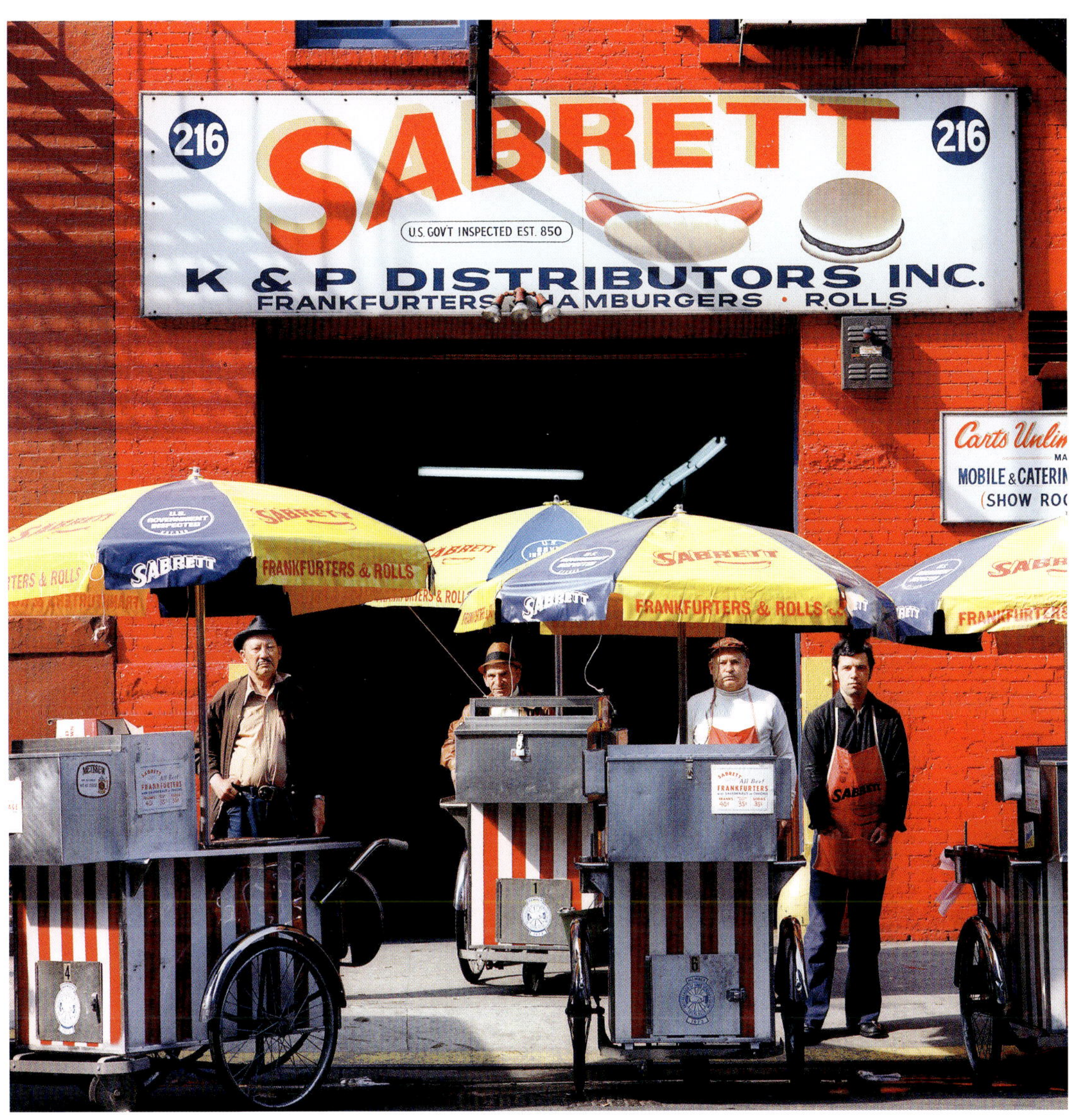

K & P Distributors, Inc., Sabrett Food Products Corporation, New York, New York, 1972-75

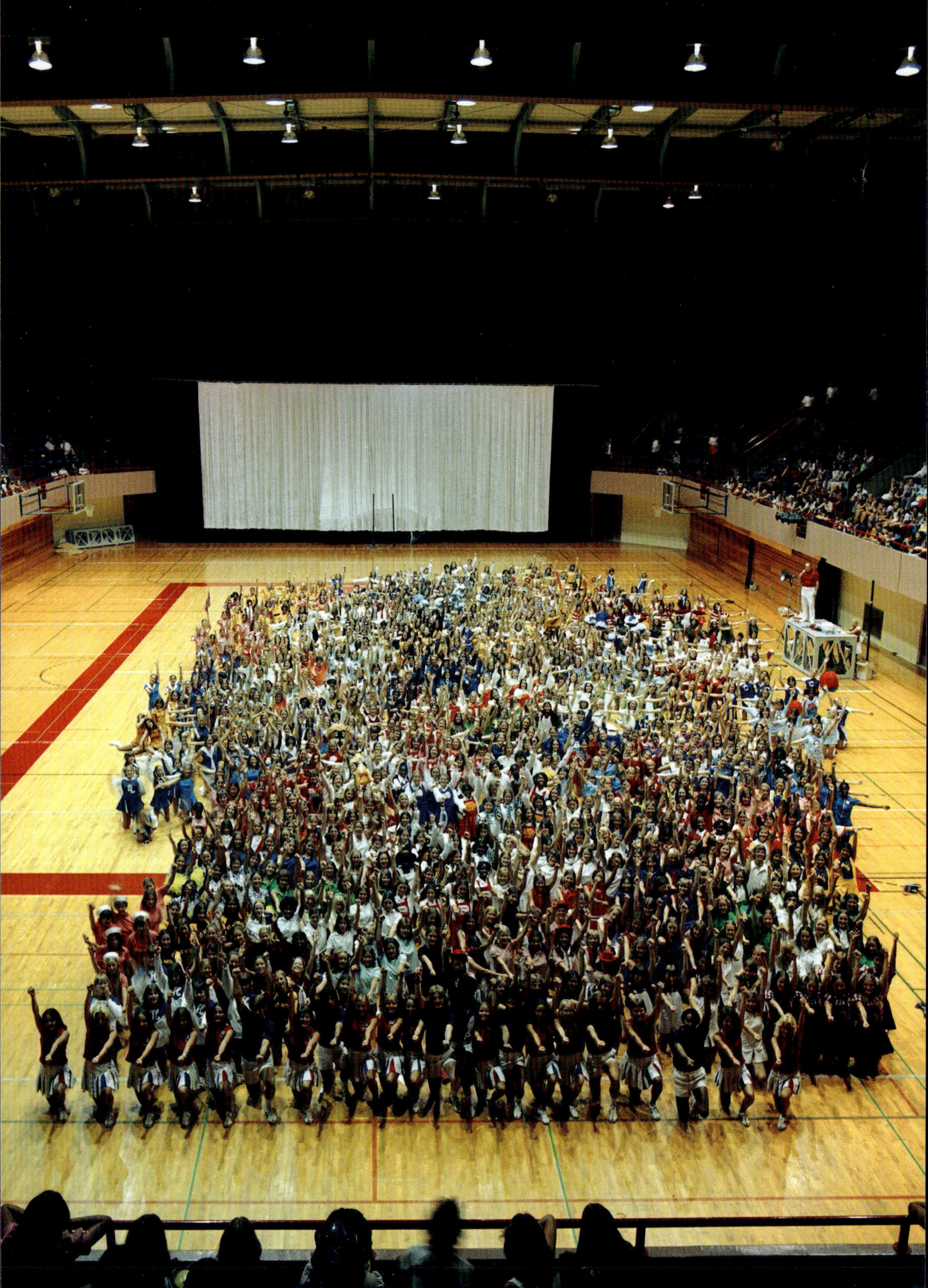

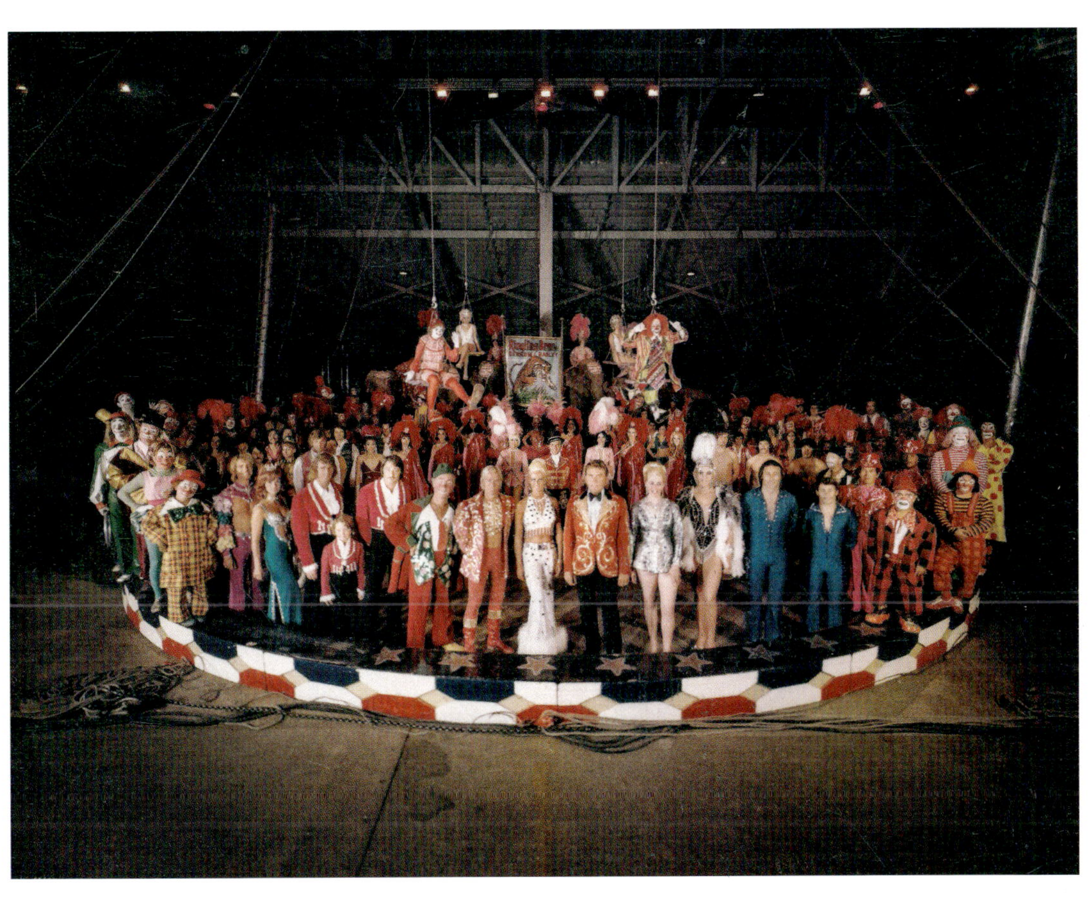

Ringling Brothers and Barnum & Bailey Circus, Washington, D.C., 1972-75

National Cheerleaders Association, Dallas, Texas, 1972-75

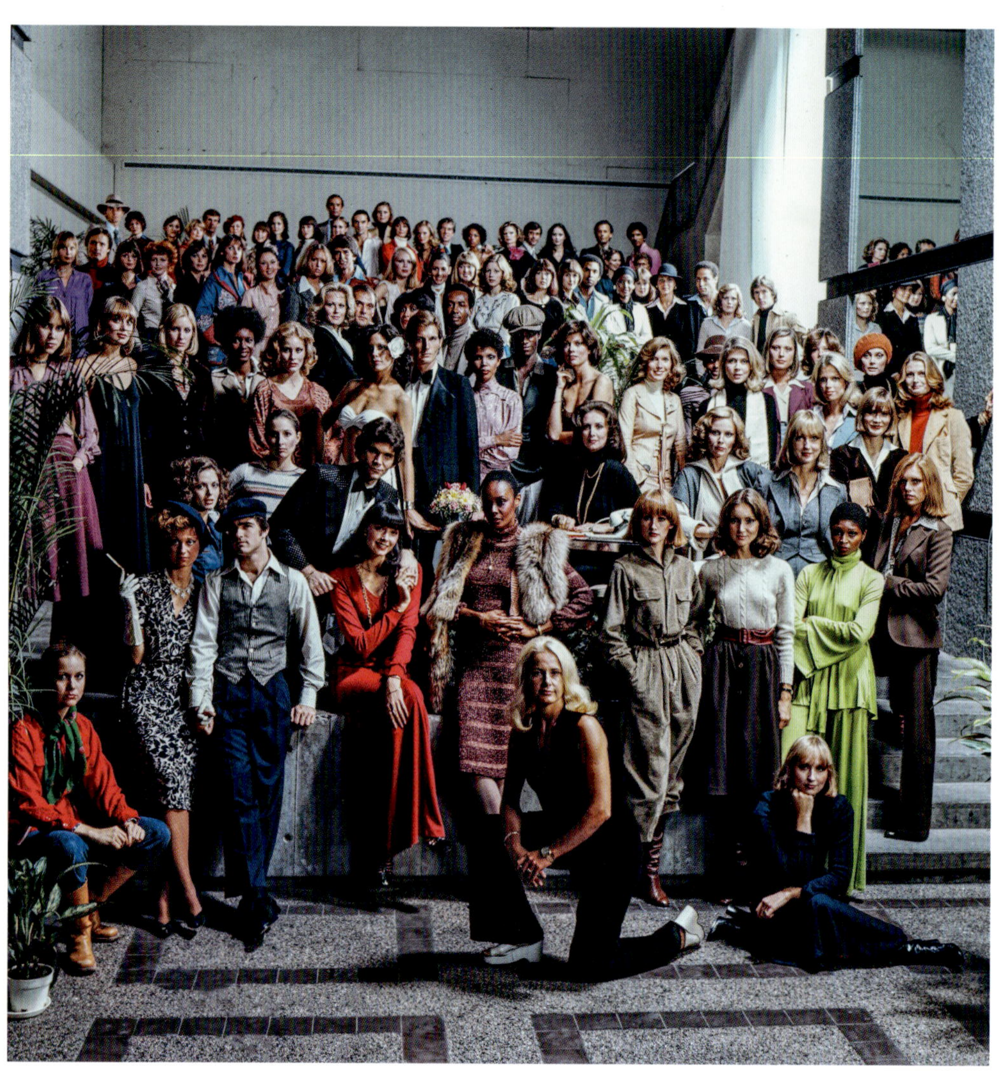

Wilhelmina Models, Inc., New York, New York, 1972-75

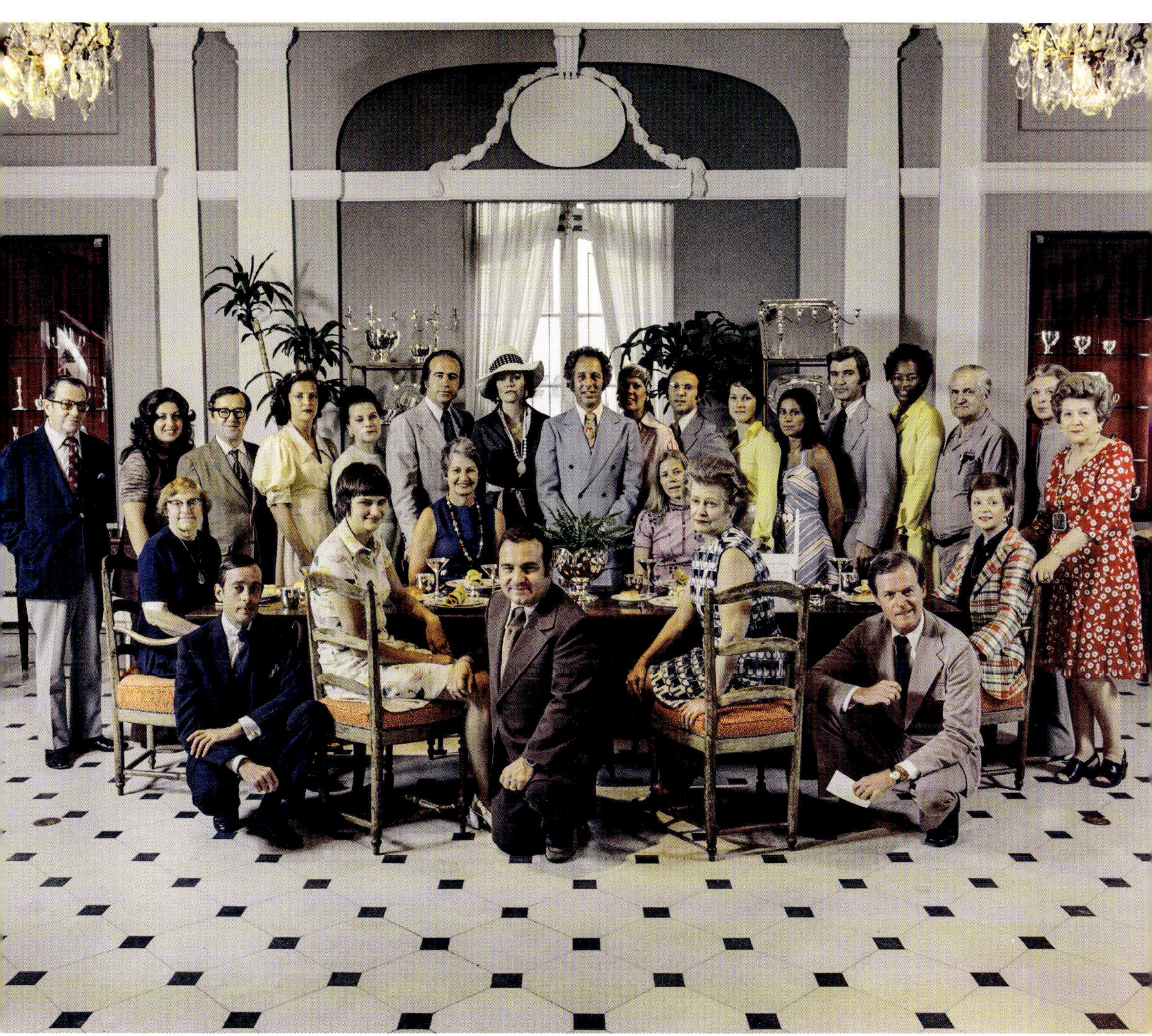

Cartler, Inc., New York, New York, 1972-75

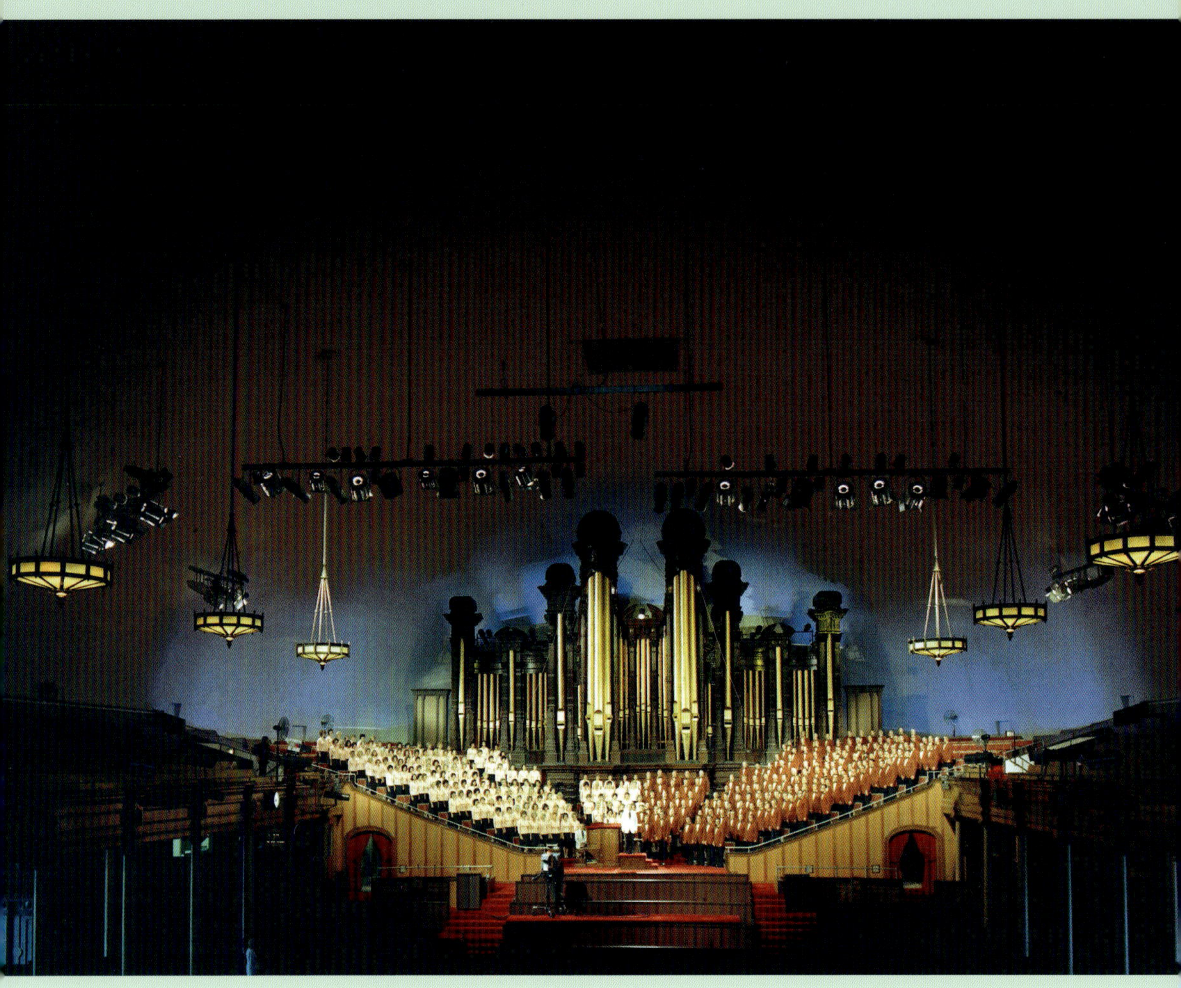

Salt Lake Mormon Tabernacle Choir, Salt Lake City, Utah, 1972-75

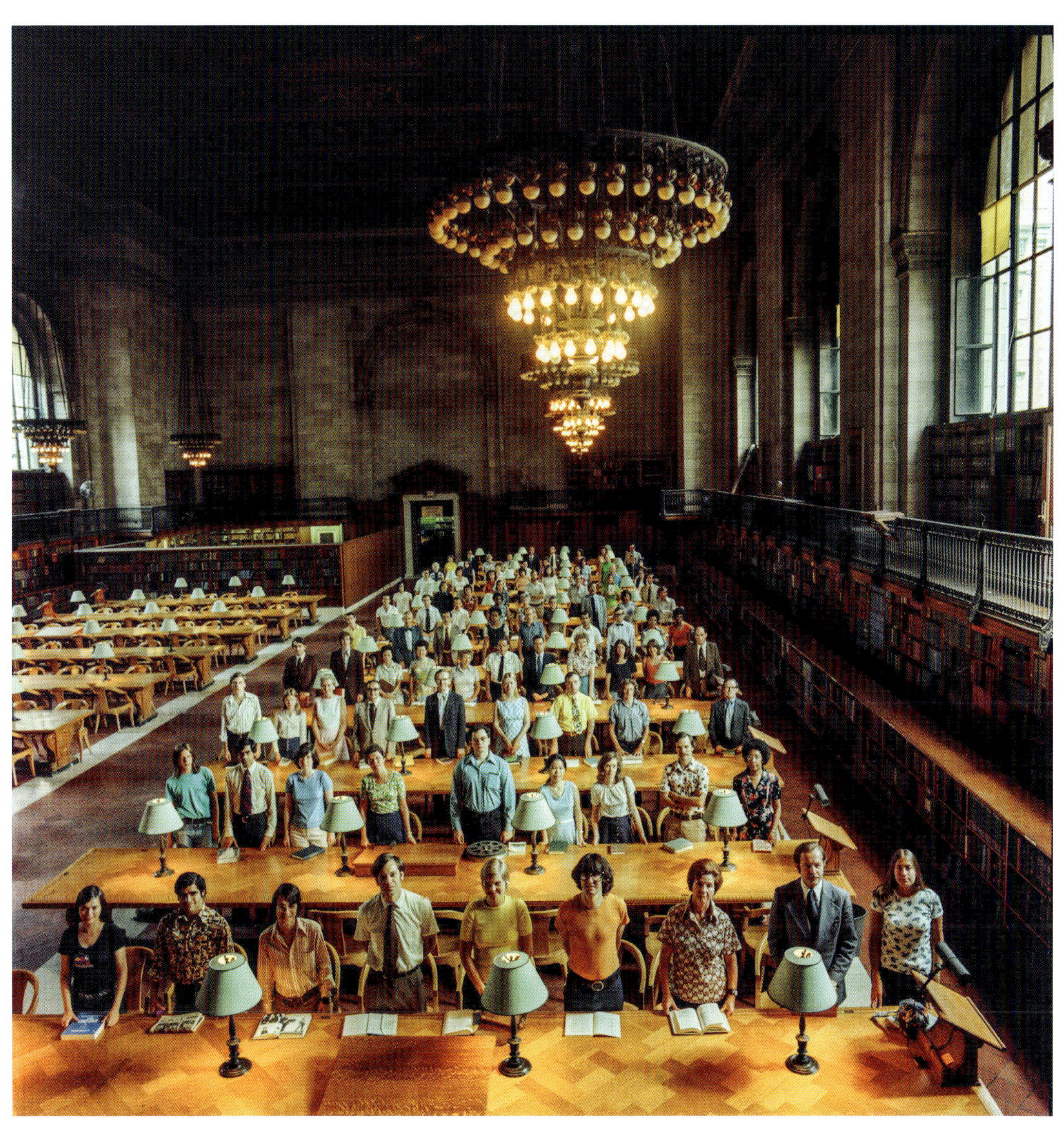

The New York Public Library, Astor, Lenox,
and Tilden Foundations, New York, New York, 1972-75

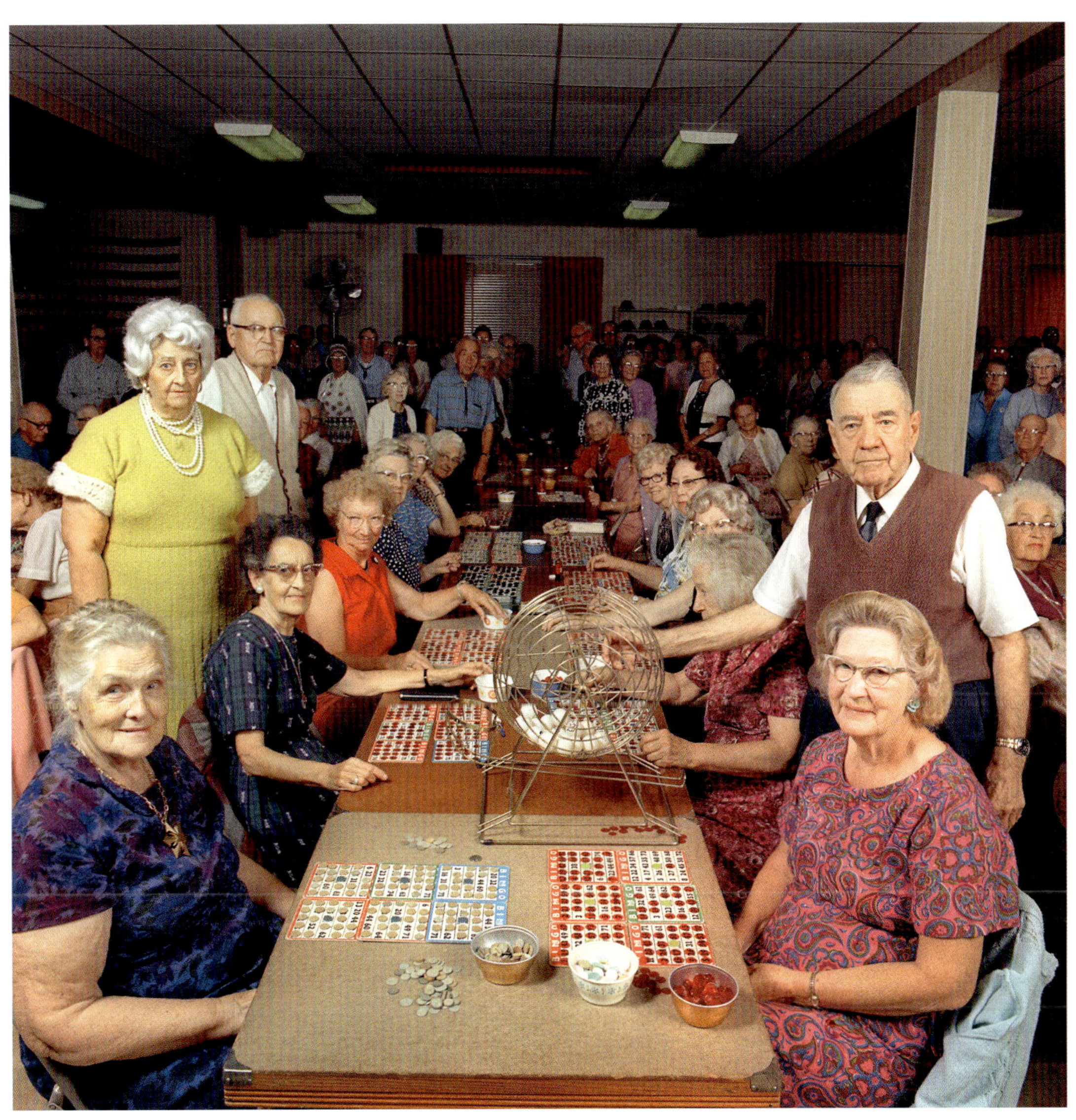

Bingo Club of the St. Petersburg Shuffleboard
and Duplicate Bridge Club, St. Petersburg, Florida, 1972-75

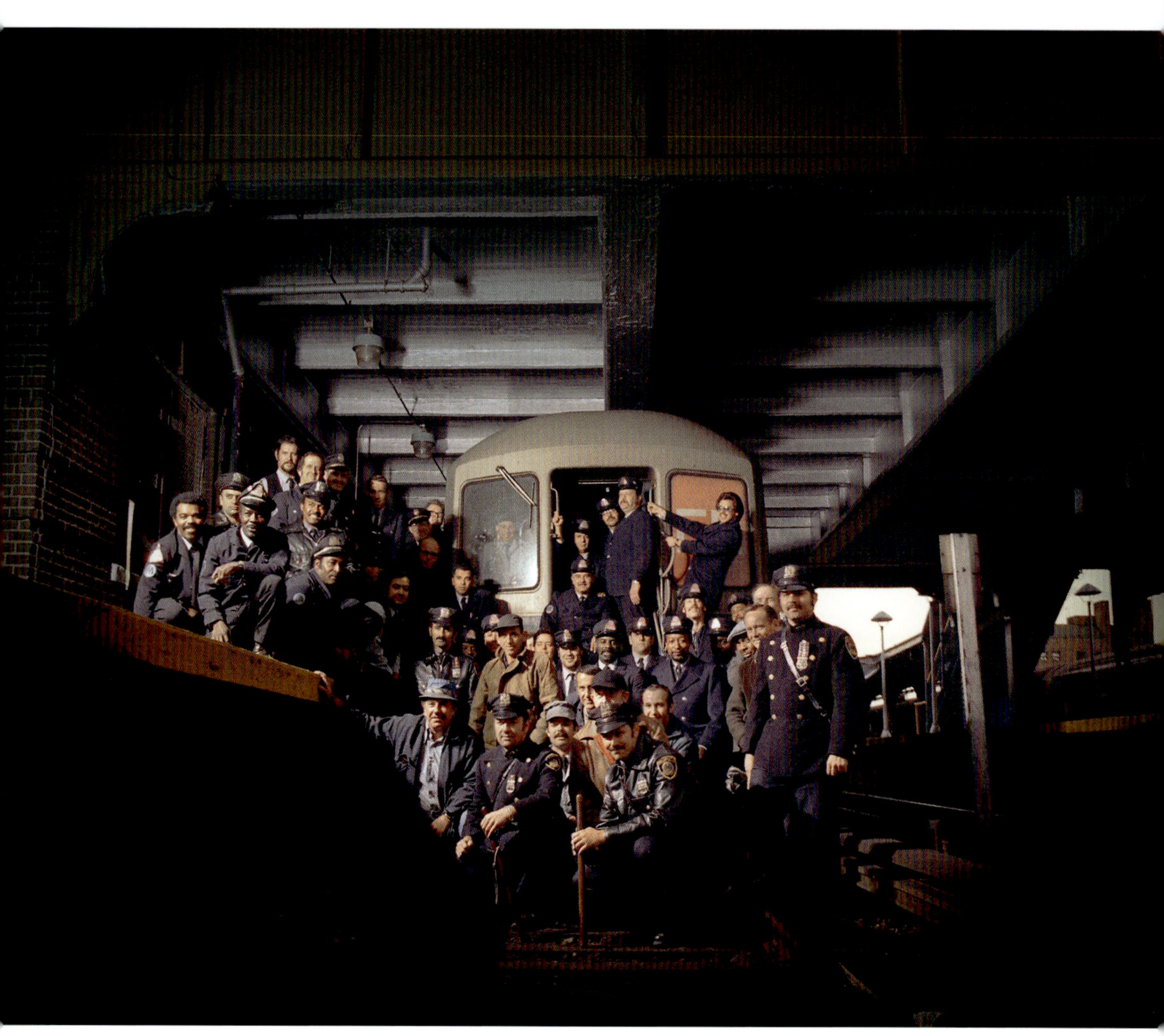

New York City Transit Authority, Brooklyn, New York, 1972-75

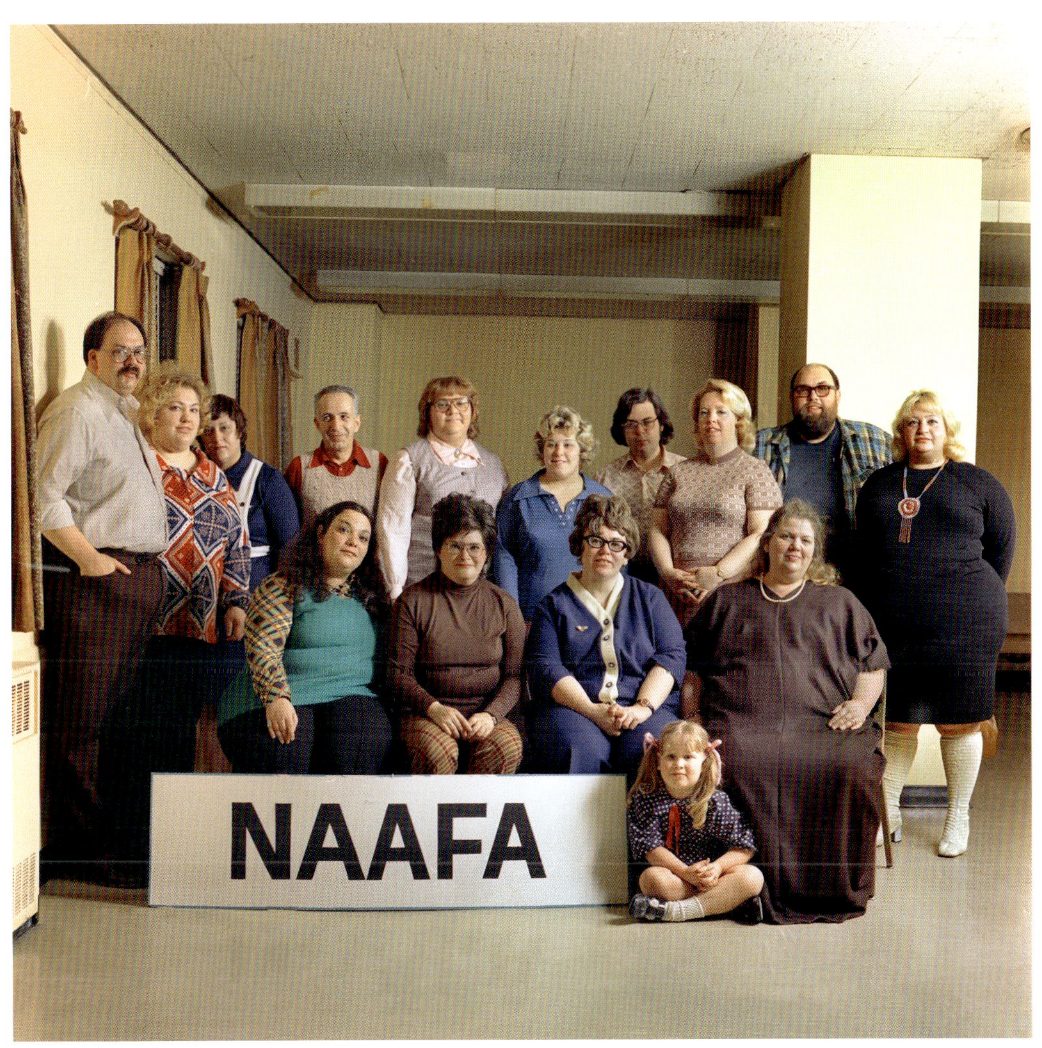

National Association to Aid Fat Americans, Inc. (N.A.A.F.A.), Westbury, New York, 1972-75

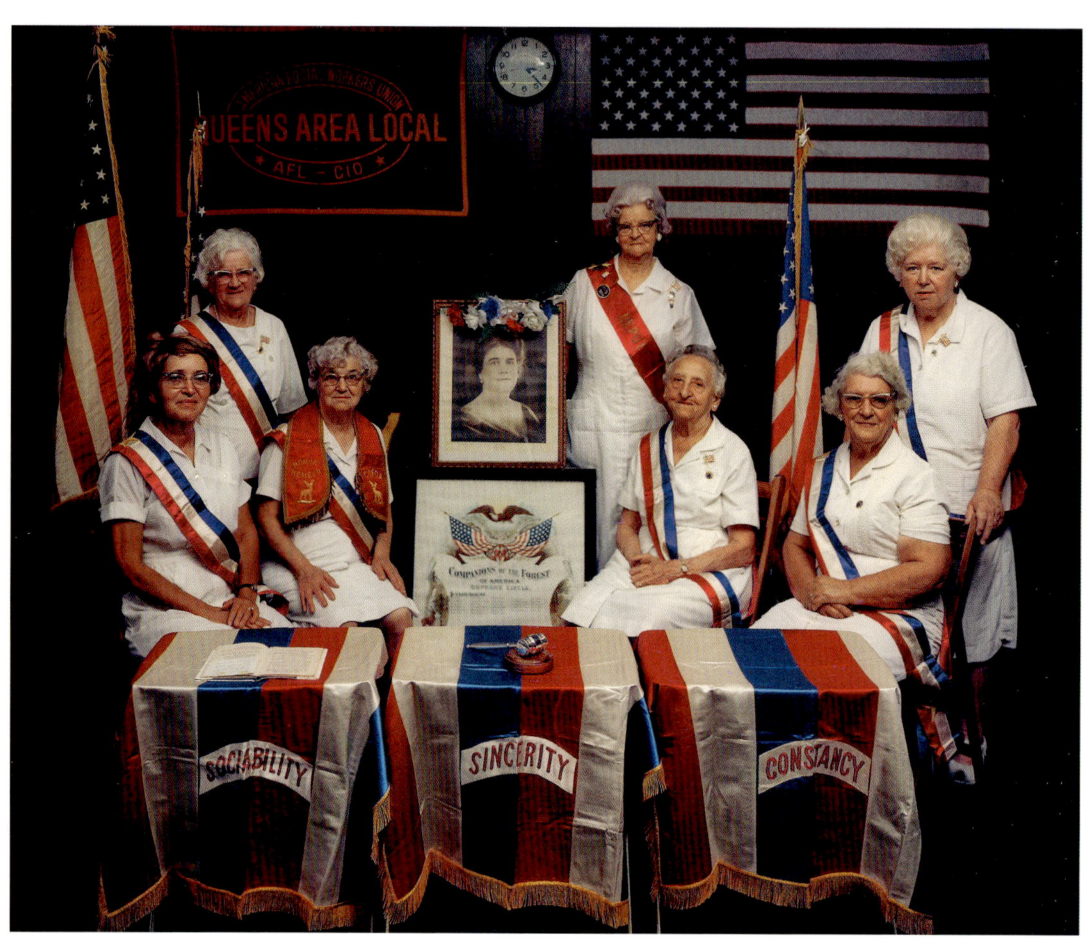

Lady Dorothy Circle #1460, The Companions of the Forest of America, Jamaica, New York, 1972-75

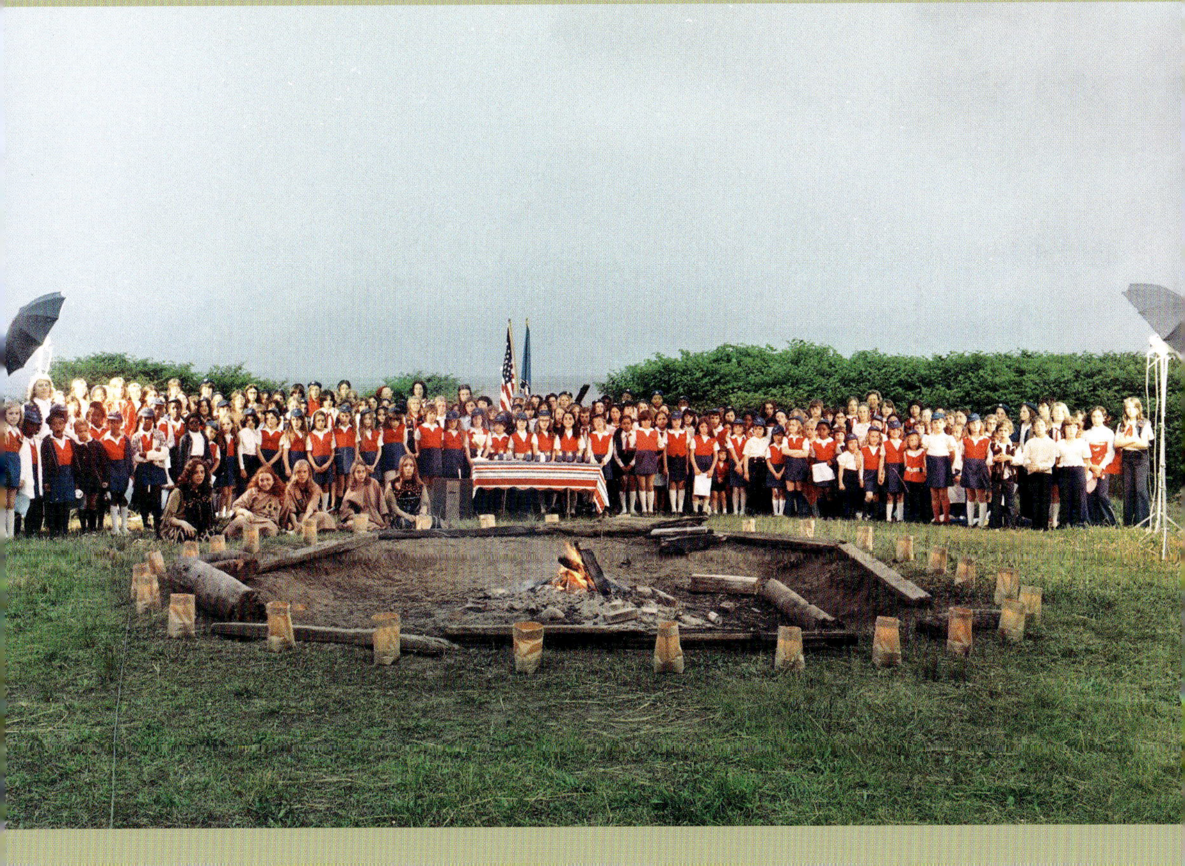

Staten Island Council Campfire Girls, Inc., Staten Island, New York, 1972-75

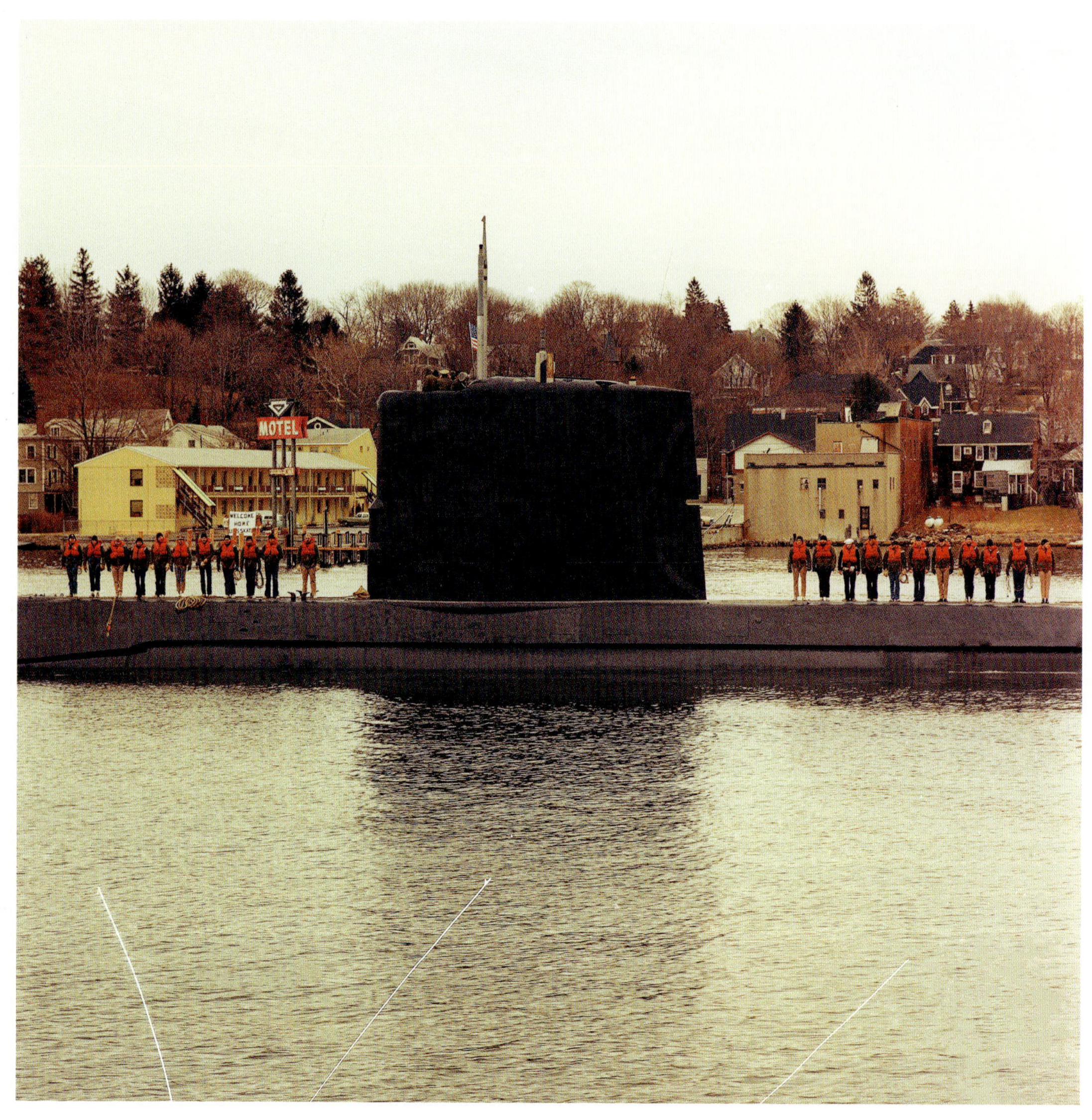

S.S. Skate, Groton, Connecticut, 1972-75

RIGHT PAGE
Cinema St. Marks Corporation, New York, New York, 1972-75

OVERLEAF
The Troc Theater, Philadelphia, Pennsylvania, 1972-75

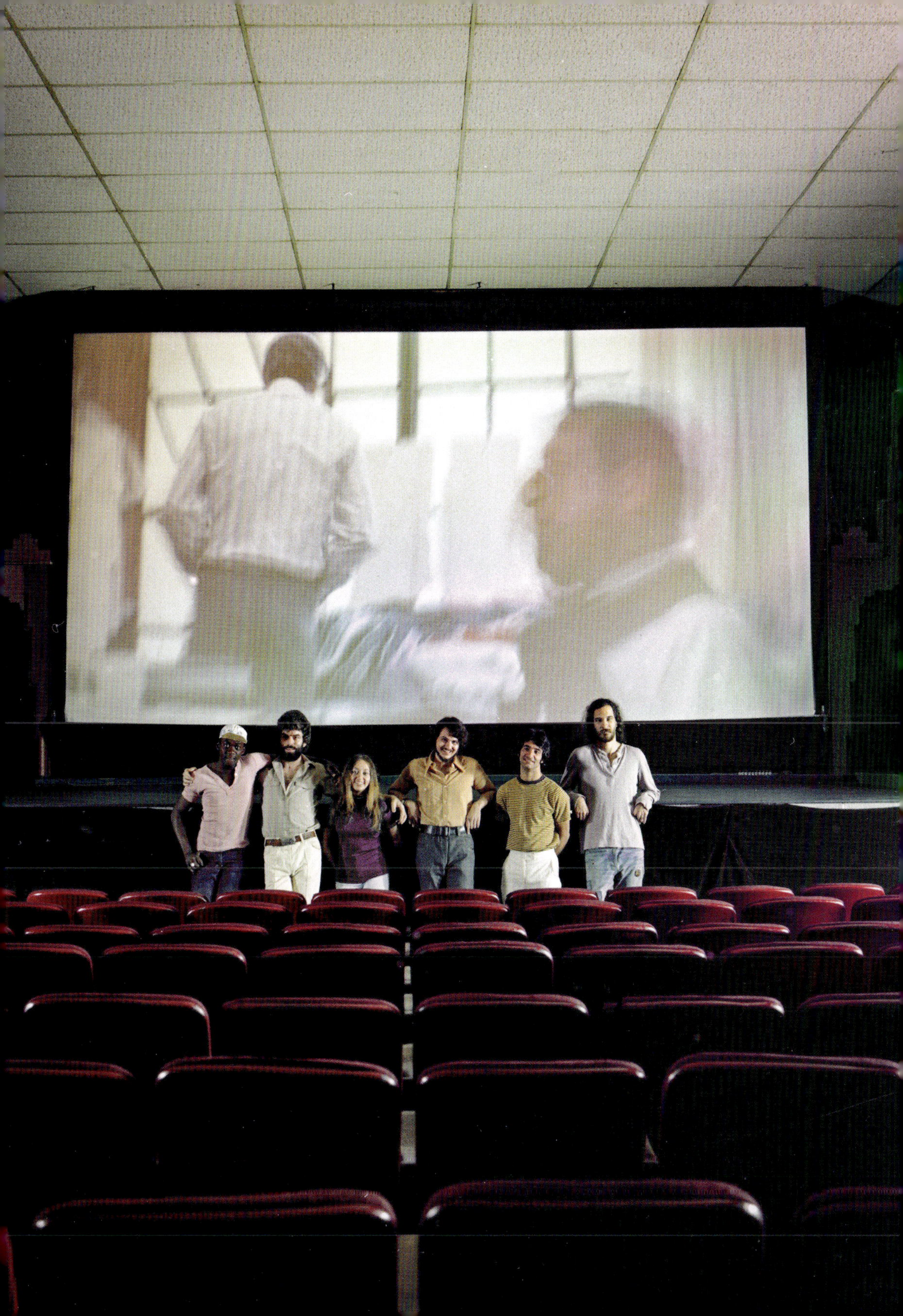

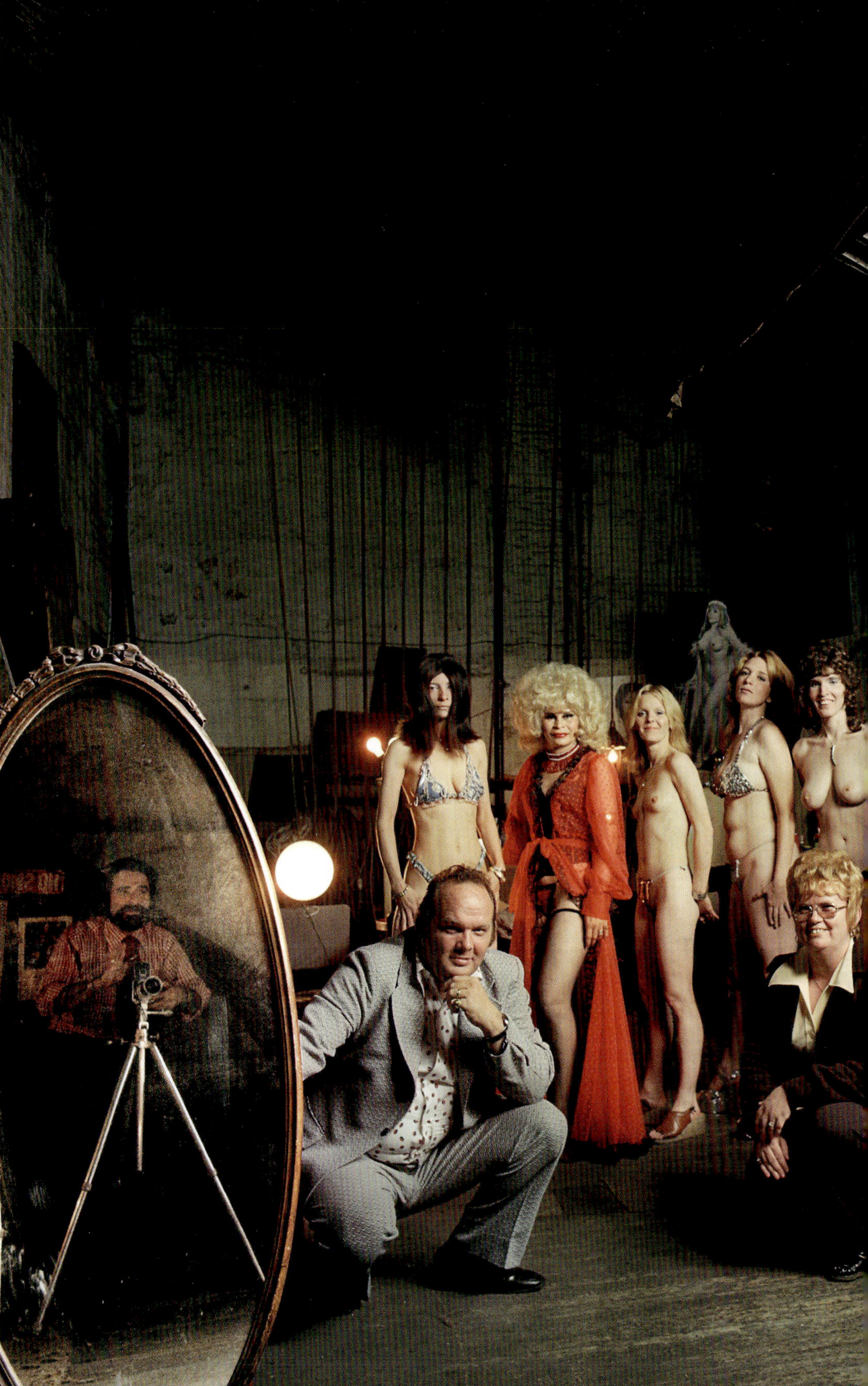

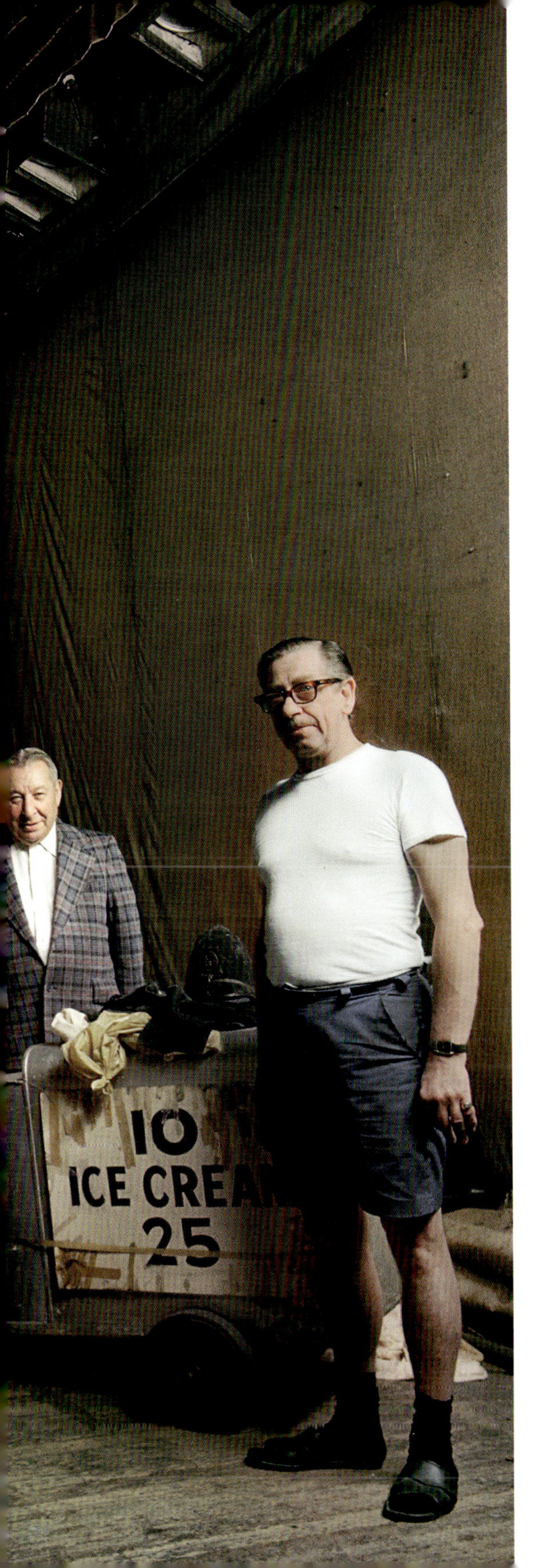
10
ICE CREA
25

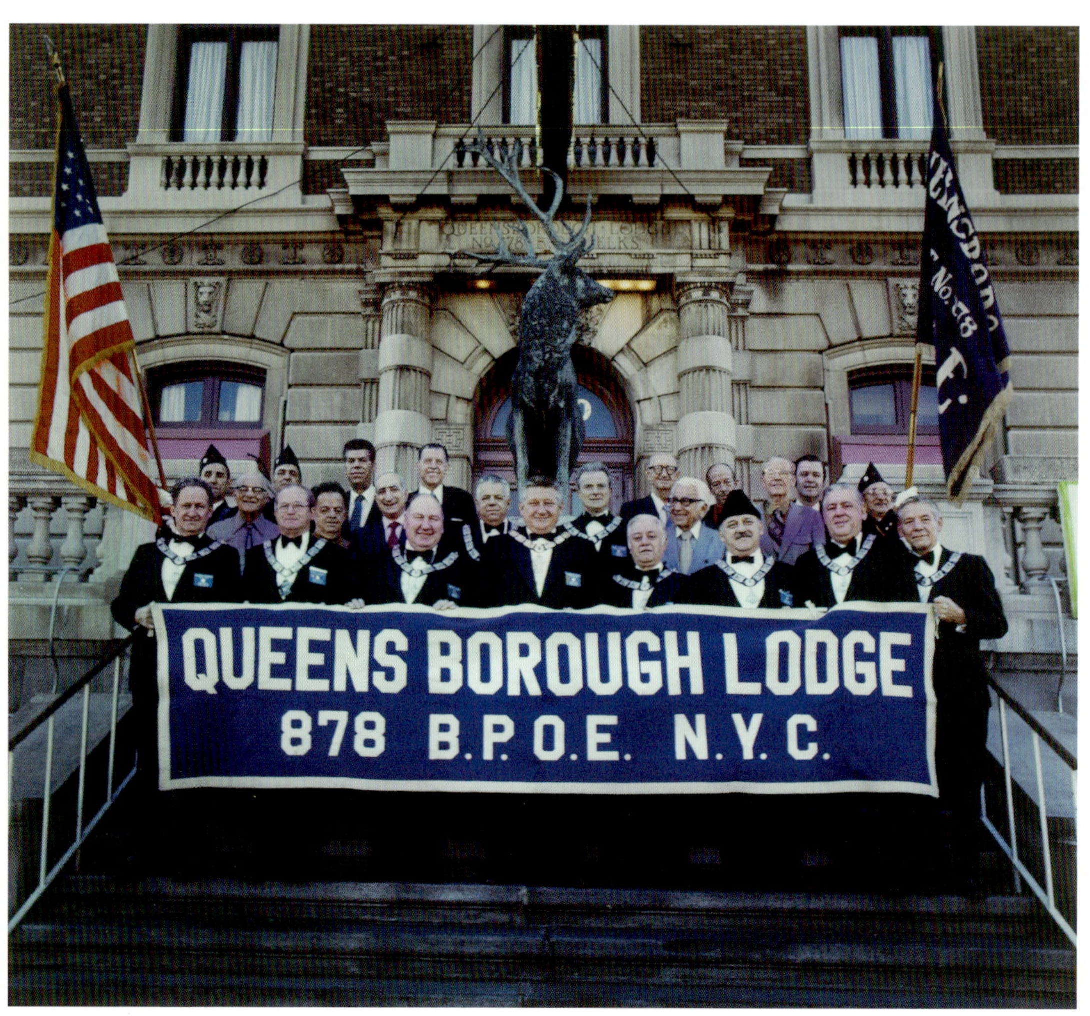

Queens Borough Lodge No. 878 B.P.O. Elks, Elmhurst, New York, 1972-75

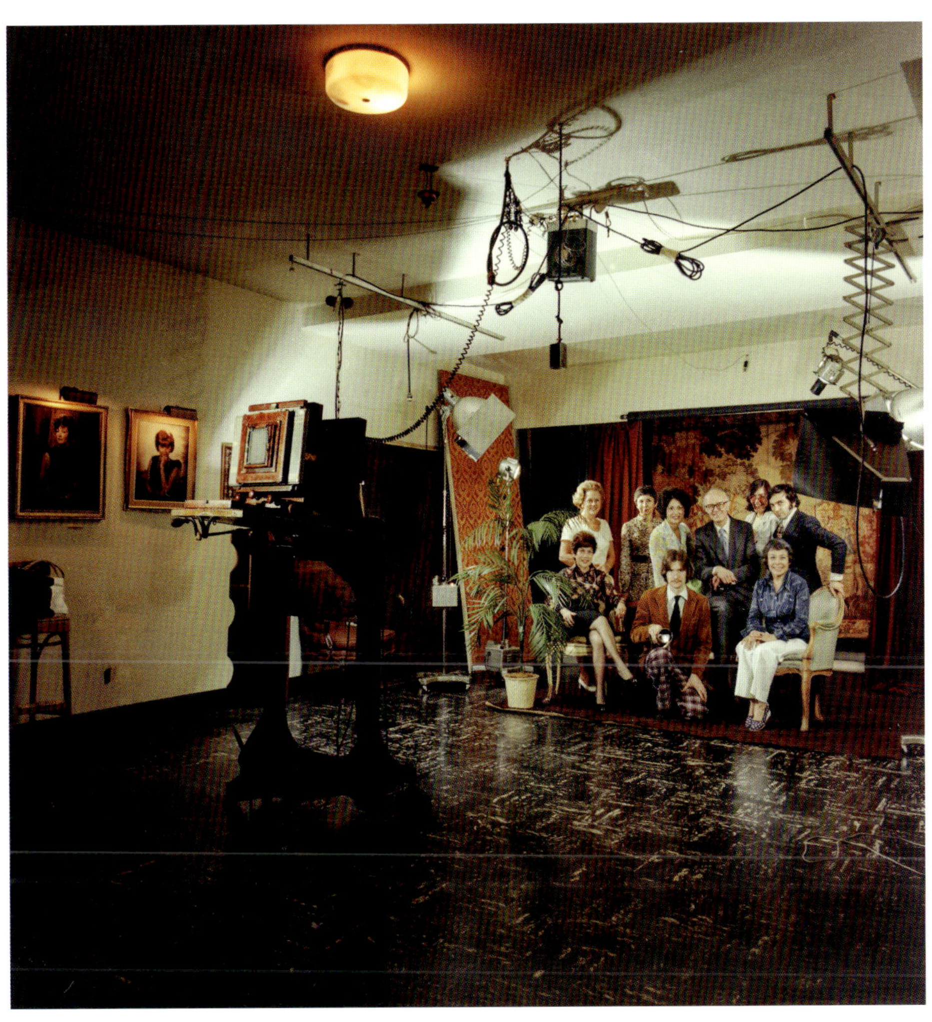

Bachrach Studios, New York, New York, 1972-75

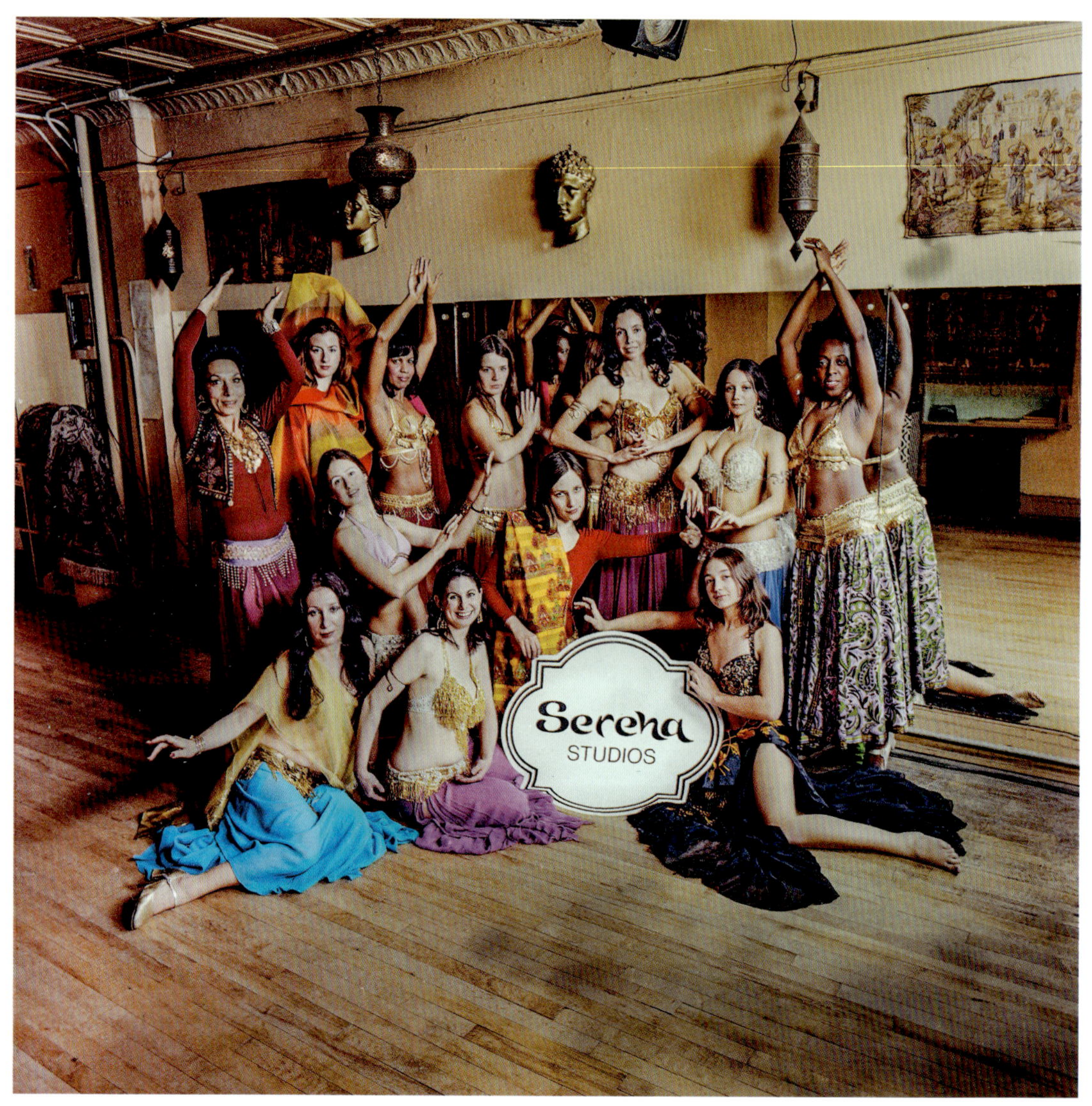

Serena Studios, Inc., New York, New York, 1972-75

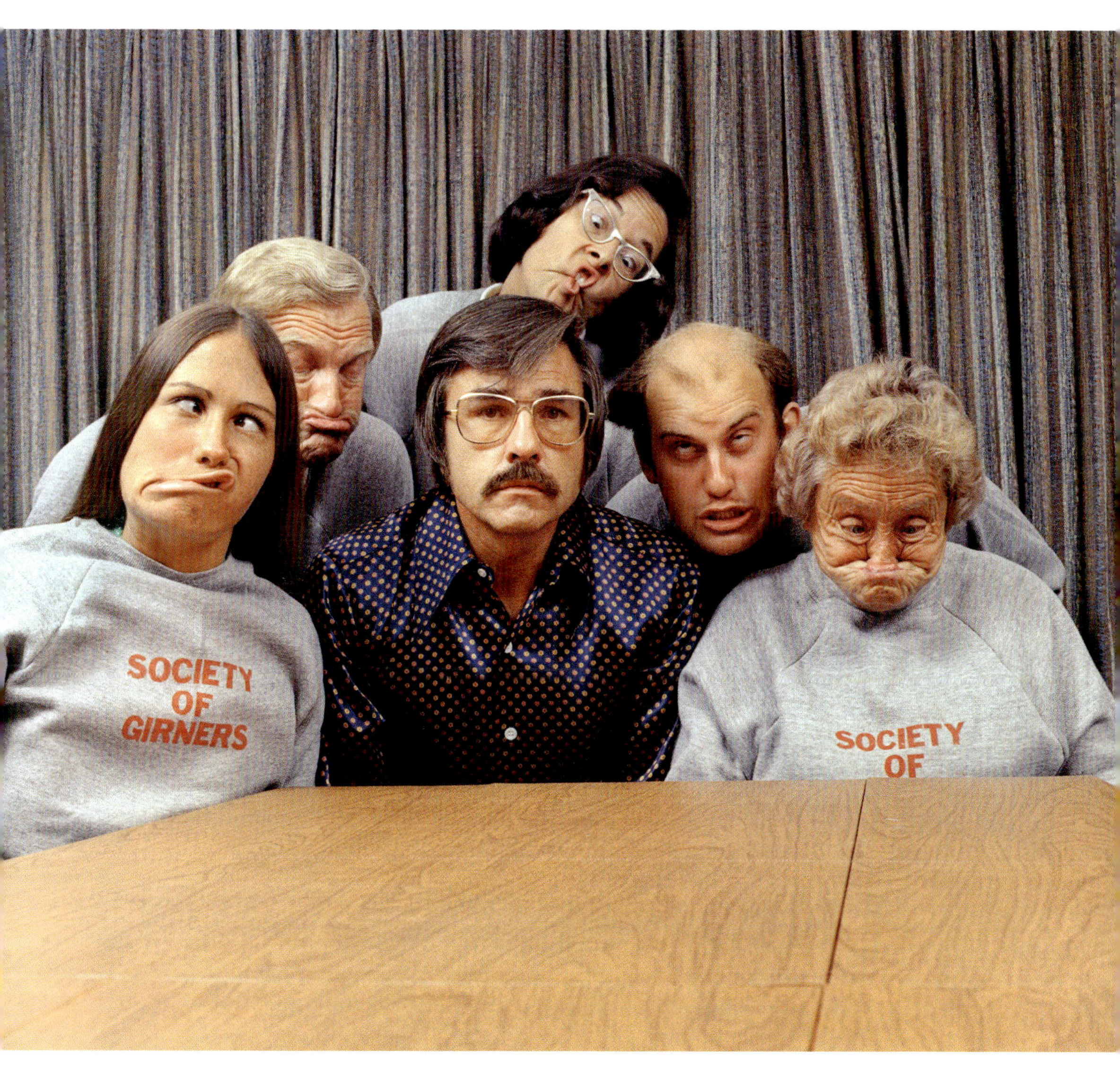

Gary Owens Society of Girners (G.O.S.O.G.), Hollywood, California, 1972-75

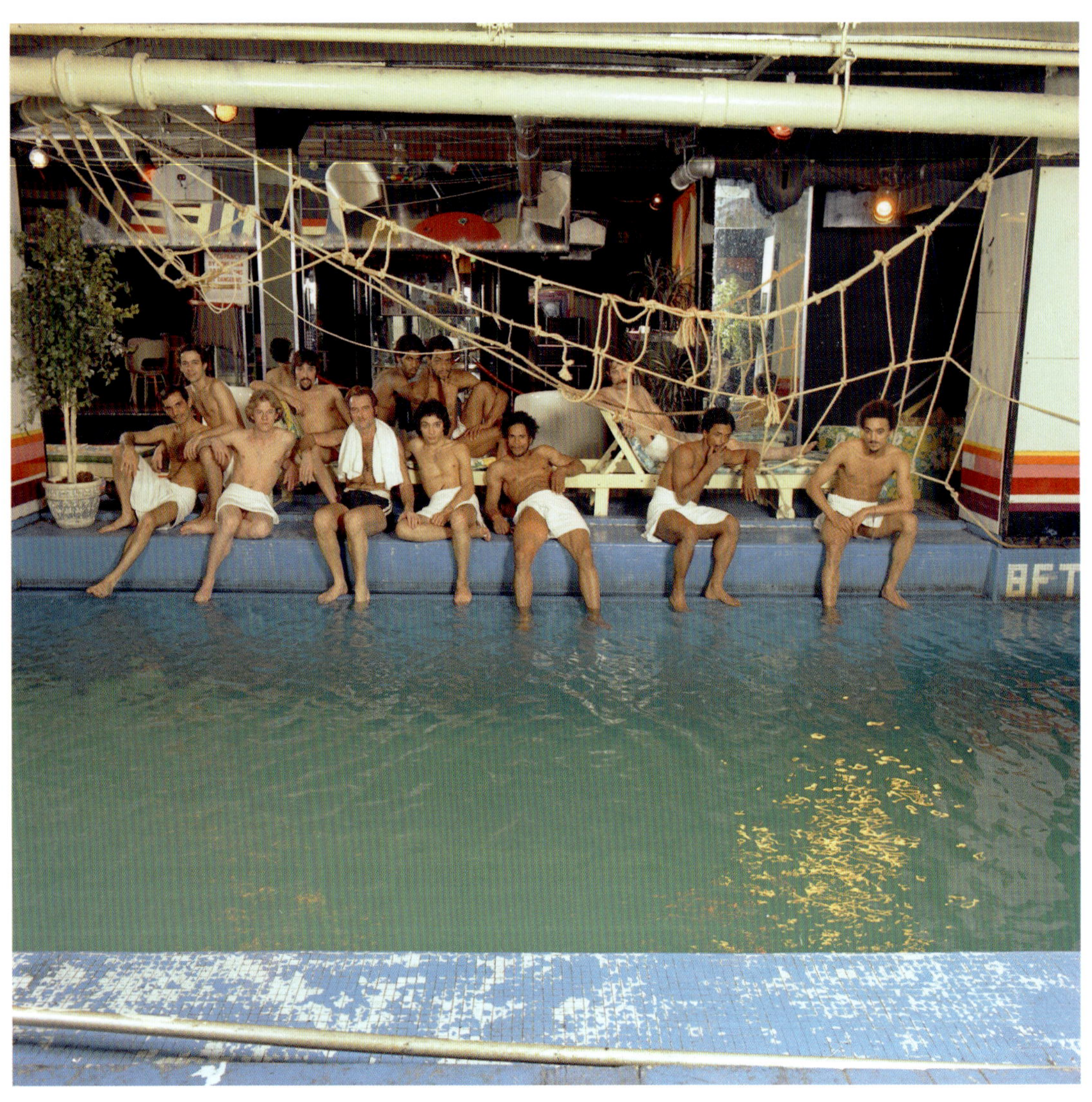

Continental Baths, New York, New York, 1972-75

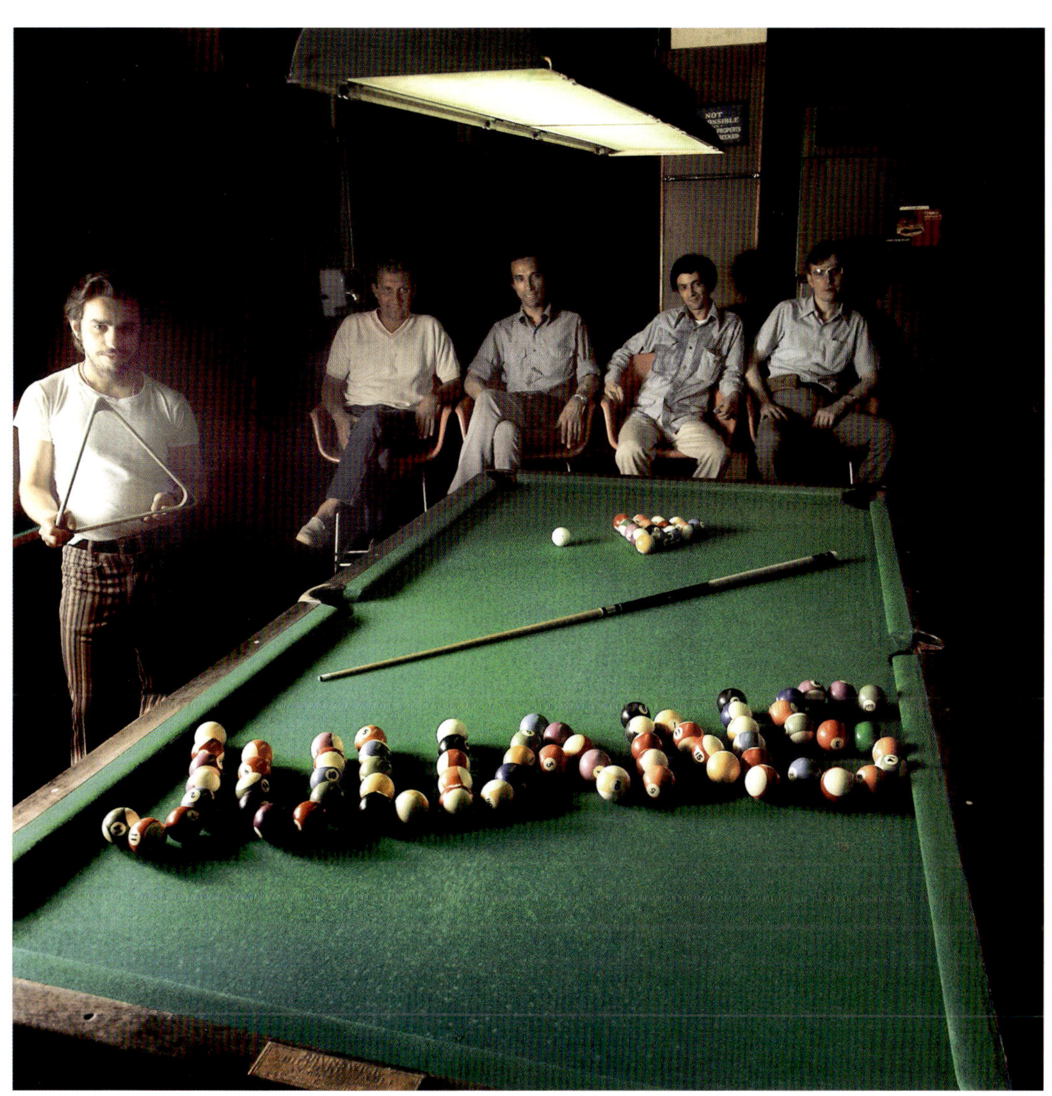

Julian Billiard Academy, New York, New York, 1972-75

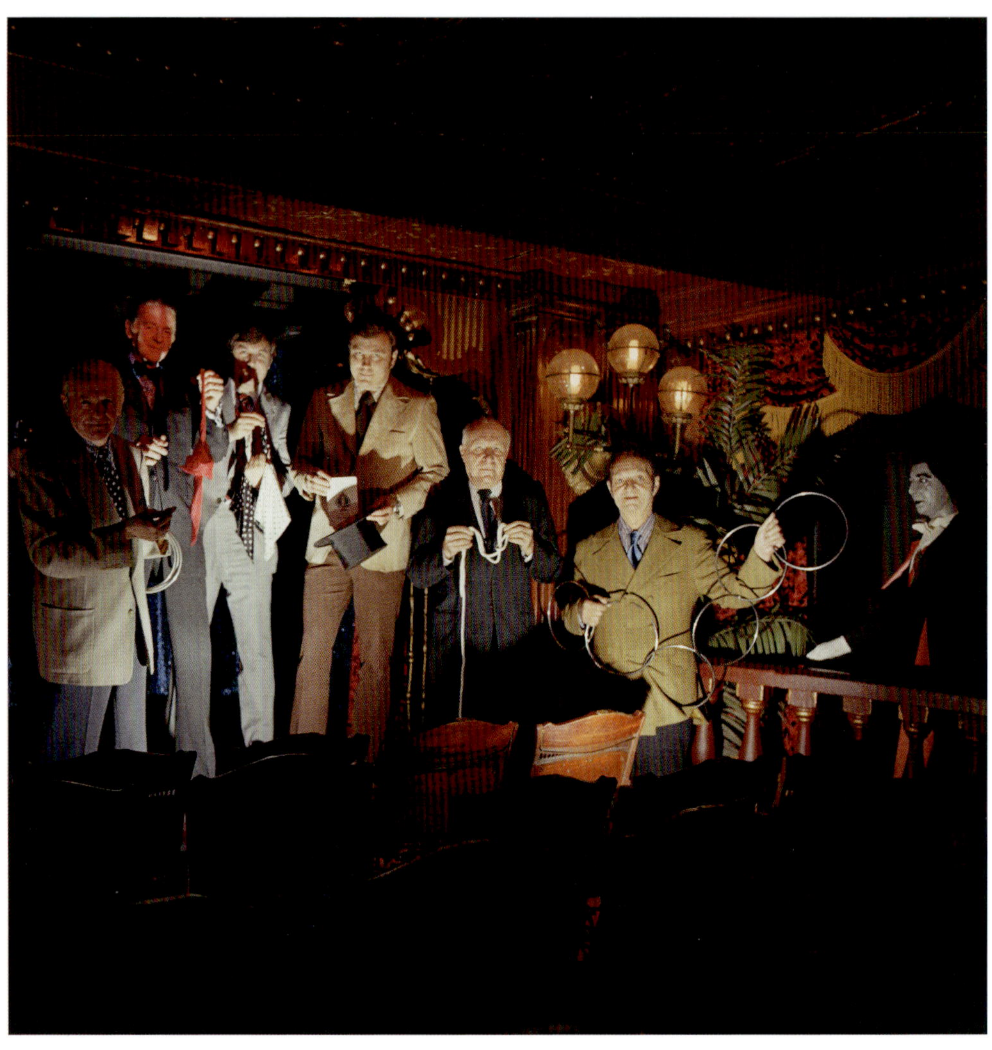

The Magic Castle, Hollywood, California, 1972-75

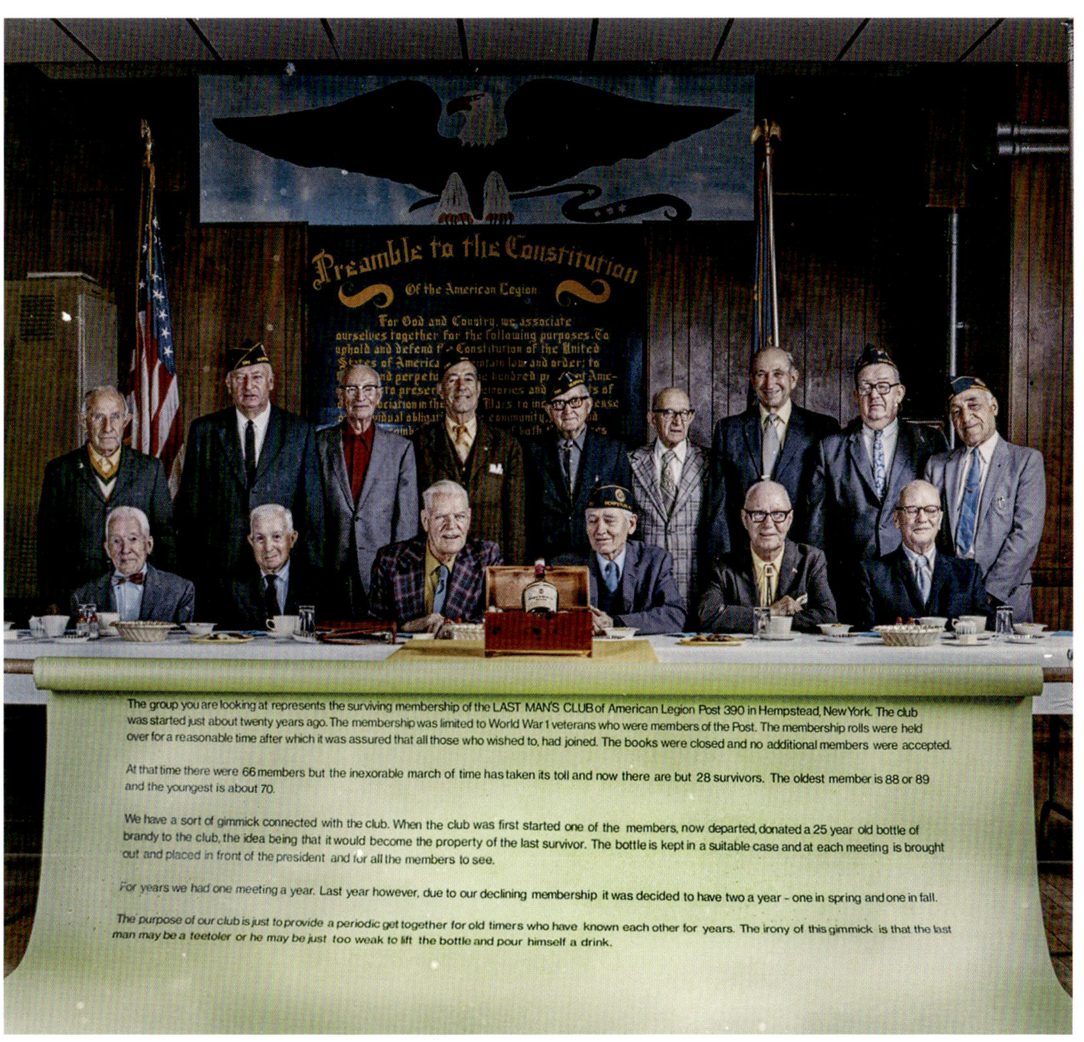

The Last Man's Club, Hempstead Post 390, American Legion, Hempstead, New York, 1972-75

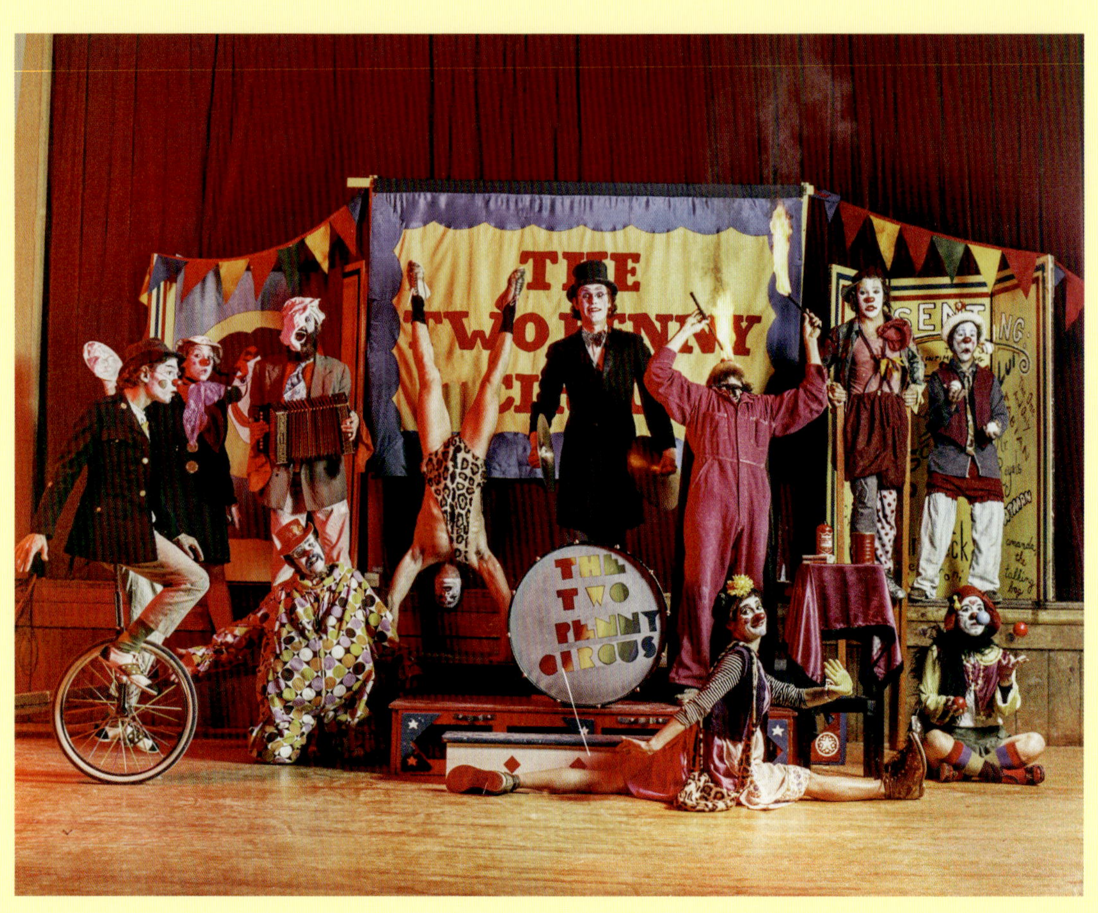

The Two Penny Circus, Goddard College, Vermont, 1972-75

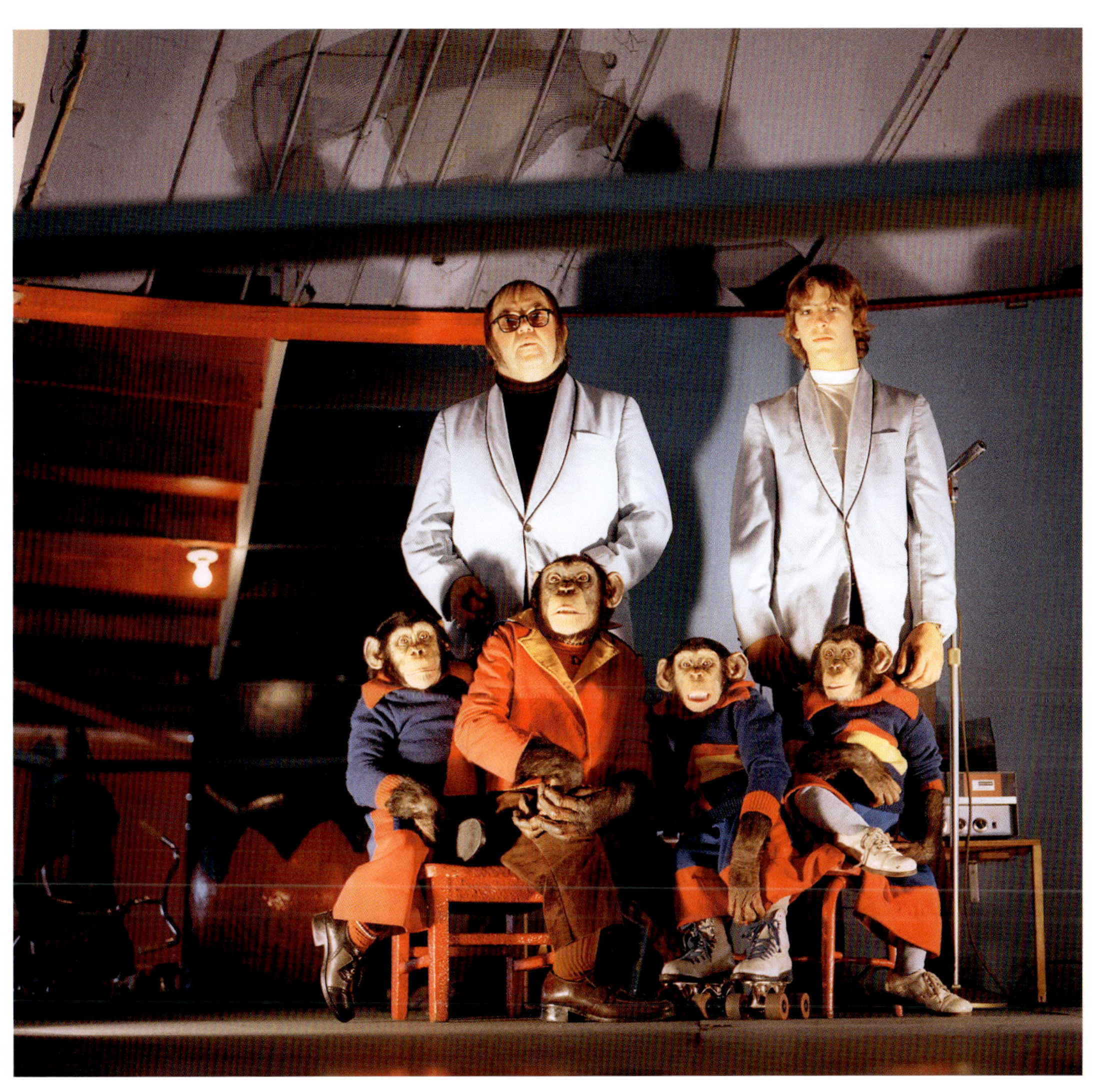

Lipko Comedy Chimps, Zanesville, Ohio, 1972-75

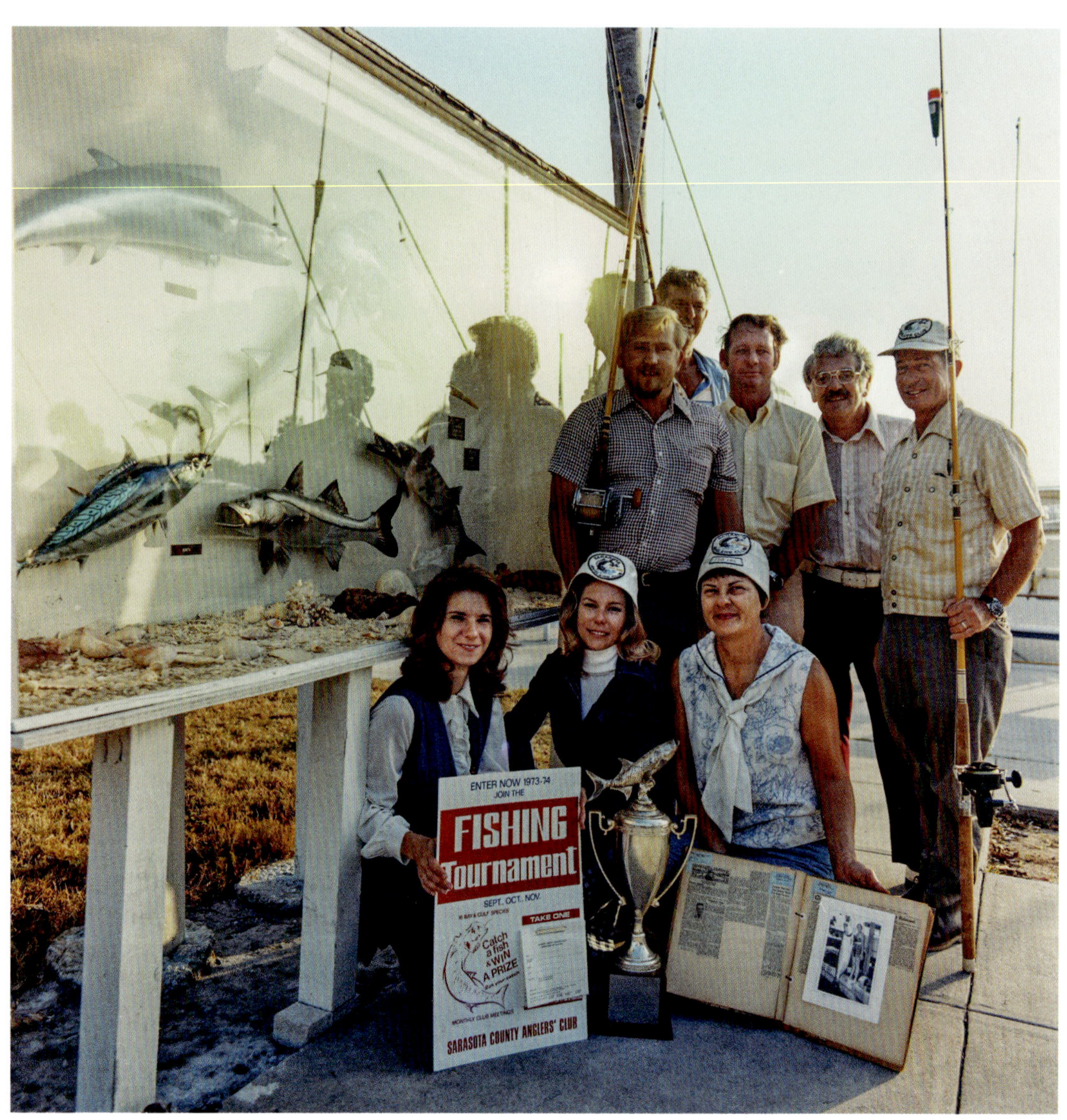

Sarasota County Anglers Club, Sarasota, Florida, 1972-75

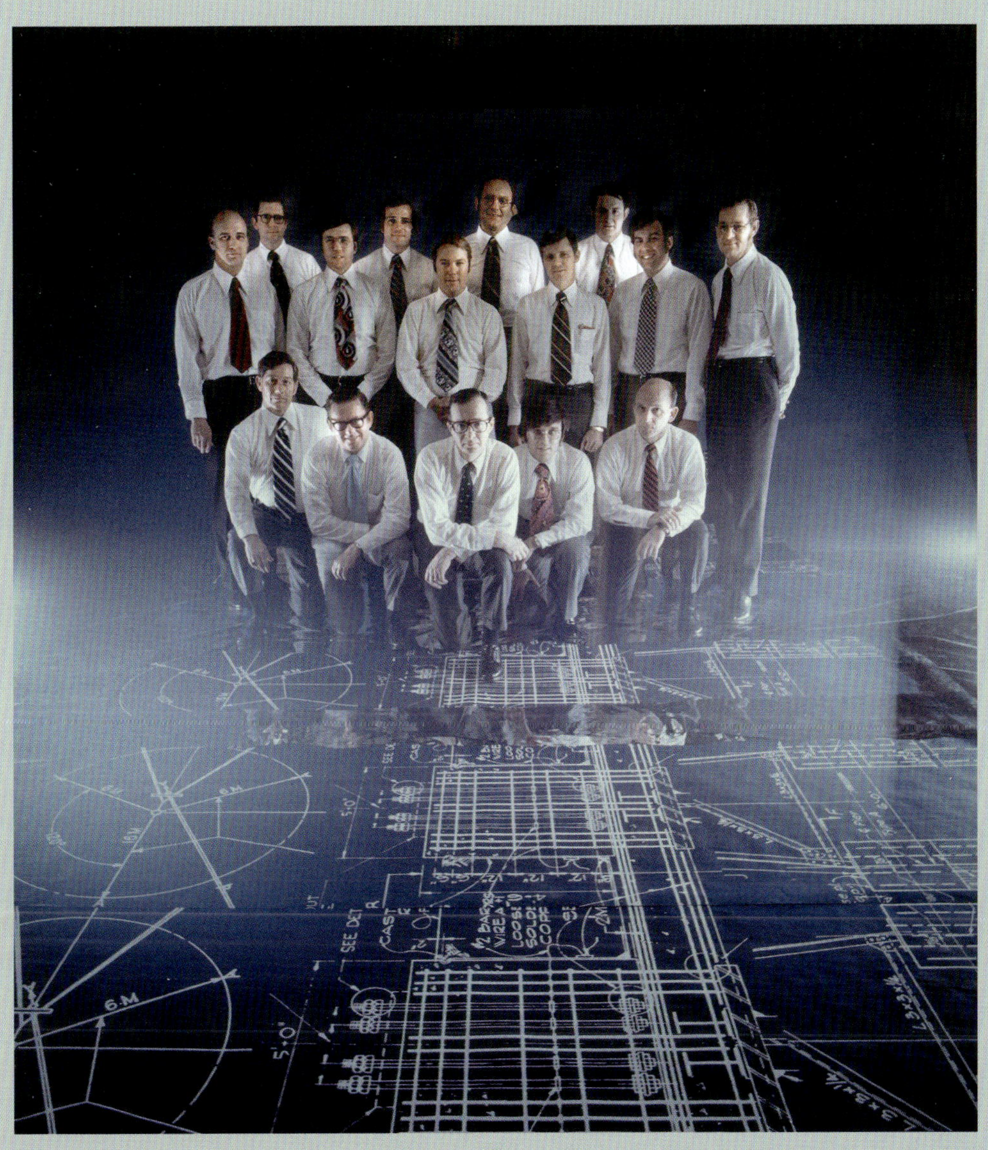

Product Managers, A.I.&I. Long Lines, Somerset, New Jersey, 1972-75

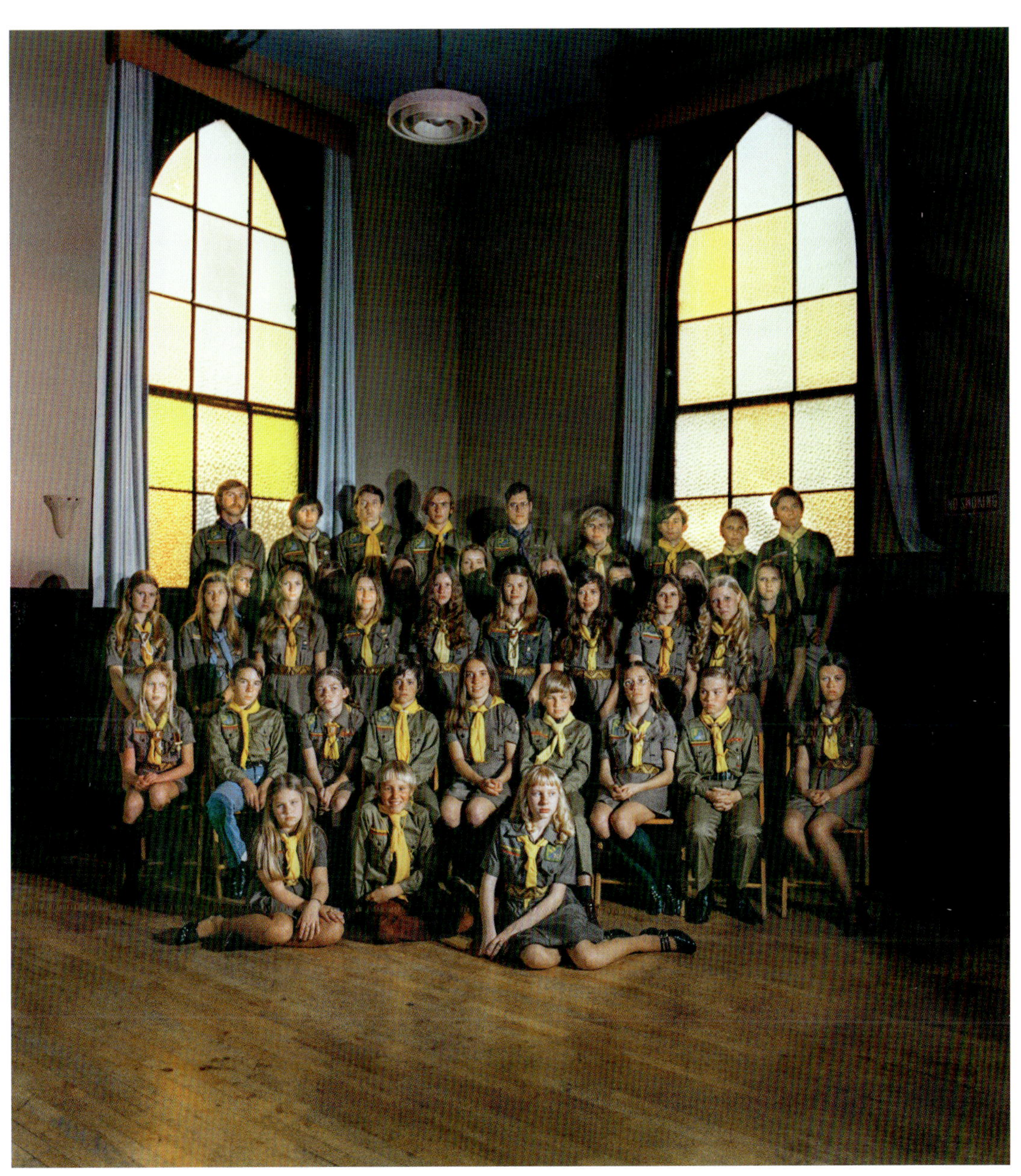

Lithuanian Scouts Association, Inc., Rancho Palos Verdes, California, c. 1972-75

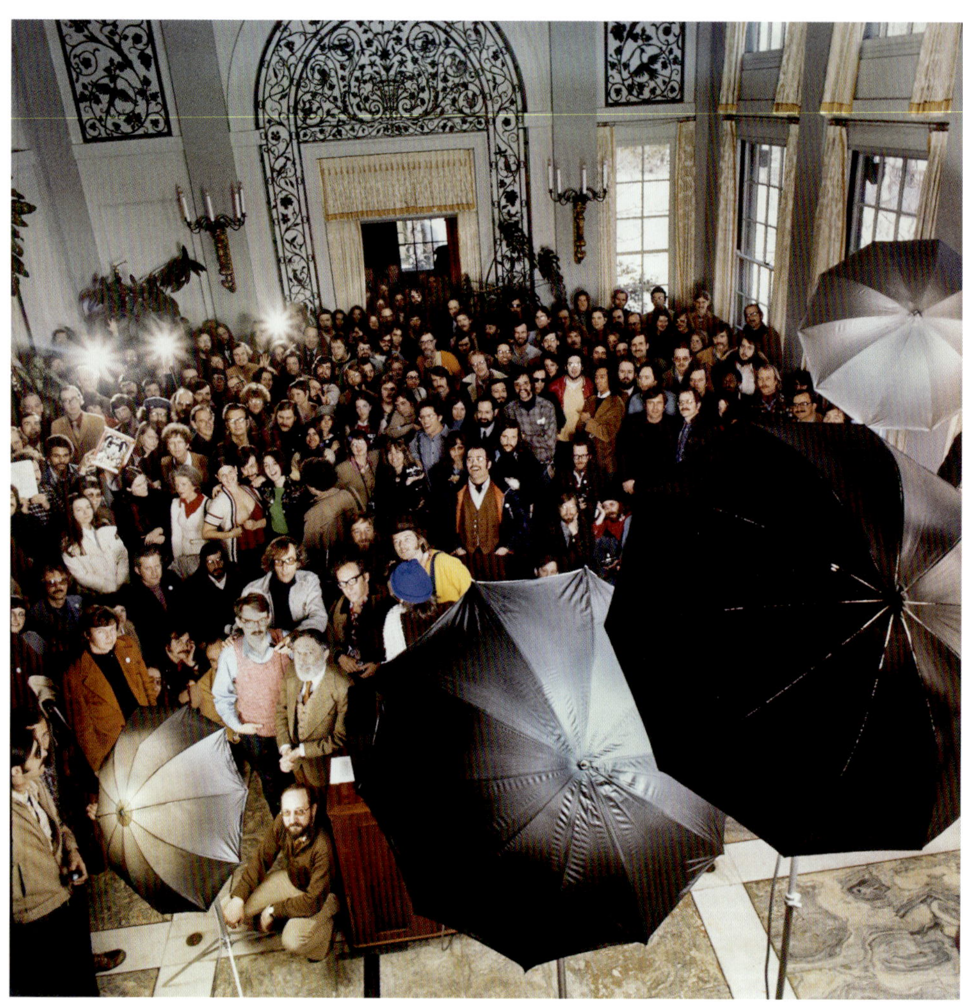

Society for Photographic Education (S.P.E.), New York, New York, 1972-75

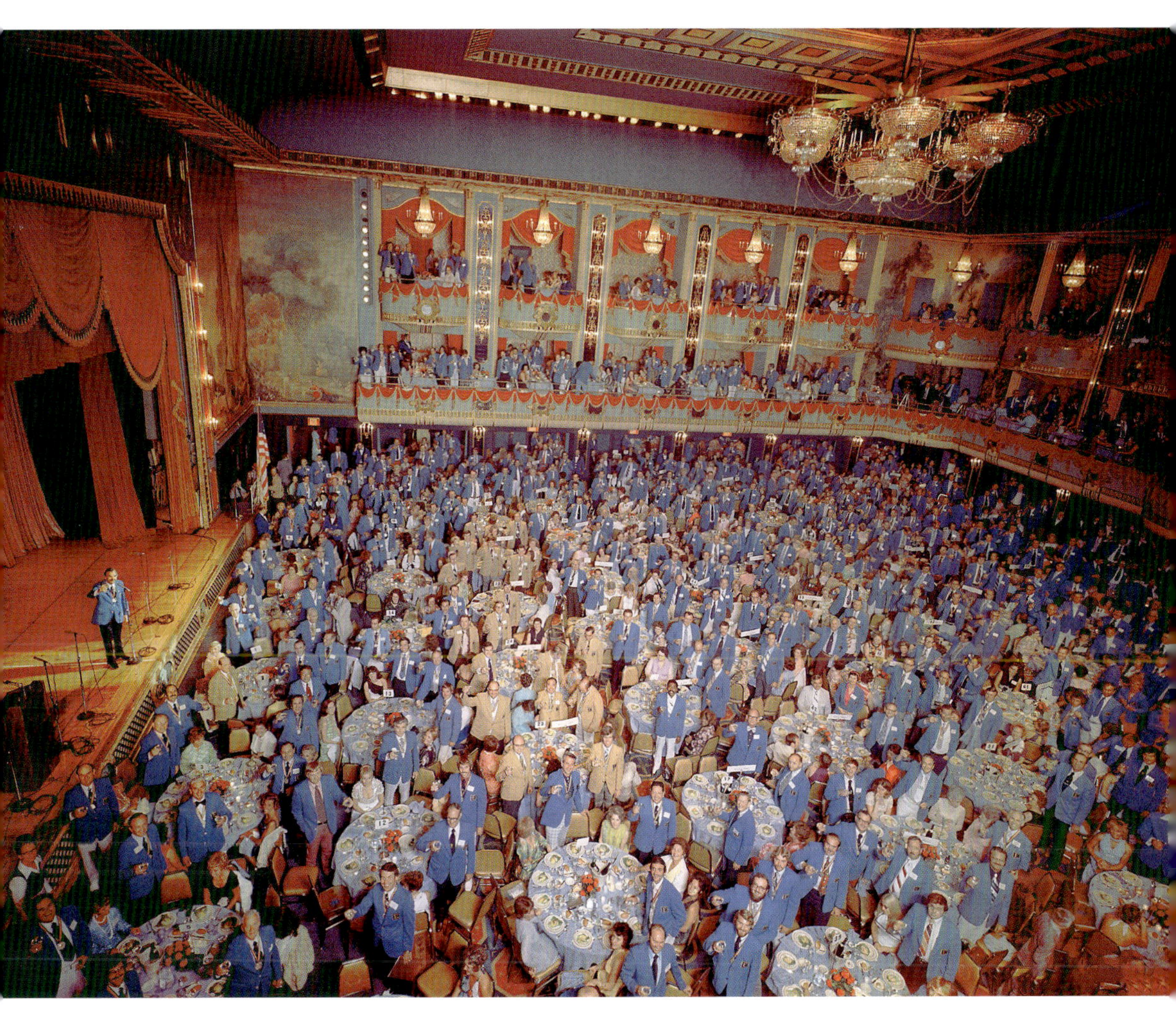

Electrolux, A Consolidated Foods Company, Stamford, Connecticut, 1972-75

OVERLEAF
Pugs, New York, New York, 1991

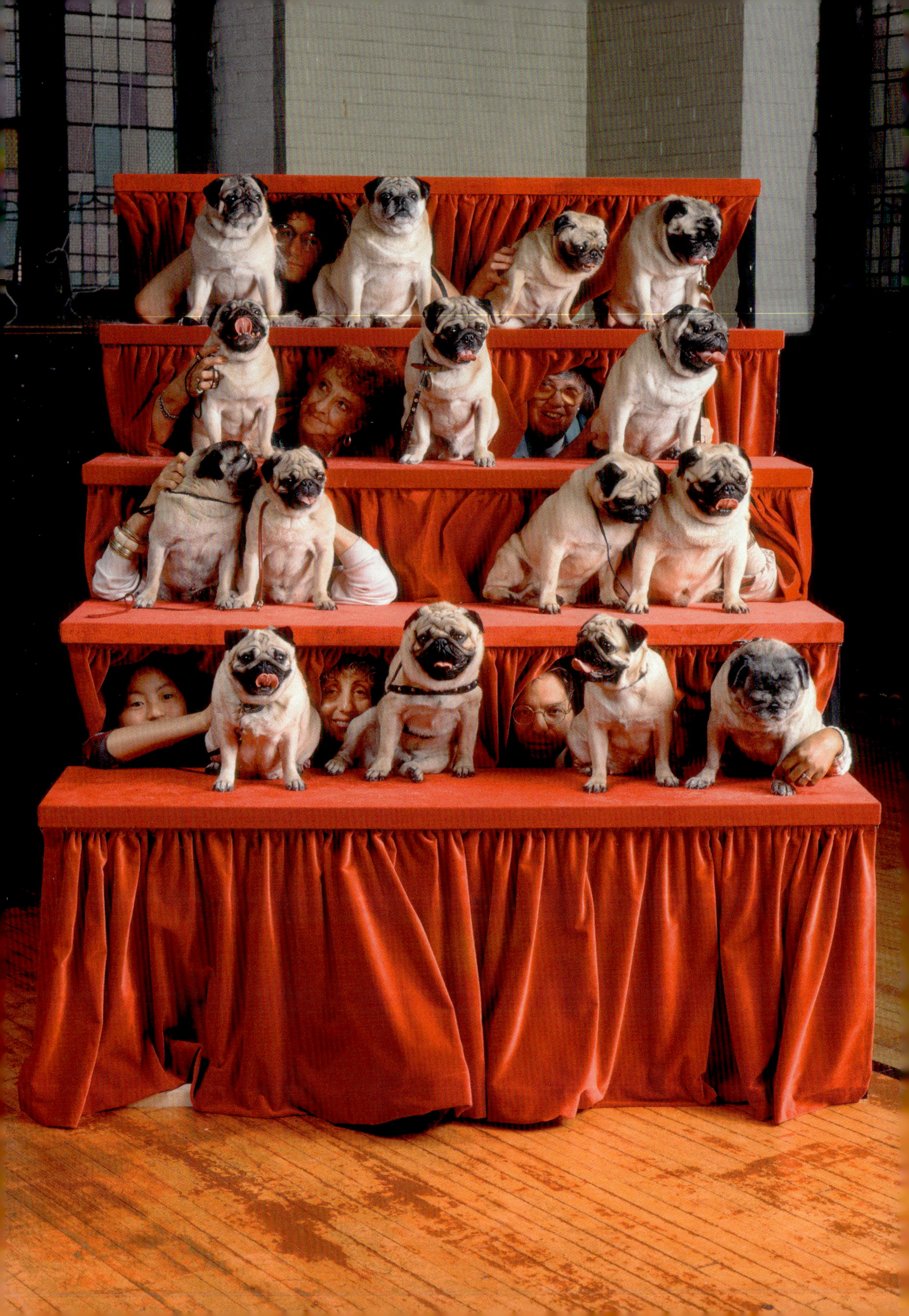

Fifty Years of Group Portraits
Kevin Moore

Neal Slavin won a National Endowment for the Arts grant in 1972 with a proposal titled "Group Portraits of American Organizations." He pursued this project for three and a half years, traveling, researching, and photographing all kinds of groups: clubs, labor unions, professional associations, as well as more recherché subcultures, such as male bathhouse members, pool sharks, and strippers. The series was published in 1976 as *When Two or More Are Gathered Together*—a title seeming to call for an answer. What happens when two or more are gathered together? Slavin's response was a boisterous series of 65 photographs, each accompanied by an information page detailing aspects of the groups pictured, including size of membership, officers, mission, eligibility, history, and outstanding achievements. "I envision a work that communicates the desire to belong in America in the mid-1970s and the conflicts caused by that wish," Slavin wrote in a "Memo" dated June 5, 1973, which served as an introduction to the book. "In short, I want to photograph groups—they are the American icon."

A preview of the book was published in the May 1974 issue of *Camera*, which debuted a selection of images and an interview with the artist. In that interview, Slavin makes an unexpected reference to French sociologist Alexis de Tocqueville, who observed in his 1838 book *Democracy in America* that the citizens of the young country had a mania for forming associations. Tocqueville asserted that, for Americans, associations were an expression of a new social order, an advancement beyond the rigid hierarchies of Old Europe. By forming groups of all kinds, be they "religious, moral, serious, futile, restricted, enormous, or diminutive," Tocqueville opined, Americans were doing the essential work of forging democracy. While Tocqueville identified many problems with American democracy—notably, the oppression of Blacks and women—he saw groups as a uniquely innovative aspect of American society. Groups were, as Slavin later put it, "the American icon."

If Slavin's project had a ring of formal research, this might be explained by the fact that he had had a string of academic successes during the preceding years, studying Italian Renaissance painting at Oxford University and winning a Fulbright scholarship to Portugal. The Fulbright resulted in Slavin's first book of photographs, *Portugal*, published in 1971. But the serious tone of "Group Portraits of American Organizations" was by design. In a departure from black-and-white reportage, which was his medium in the Portuguese book and the lodestar of art photography at the time, Slavin conceived of his new series as a conceptual art project driven by method, parameters, and outcomes. First, he established a rudimentary set of guidelines, asking each group to wear uniforms and to bring to the shoot symbolic props or objects (if they had any) and to choose a meaningful location. And he had them fill out a nine-part questionnaire. Then Slavin did something unexpected: he asked them to pose themselves, reasoning, "no outsider knows the status and rank of each individual as well as the membership does." At that point, the portrait was in their hands.

While the method purported to be rational, even official, the results most often were not, and therein lies the allure. Into an arena of rigorous sociological investigation, Slavin invited chaos. Group members spontaneously waved, saluted, or flexed. Or they girned (made faces), squatted, and embraced, depending on their dynamic. Some are having fun and their actions, naturally, are funny (both funny ha-ha and funny peculiar). But the funniest images are arguably the ones approached in a spirit of resolute sobriety, made quirkier by details of dress or setting: expressionless Star Trek conventioneers in garish homemade costumes; the Third Basic Combat Training Brigade with faces hidden beneath grotesque gas masks; members of the International Twins Association wearing identical outfits.

The extended captions are also funny in just the same ways. These short texts, presented in the style of a dry corporate report, pulsate with the same riotous content as the pictures. The Disabled Veterans, for example, offer an award for "Amputee of the Year." The Twins Association is governed by "Co-Presidents Dale and Dean Vaughn" and "Co-Vice-Presidents Torry and Terry Collinson." The Elks Lodge has an "Exalted Ruler," an "Esteemed Leading Knight," and an "Esteemed Loyal Knight." Some of the groups are simply funny in the peculiar sense. Into this category fall the dwarf lady wrestlers, the chimp trainers, and the circus clowns, modern-day extensions, perhaps, of the traveling freak show, described by one unkind reviewer in the 1970s as "bizarre and off-putting groups." (Slavin, who embeds within the groups, remains adamant on the point that, yes, the portraits have humor but the humor is communal—shared within the group.)

But there are more layers to these photographs. Indeed, many are not funny at all and embody serious social purpose. There are coalitions for women's labor, whose focus is on legislation for equal rights and pay. The Cemetery and Greens Union not only offers scholarships to the children of workers, the president did a fourteen-day hunger strike and jail time over a contract dispute. More poignant, perhaps, is the Lady Dorothy Circle, whose original purpose was conservation and charity work but whose recent mission is to take care of their elderly members. And the Last Man's Club, founded by World War I veterans, meets once a year for a dinner where members swap stories and then "quietly leave," pondering who among them will be the last man and the last of the group.

Some of the groups have pulled off some astonishing achievements. The Associated Blind designed the American flag in Braille. The S.S. *Skate*, a nuclear-attack submarine, steamed under pack ice to the North Pole, where she surfaced to "commit the ashes of the famed explorer Sir George Hubert Wilkins to the Arctic." Or how about the remarkable history of Warner Communications, represented by its Women's Intramural Softball Team? The company started as a funeral business, got into parking lots, then into cleaning, publishing, and construction, eventually acquiring talent agencies and Warner Brothers and monopolizing the entertainment industry.

An undeniable nostalgia pervades the photographs, most evident in the ill-fitting, brightly colored clothes, the gaudy interiors, and the outdated cars. While other photographers, such as Diane Arbus and Elaine Mayes, had treated similar subjects, Slavin chose color. At the time, the choice was radical enough that Slavin felt compelled to justify it, noting in the book's introduction, "A gold trophy can mean something different from a silver trophy and the distinction cannot be rendered in black and white." Color now seems an essential element of Slavin's project, as it not only distinguished between gold and silver, it drove headlong into the carnivalesque details of the sexually-liberated, politically-agitated 1970s. Walker Evans had famously described color as "vulgar." Slavin's response, taking in the social landscape of the 1970s, was "color is the solution."

Color photography was uncharted territory, at least in terms of its use in the rarefied world of art photography. Numerous photographers were at work testing the potential of color during the 1970s and the decade before: Garry Winogrand, Helen Levitt, and Mitch Epstein explored color in street photography; Stephen Shore investigated color photography's vernacular associations in postcards and drugstore prints; Robert Heinecken tested color as a medium of advertising and propaganda; and William Eggleston used color to explore tender and banal moments in the American South. But color held negative associations among the art photography cohort, inescapably conjuring commercial uses in advertising and popular culture, movies and television, family snapshots, vacation slideshows, and—tricky for Slavin—the Sears Portrait Studio. Black-and-white photography was still the medium of serious moral purpose, the messenger of news, social injustices and probing human insights. Color had a nuance of entertainment, fantasy, or, just the opposite, everyday life, nothing special at all.

Slavin distinguished his series as art in several distinct ways. First, he declared it so, applying for an NEA grant and emphasizing the project's rigorous method and sociological intent. This was not commercial studio portraiture but a serious study, using photography as an essential tool. Slavin's prospectus ("Memo") reads like a science brief, with headings such as "Stereotypes and Clichés," "Method," and "Possible Outcome." Close readers may have detected a hint of irony in the wording, but the value remained the same: to discover, in pure visual terms, the ways people negotiated their individuality with their desire to belong. Second, the complexity and scale of Slavin's orchestrations were mind-boggling. Not unlike film production, involving schedules, technical apparatuses, and masses of people, the photographer went to great lengths to get the single shot. He climbed ladders, boarded boats, shouted through megaphones—whatever the situation demanded. Last, there was the coaxing of subjects, all the relaxing, seducing, and encouraging that portrait photographers since the early days of the medium have had to master in order to get their subjects to perform some version of their true selves, or simply their selves in that moment. As with any artistic endeavor, the devil is in the details, and subjects like children and animals have always been particularly devilish.

Despite subsequent success as a filmmaker, Slavin remains known as one of the great group portrait photographers and continues to be engaged to apply his skills. This new revised edition of *When Two or More Are Gathered Together* contains fifty-four additional photographs taken since the original book was published. The new subjects, ranging from stock brokers to shark feeders and civil rights activists, suggest, in subtle ways, how the world has changed over the last fifty years and how organizations have remained indicators of those changes. The very existence of the Roving Leaders, the American Gold Star Mothers, and the Downtown Independent Democrats suggests a world of ongoing struggle against social injustices and violent conflict.

As it goes, there have been minor yet necessary changes to the original book. Those intimately familiar with the first edition, or comparing the books side by side, will note that certain images have been replaced with variants, this the result of the sad reality of lost or damaged negatives. But the same sequence of the original sixty-five photographs and their commentary remains intact. Moreover, the language of groups—their names, titles, and descriptions—have significantly evolved over time as well. Words that in the 1970s were commonplace have now, to varying degrees, become offensive. For the most part, such language has been left as is, being an expression of the common attitudes of the time, also bearing in mind that this is how groups then self-identified and self-described. In that sense, this new edition of *When Two or More Are Gathered Together* hopes to challenge readers, especially younger ones, to imagine another time and mindset, a time not better nor worse than our own, but filled with the same aspirations, imagination and challenges, yet in a different historical context.

Certainly, over the last fifty years, the nature of groups has changed—how they organize, how they meet, where they meet, and what they meet for. Much of this activity now happens online, on platforms such as Instagram and TikTok. But in many cases, the online realm is a parallel space, a portal of introduction and information that interfaces with in-person assembly. No matter how they form, the reasons for groups have not changed much over time. Groups exist to express common identity, to provide companionship, offer support, and a sense of belonging. Groups also form to preserve, share, agitate, entertain, or simply to escape. In the fractured and often divisive times in which we live, exacerbated by politics, technology, and propaganda, groups have come to provide the social sustenance often missing from traditional outlets, such as jobs and families. Groups, with their processes of arguing, consensus building, and voting, are our common experience of working democracy.

Returning to Tocqueville, groups hold the essential power to maintain our democracy, for in unity there can be common purpose, common good. Groups are an expression of the fundamental values of American life, providing everyone with a place to belong, a voice, no matter their background or interests. Tyrants, whether they appear as men, money, or power, work to divide people. Americans must remember, now more than ever, that American democracy is a coalition of groups, and that groups, serious, futile, enormous, or diminutive, hold the key to our essential freedoms.

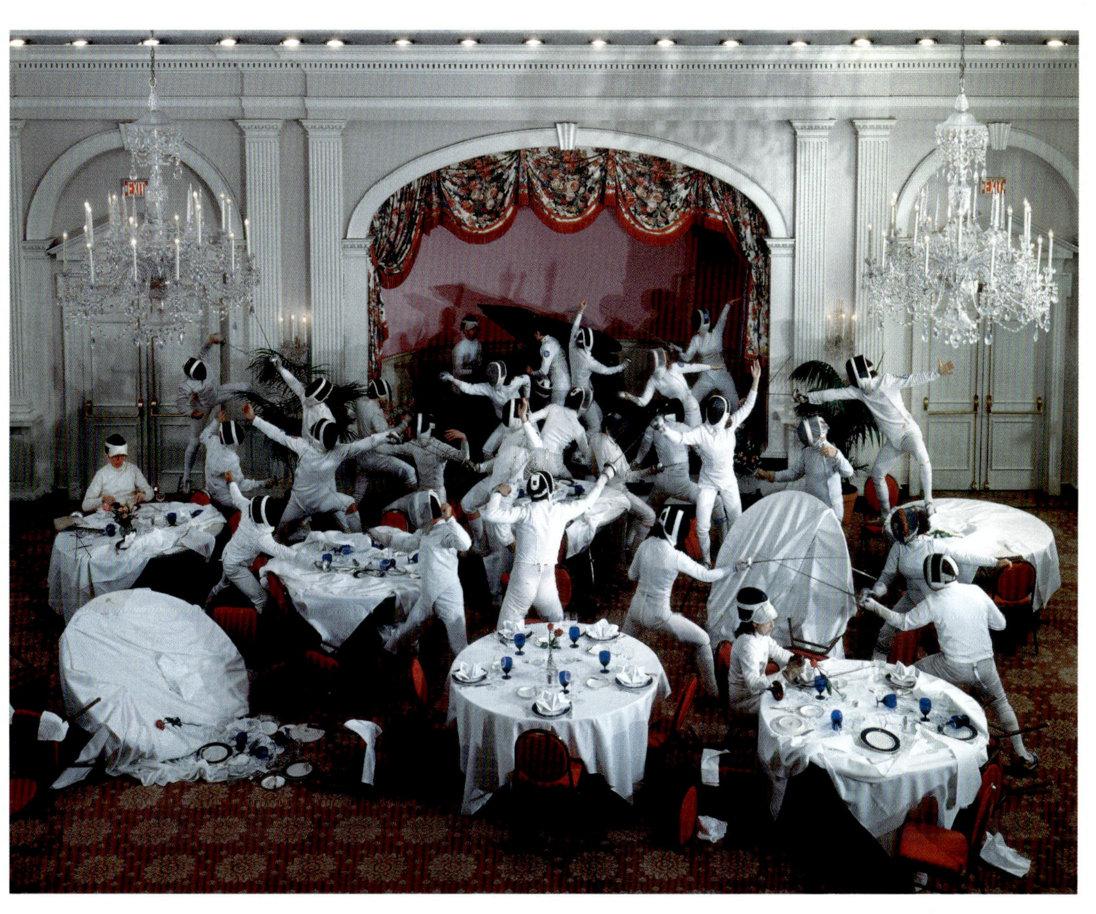

The D.C. Fencers Club, Washington, D.C., 1988

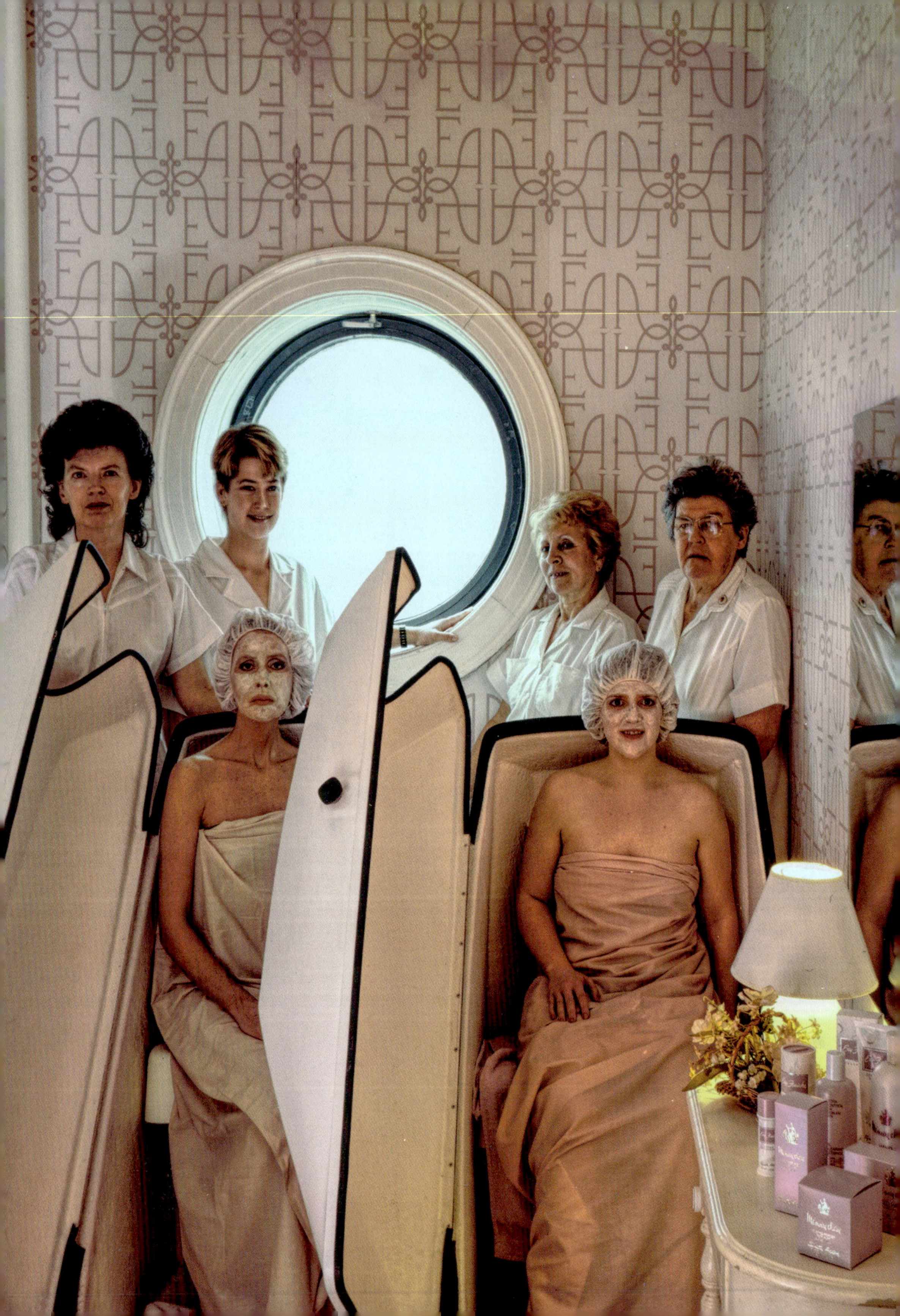

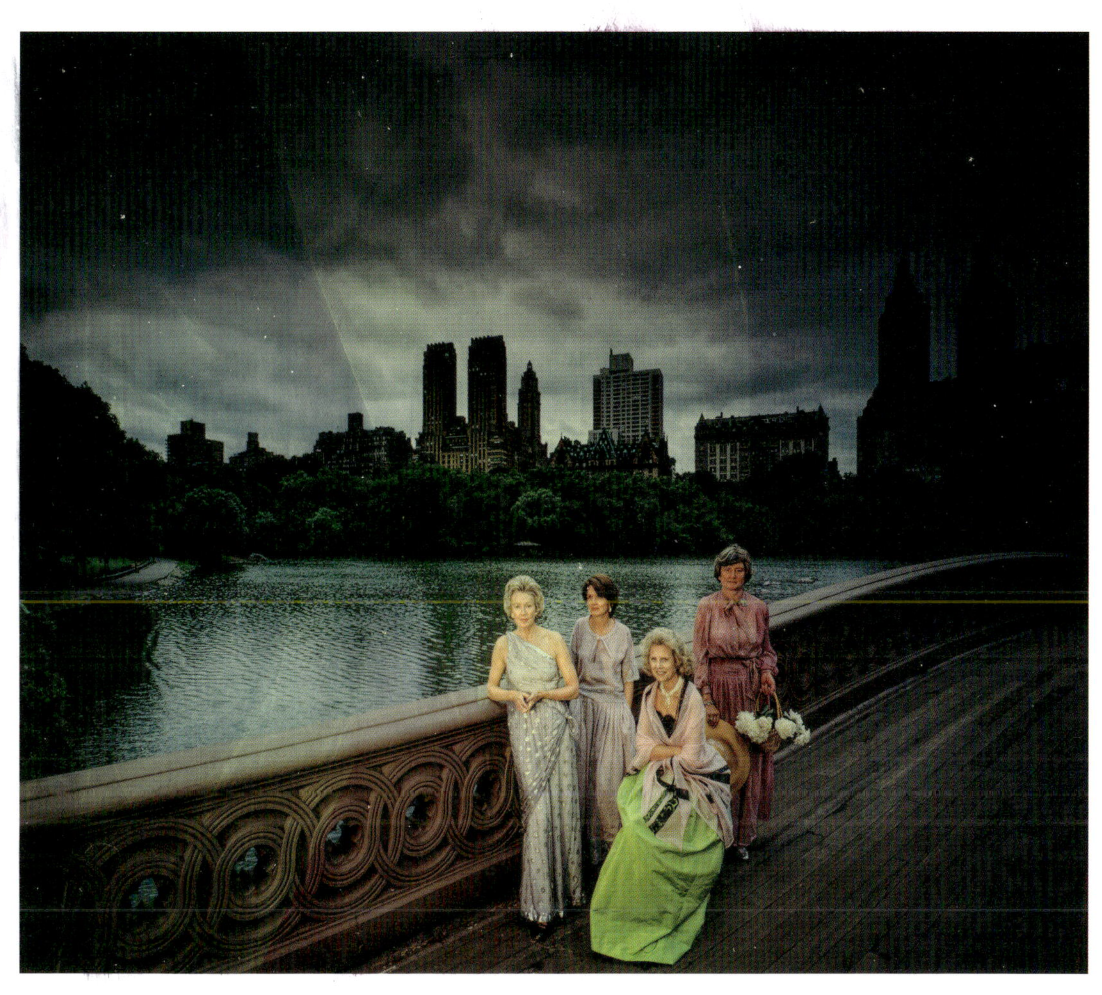

Benefactors of the Central Park Conservancy, New York, 1982

Elizabeth Arden Masseuses, Washington, D.C., 1987

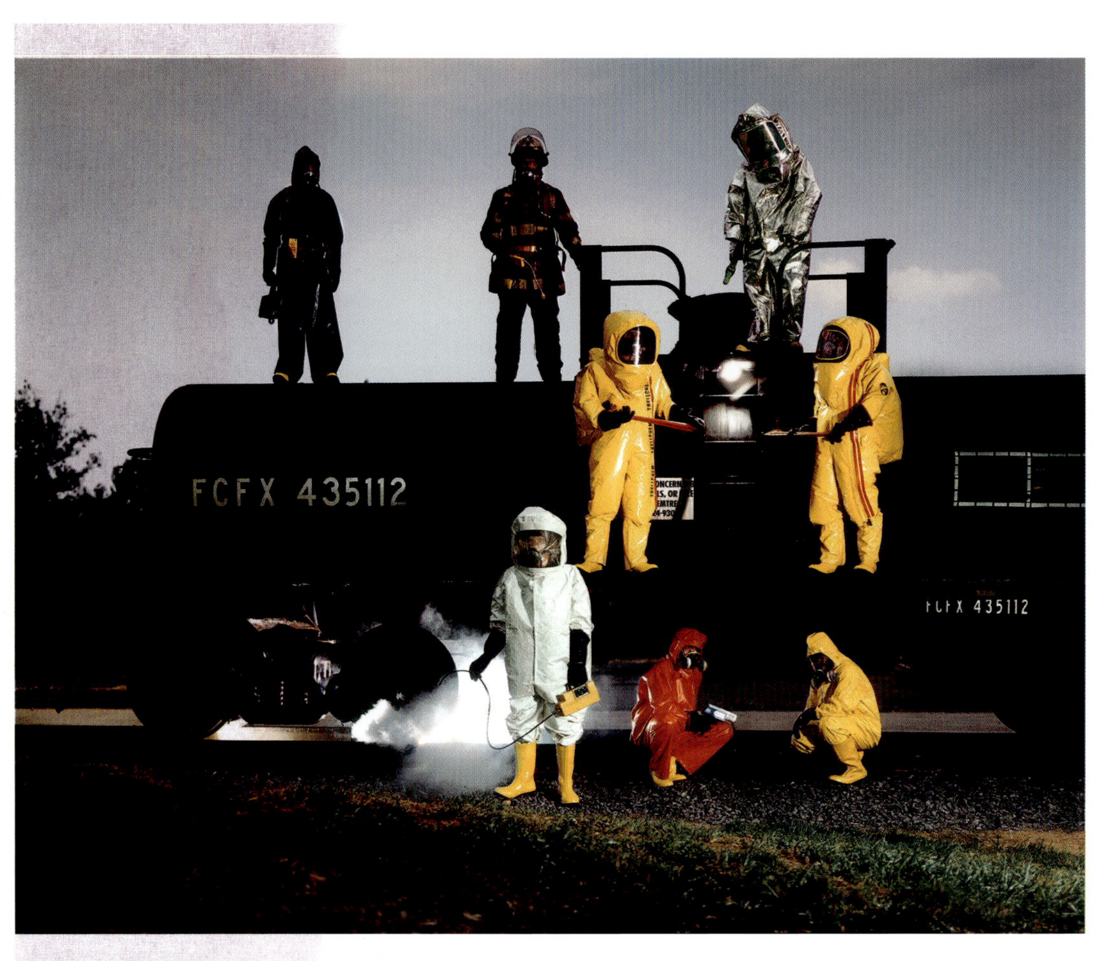

Hazardous Materials Response Team, Washington, D.C., 1988

RIGHT PAGE
Insect Scientists, New York, New York, c. 1990

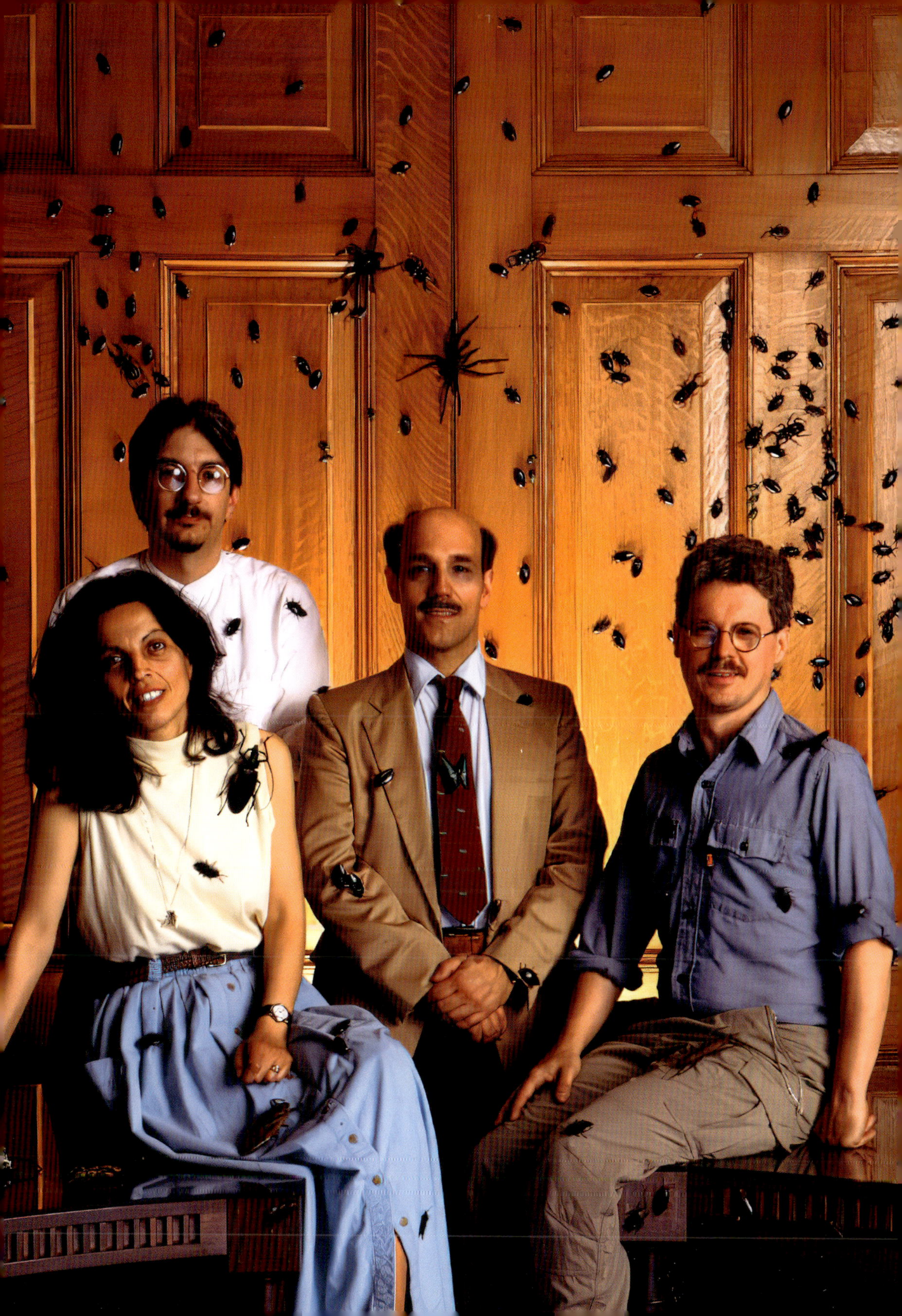

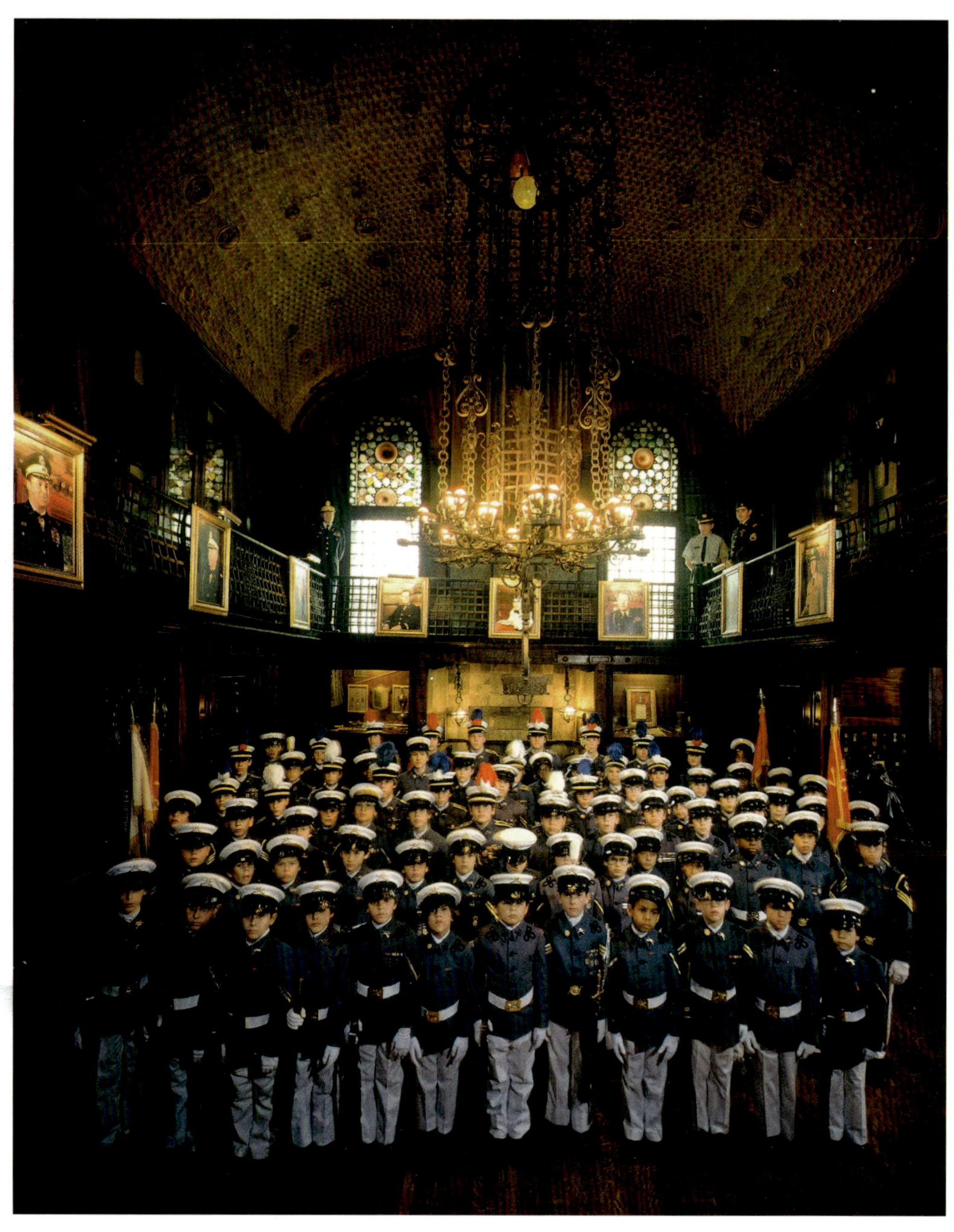

Knickerbocker Greys, New York, New York, c. 1990

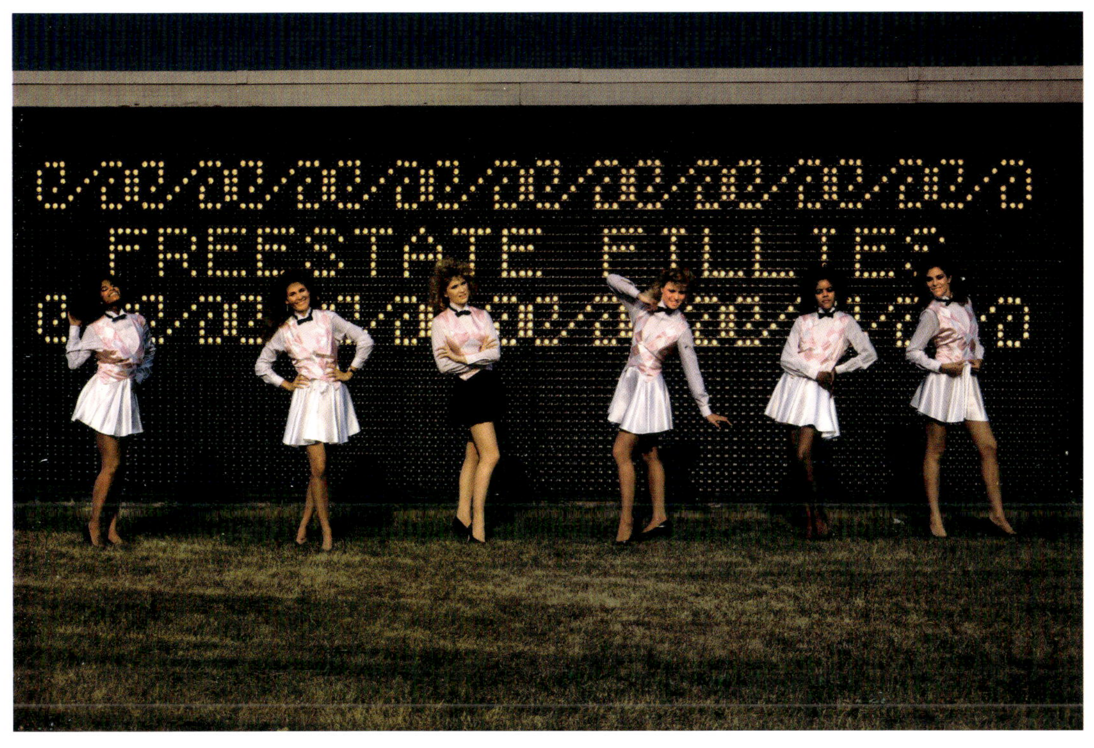

Freestate Fillies, Laurel, Maryland, 1987

OVERLEAF
New York Stock Exchange, New York, New York, 1986

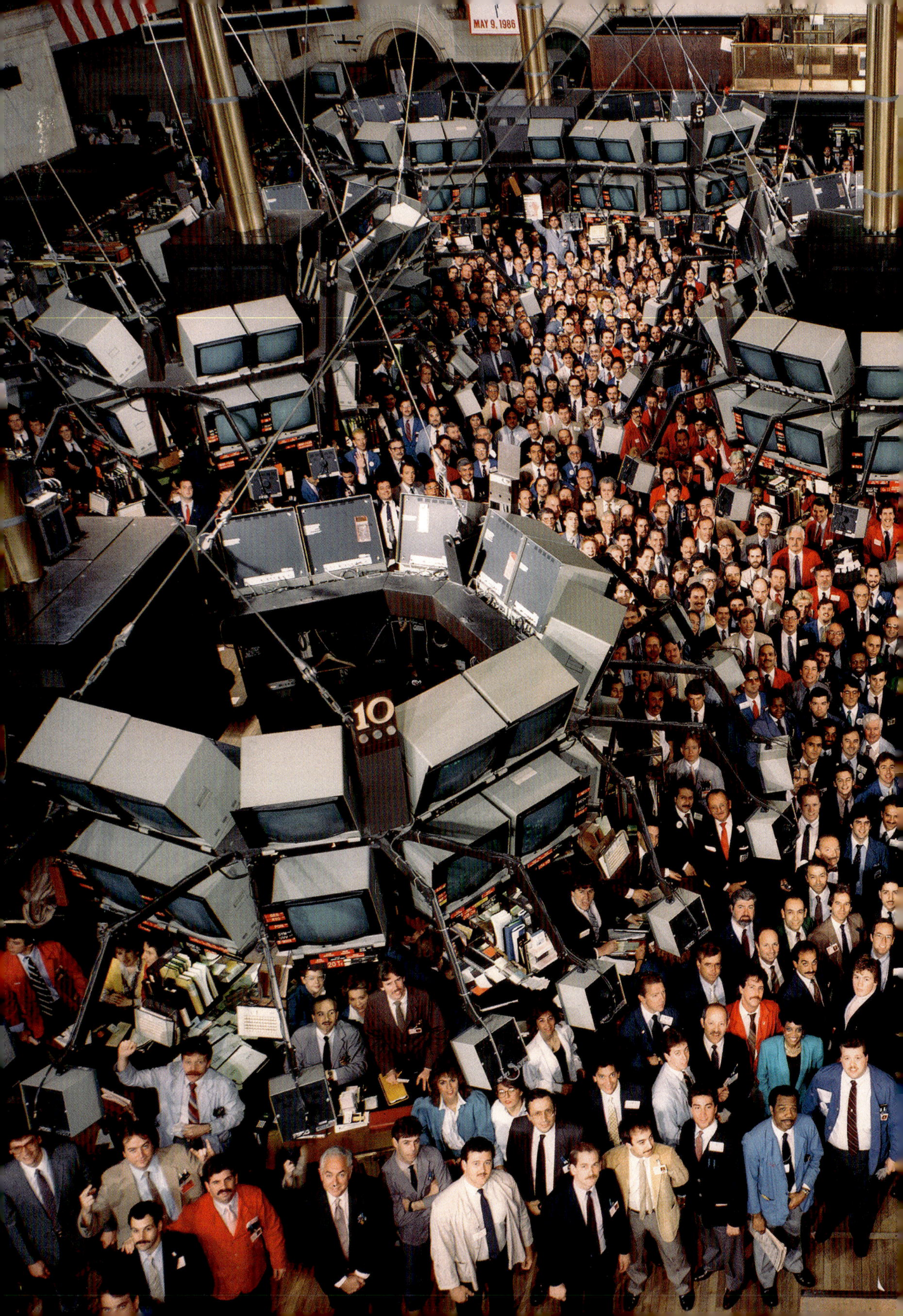
MAY 9, 1986

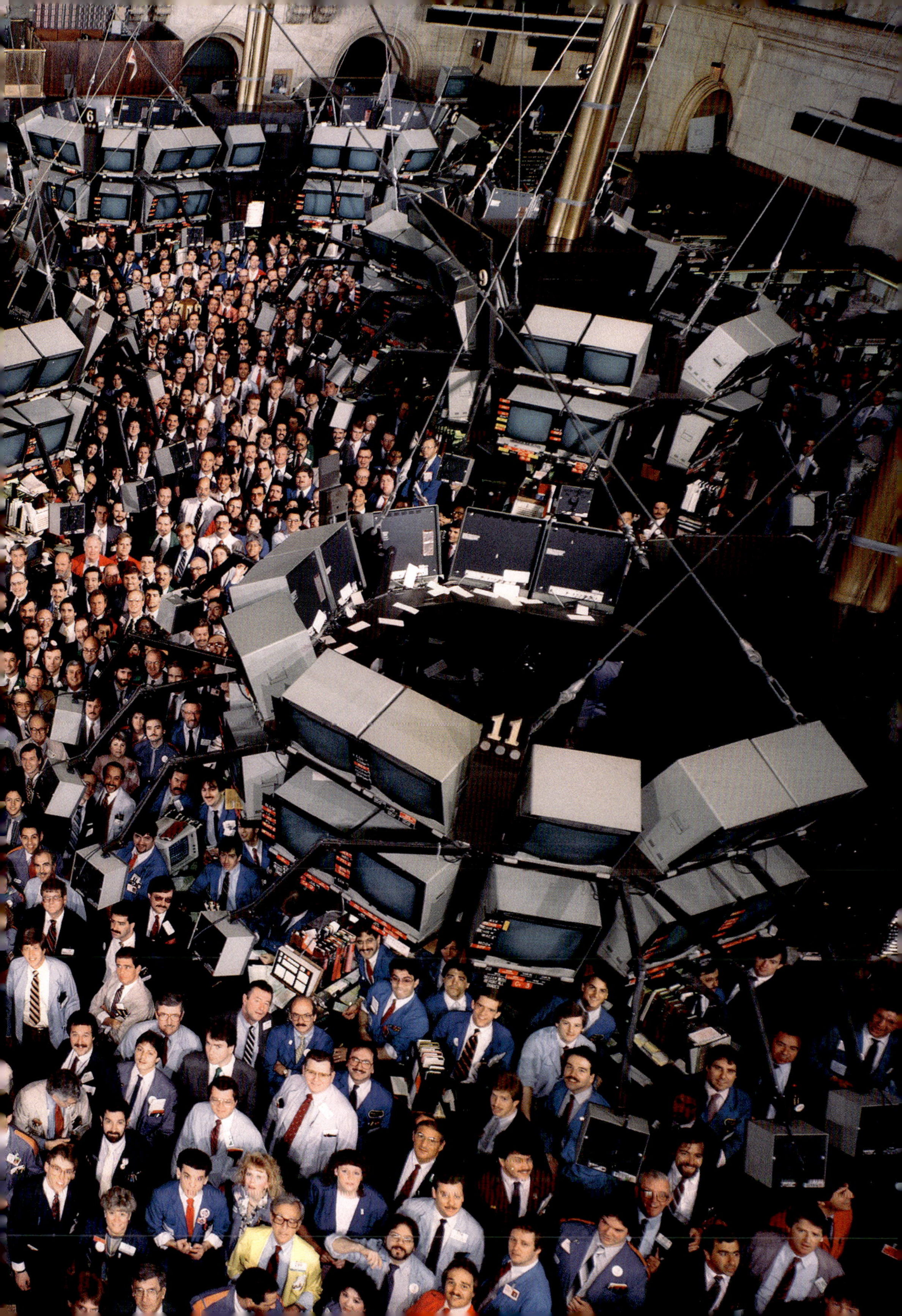

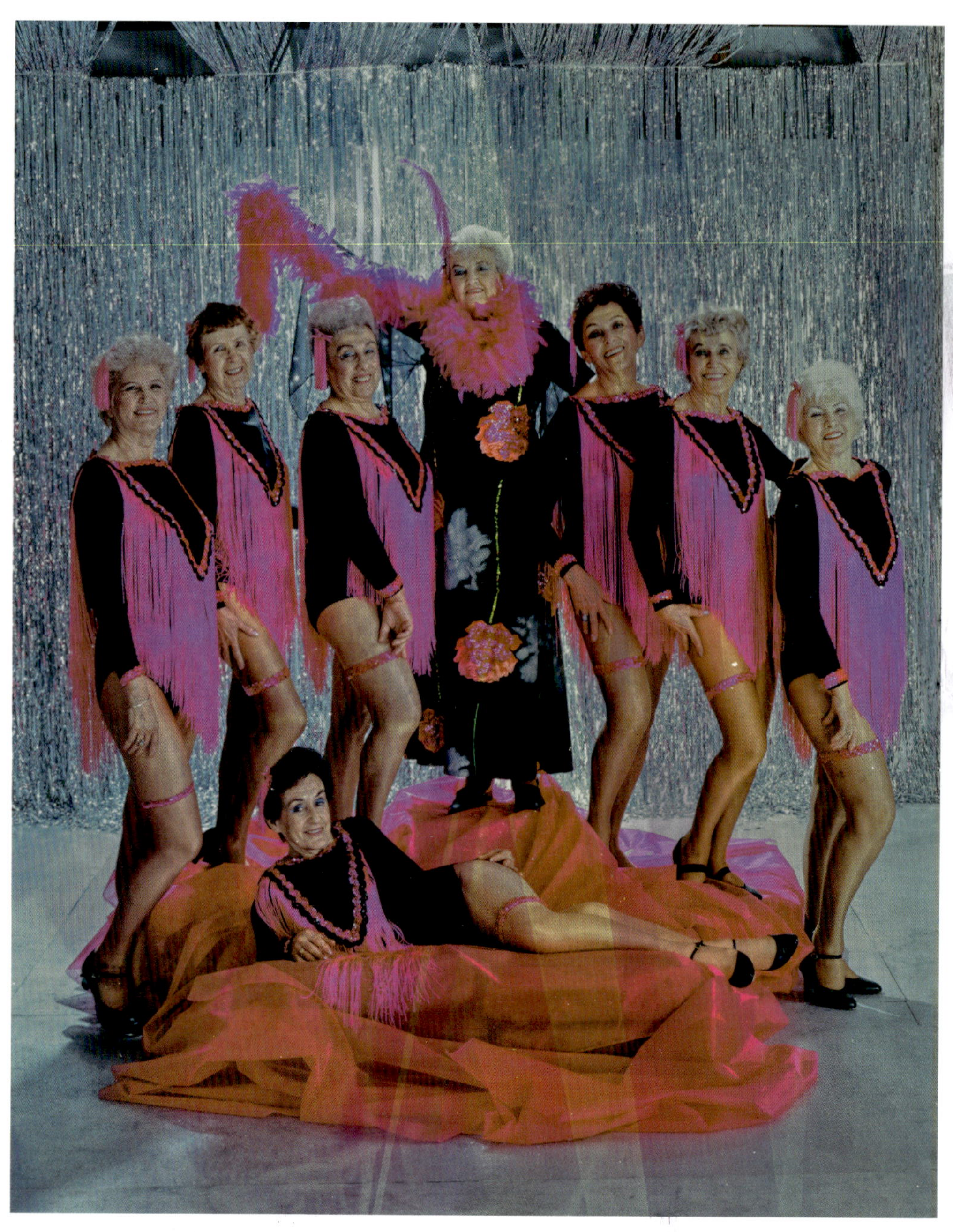

Golden Songsters, Nassau County, New York, 1989

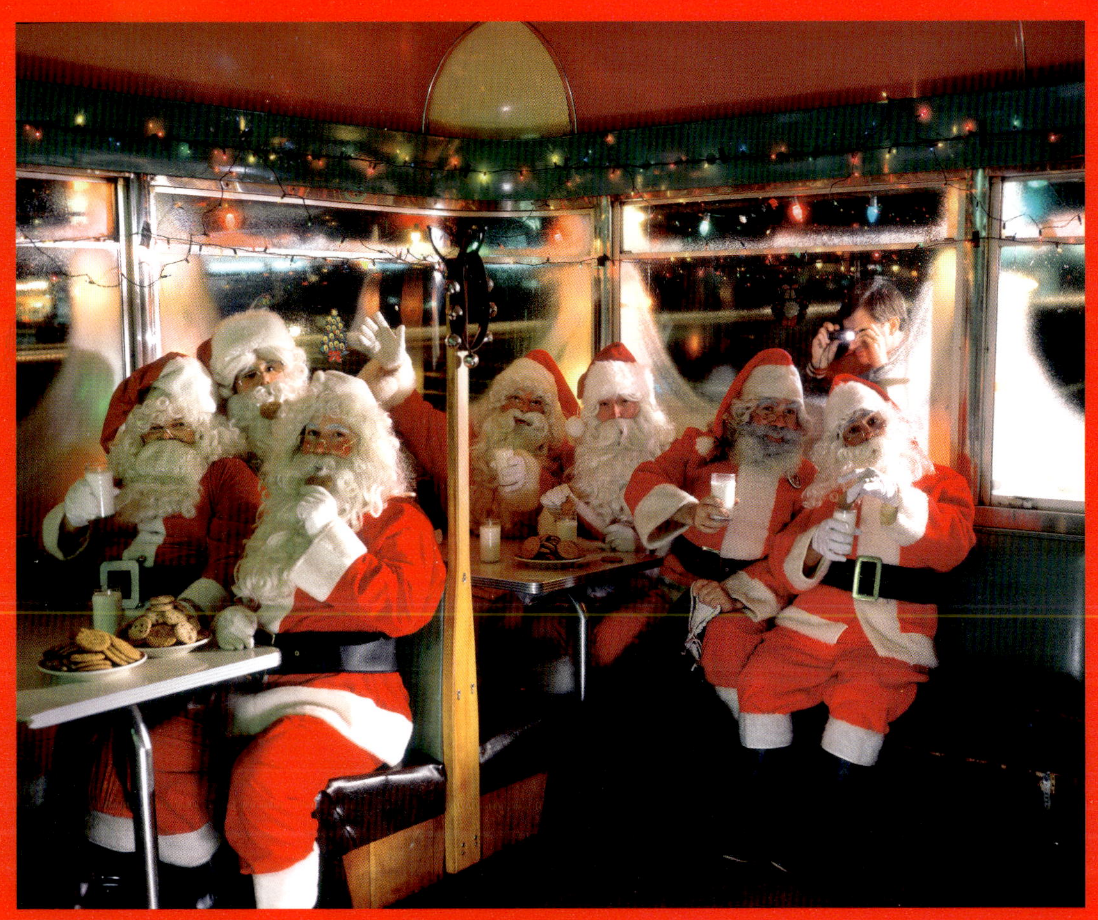

Santa's Helpers, Silver Spring, Maryland, 1987

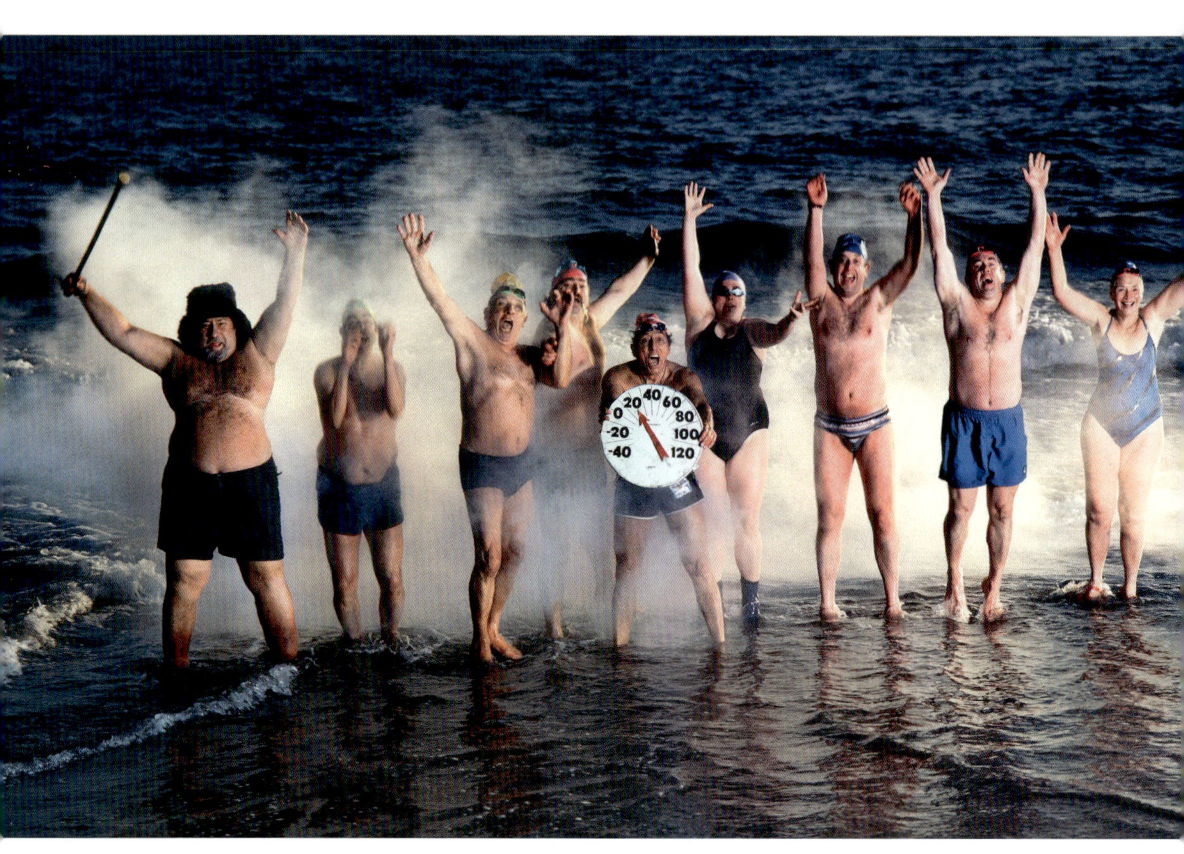

Polar Bear Club, Brooklyn, Coney Island, New York, 1972-75

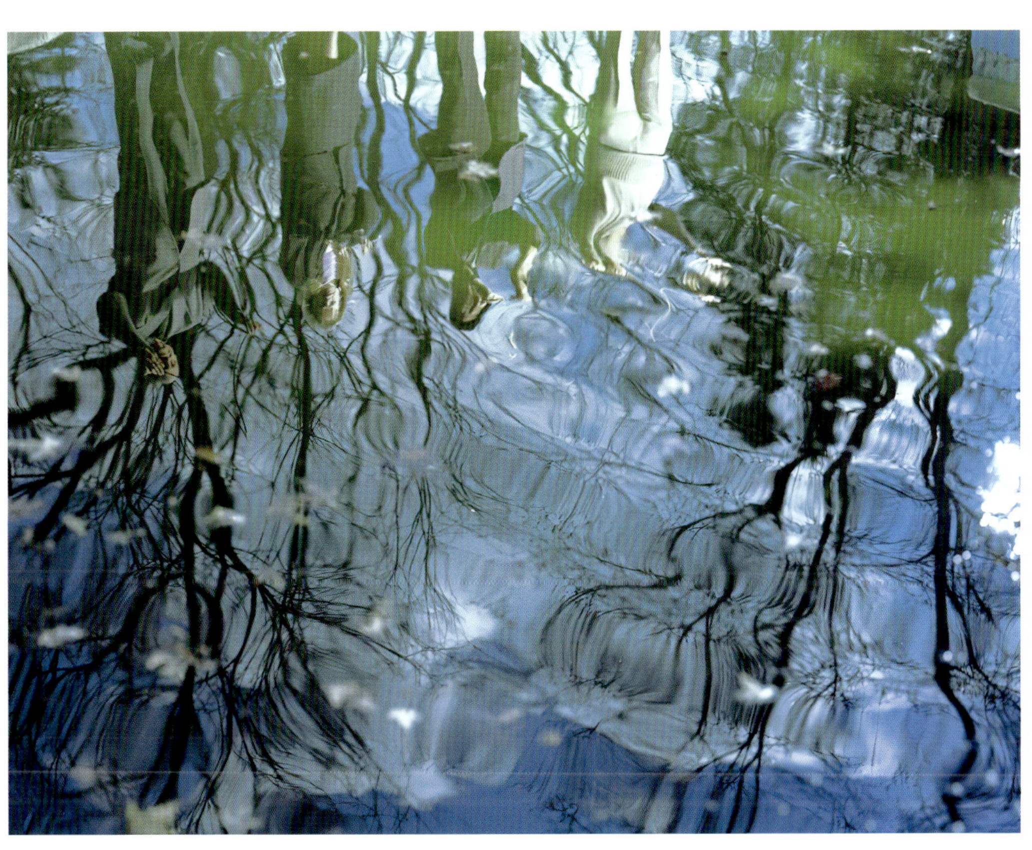

American Society of Dowsers, Leesburg, Virginia, 1988

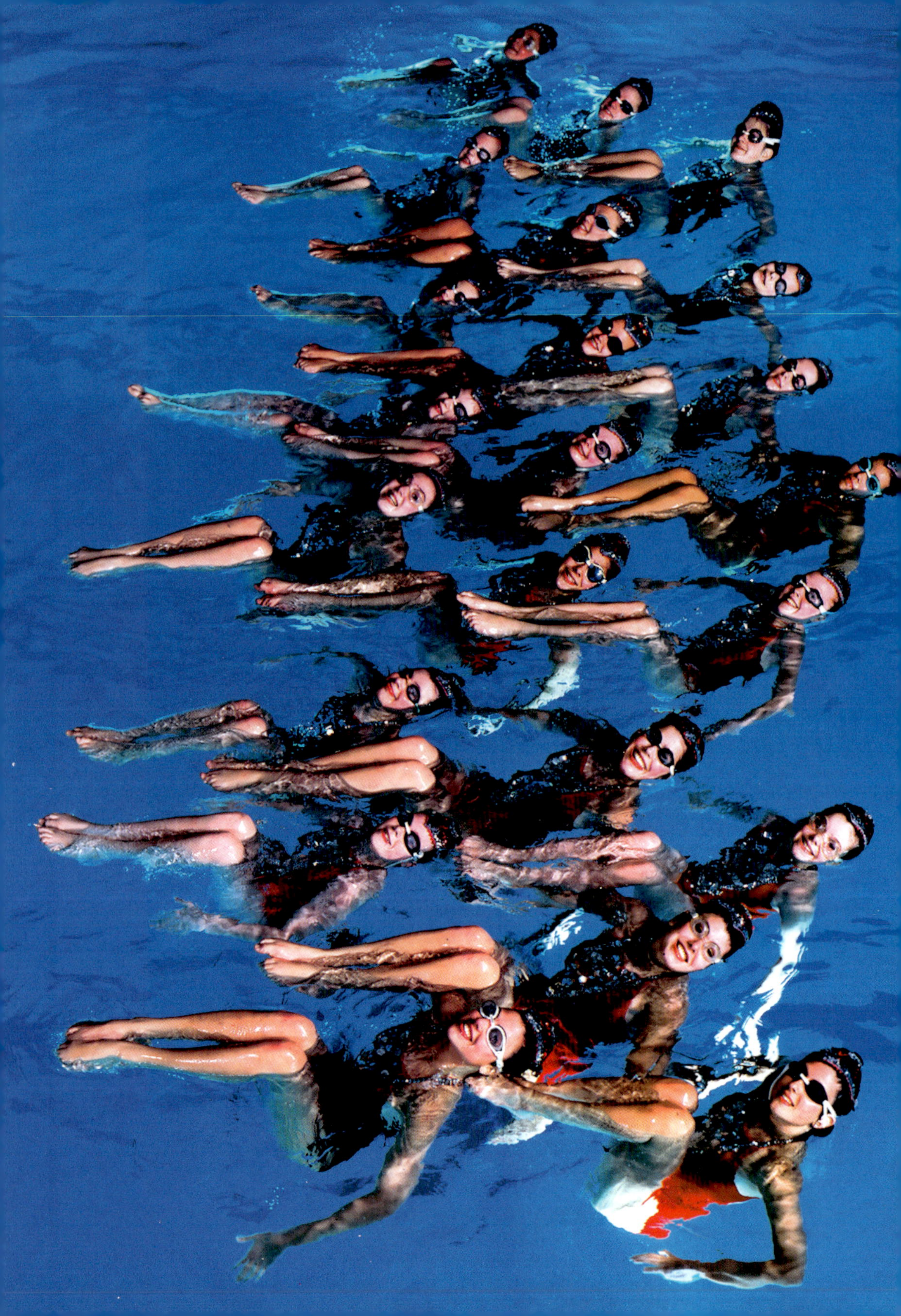

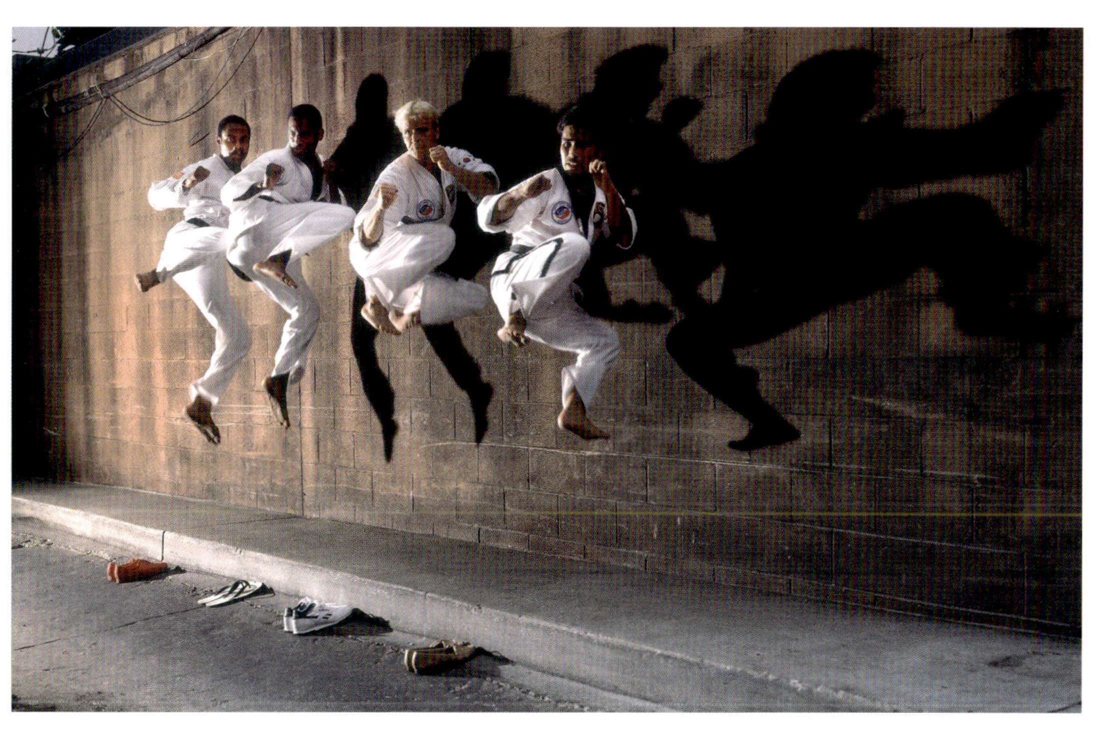

Tae Kwon Do Instructors, Washington, D.C., 1987

North Shore Aquatics Club, Long Island, New York, 1988

Lifeguards of Wild World, Bowie, Maryland, 1988

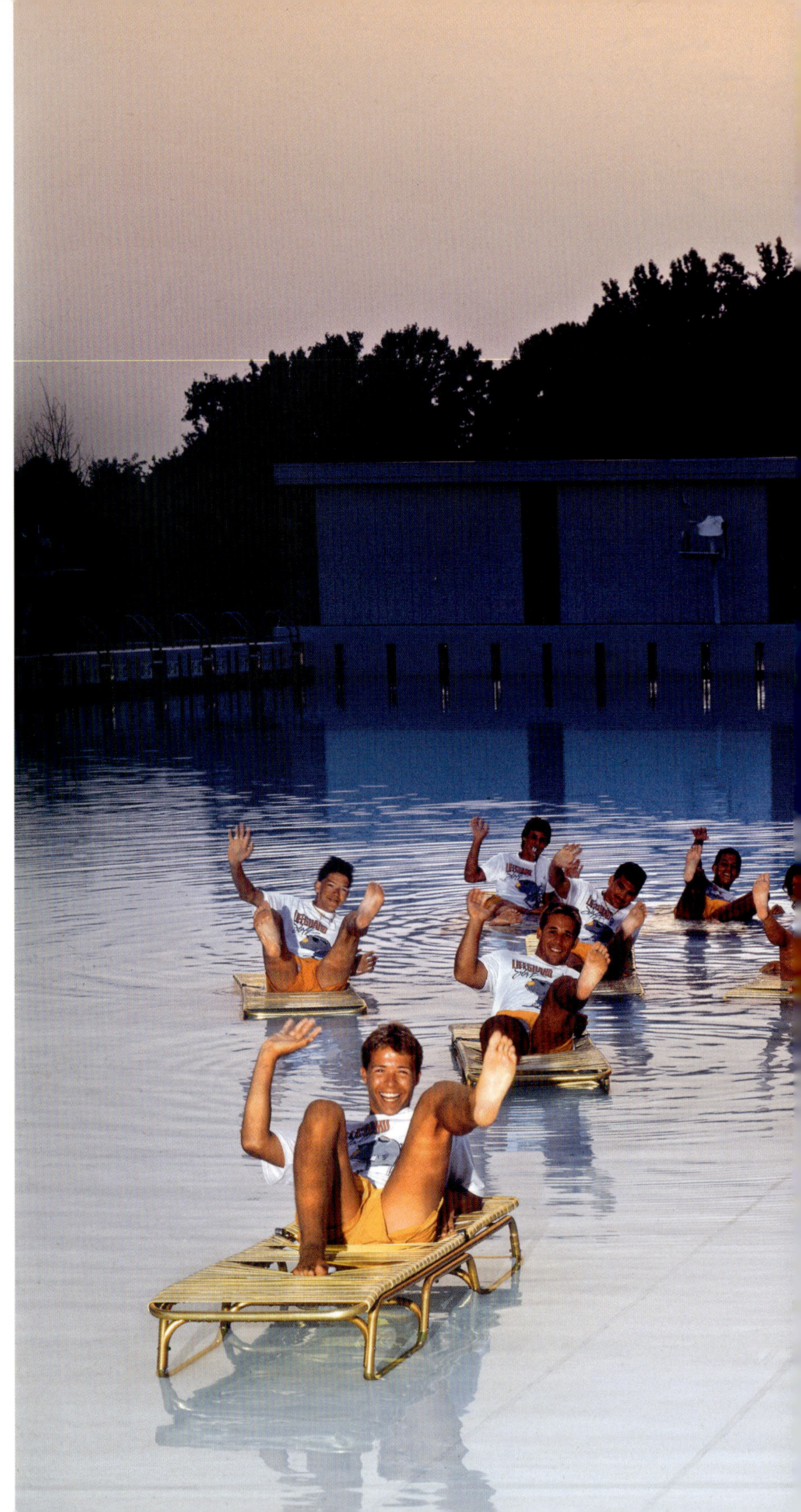

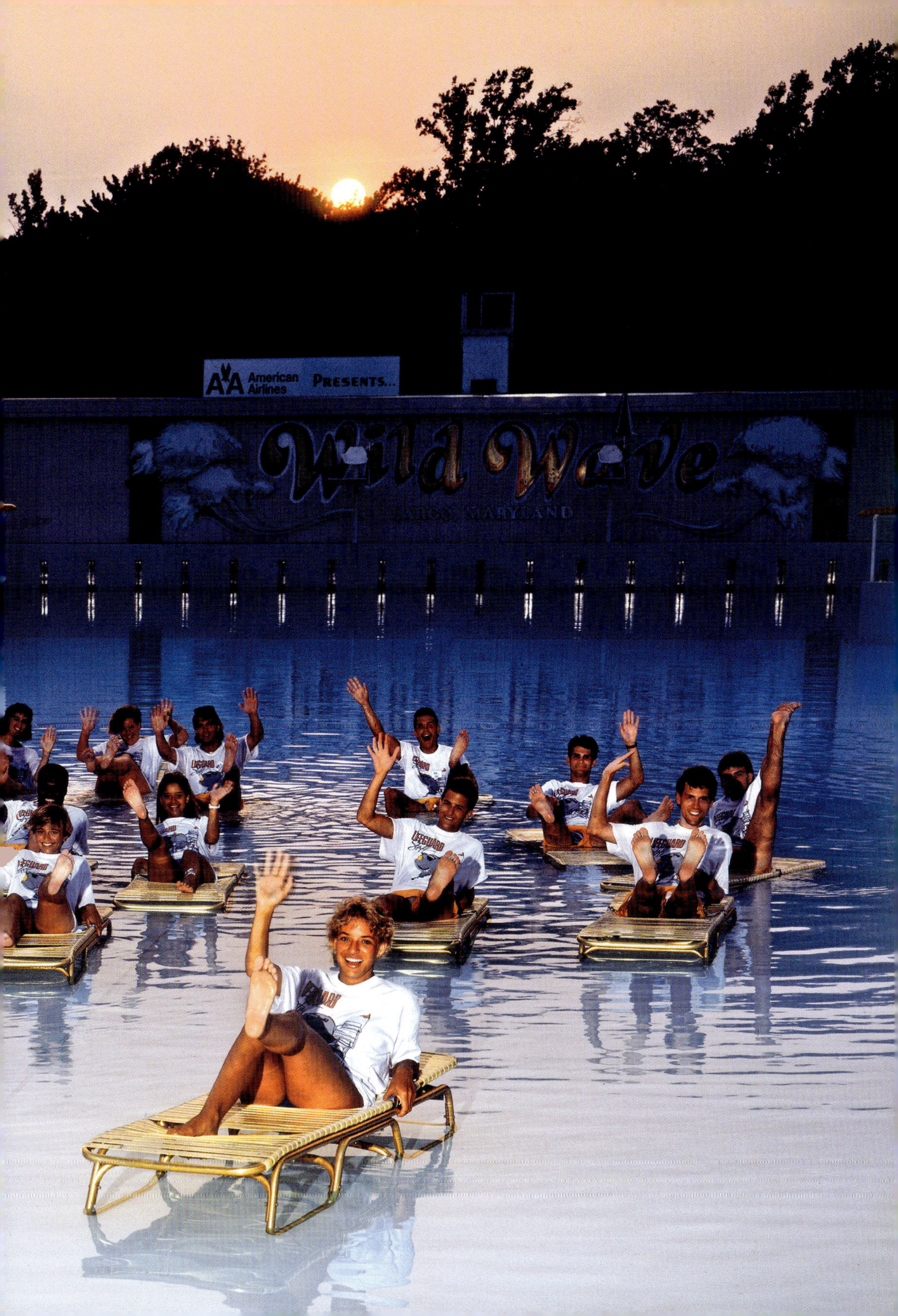
American Airlines PRESENTS...
Wild Wave
LARGO, MARYLAND
LIFEGUARD

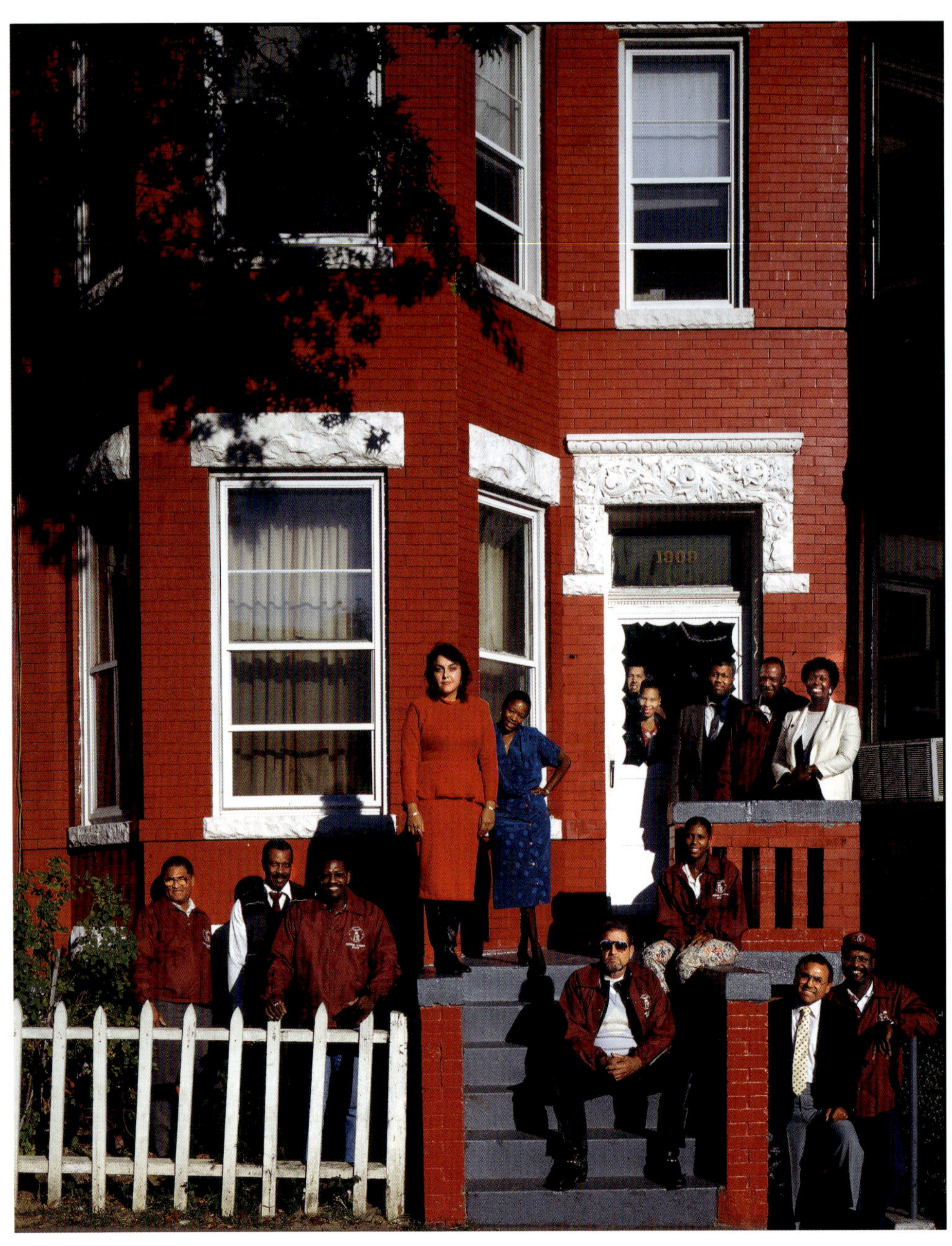

D.C.'s Roving Leaders, Washington, D.C., 1988

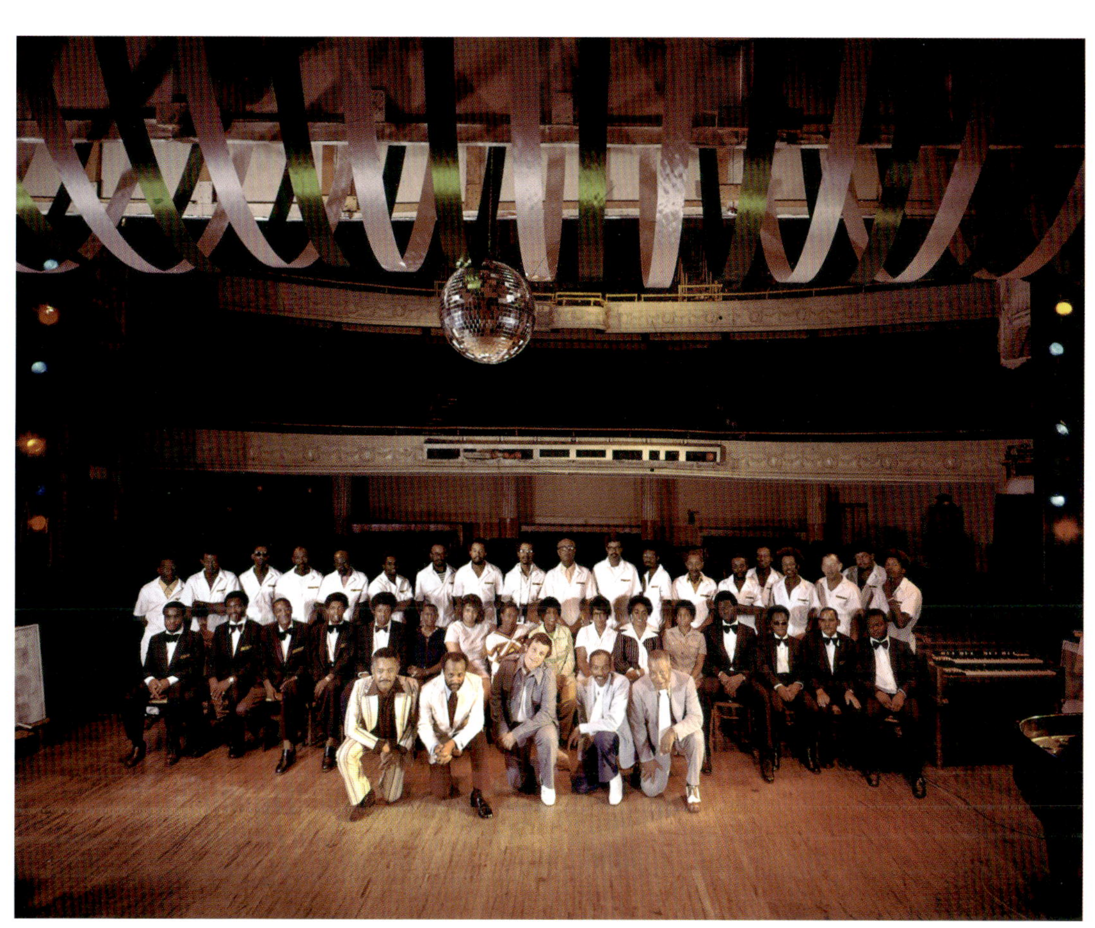

Apollo Theater, New York, New York, 1972-75

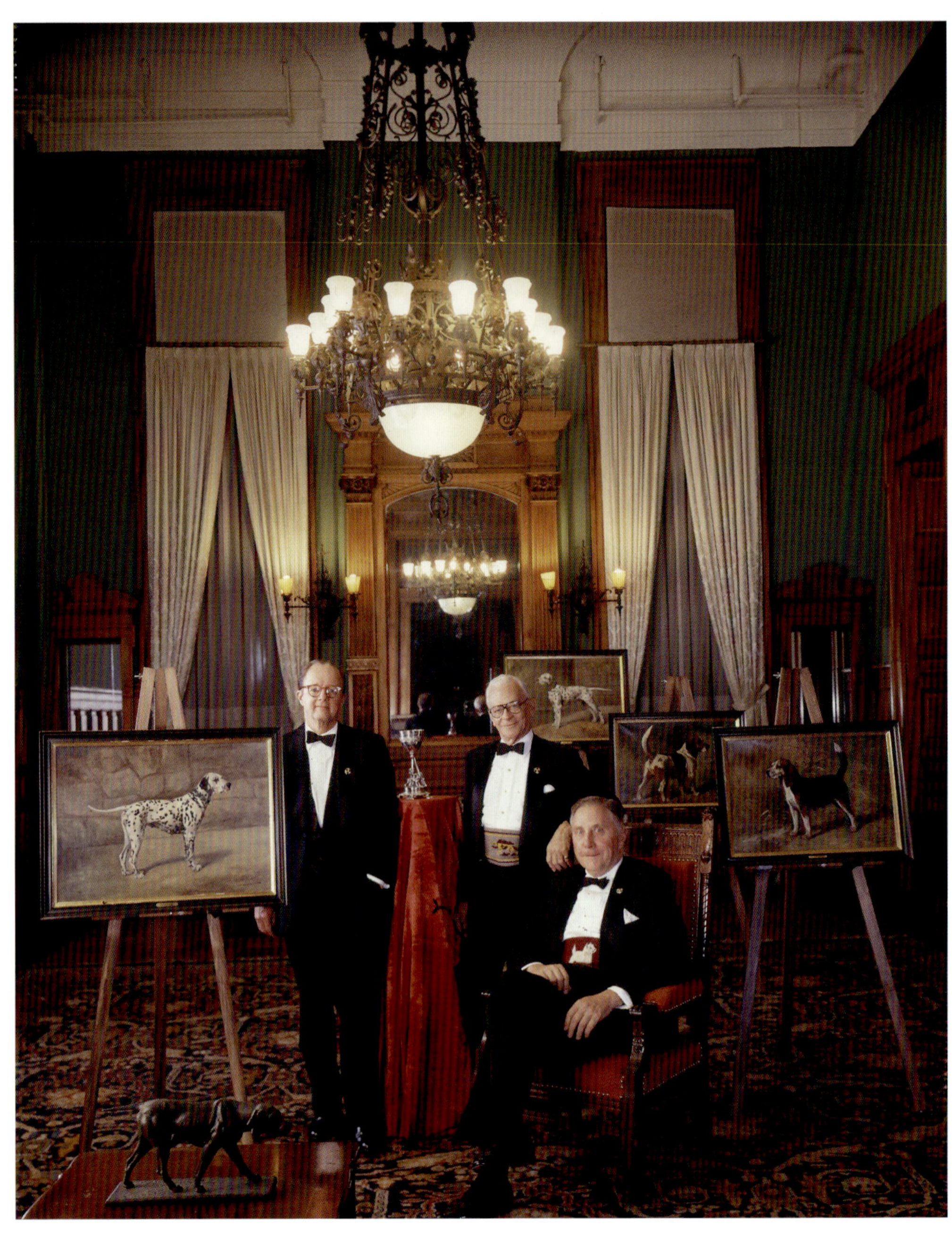

Officers of the Westminster Kennel Club Dog Show, New York, New York, c. 1990

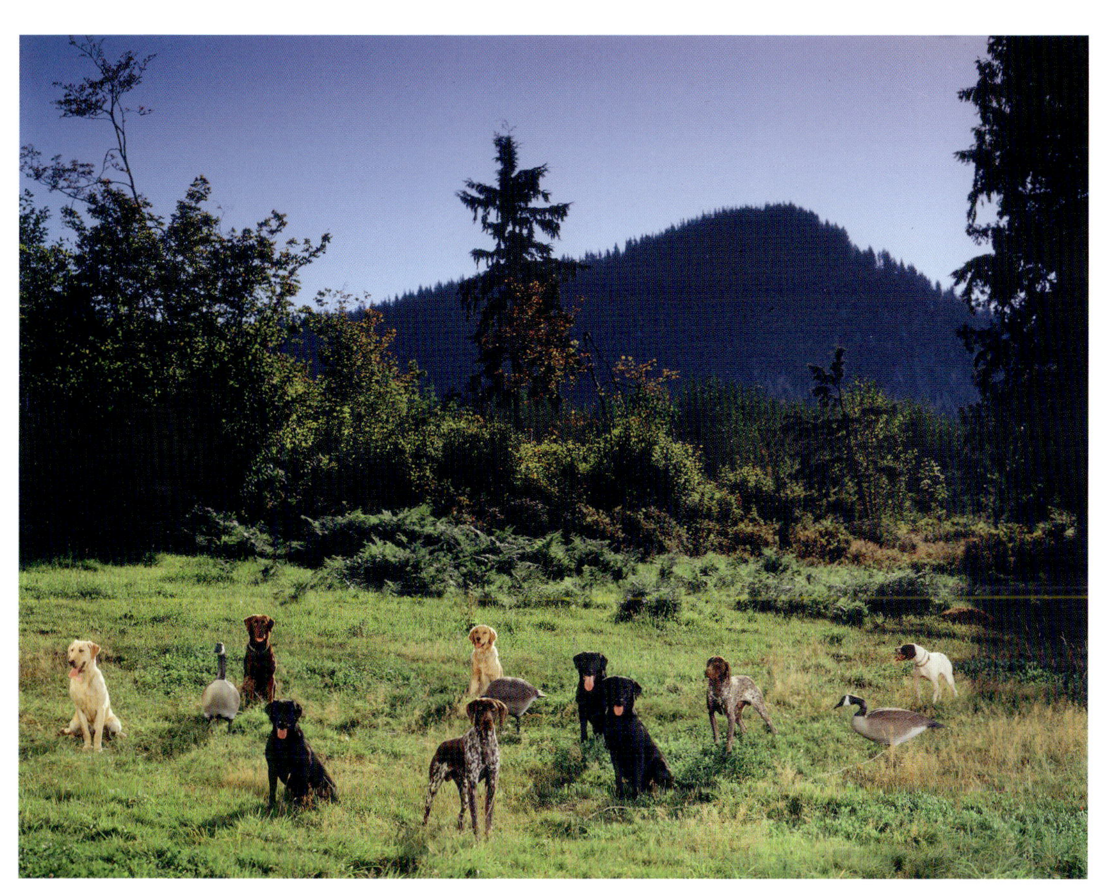

Dogs and Geese, Oregon, 1994

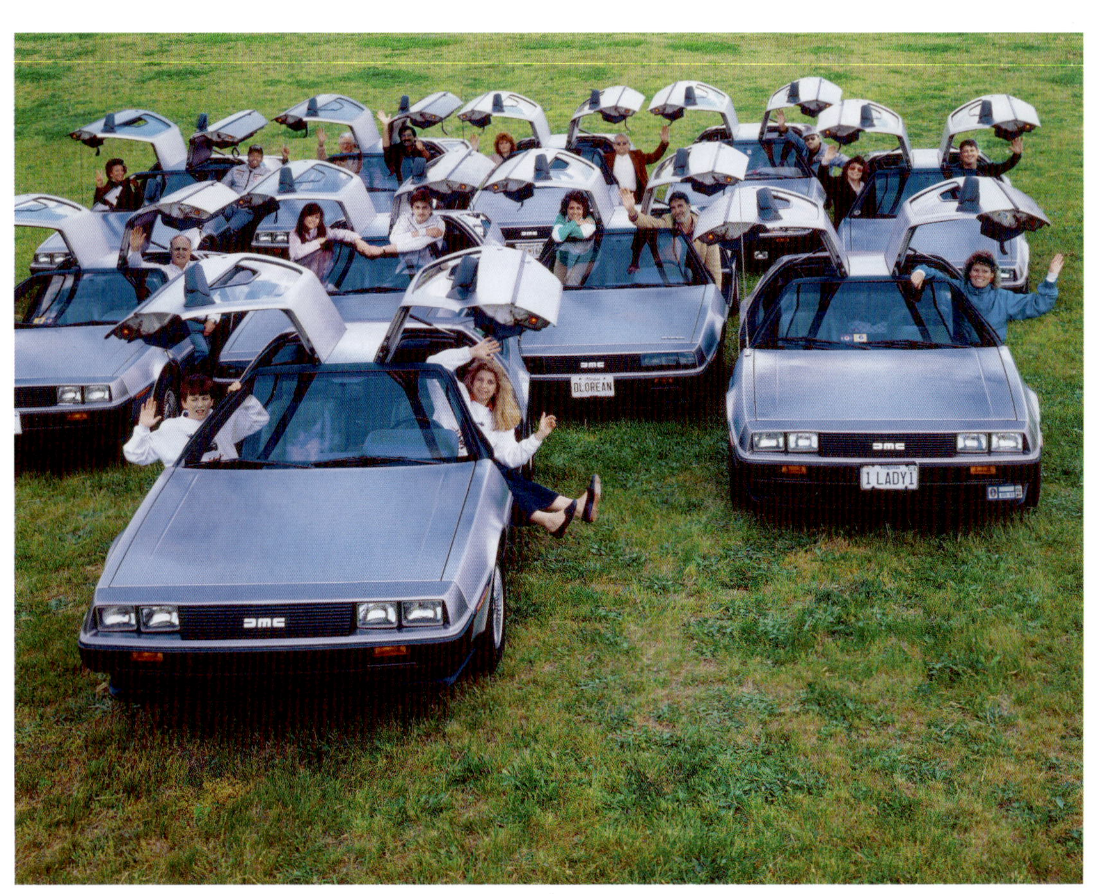

DeLorean Car Owners Association, Washington, D.C., 1988

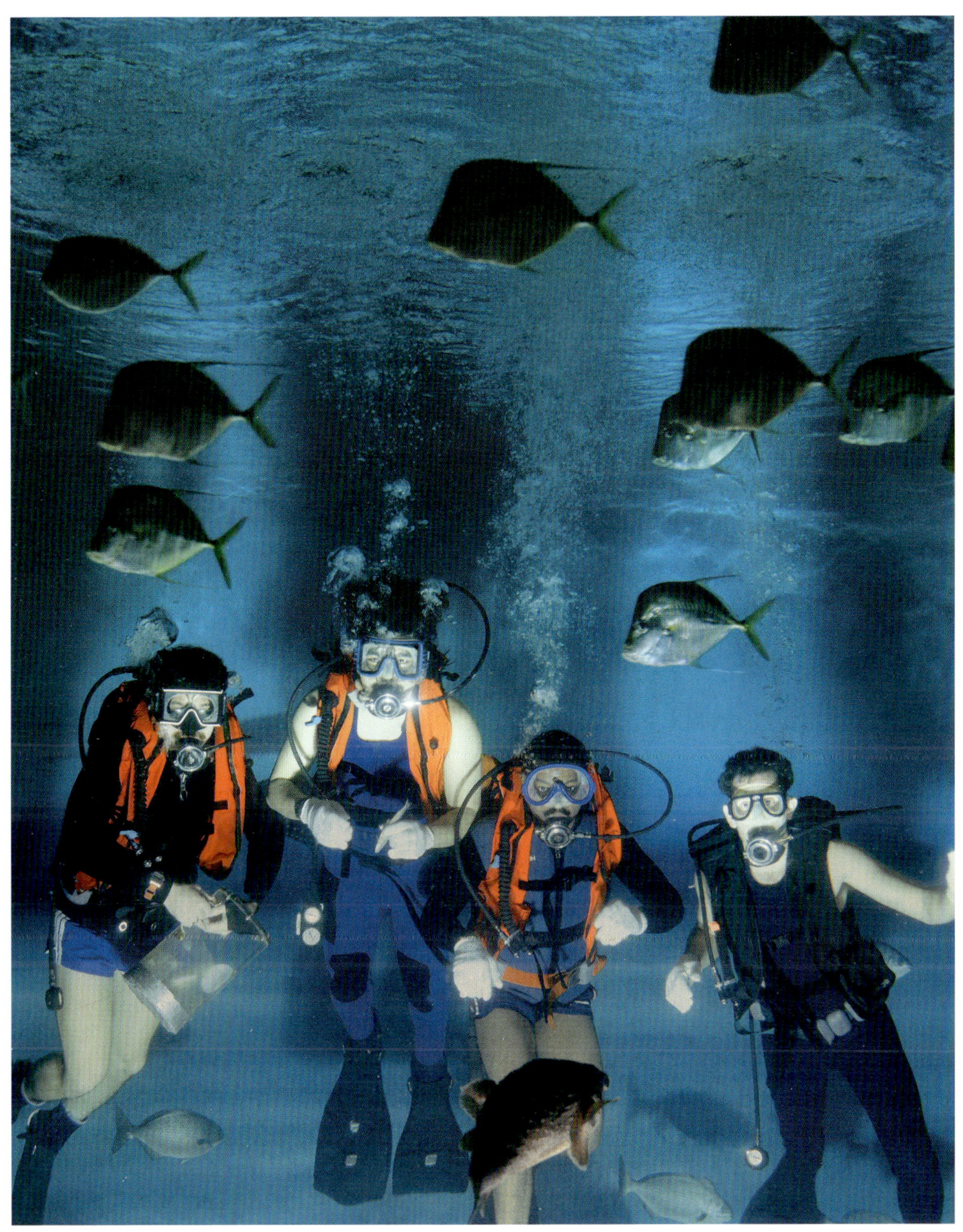

The Aquarists of the National Aquarium, Baltimore, Maryland, 1988

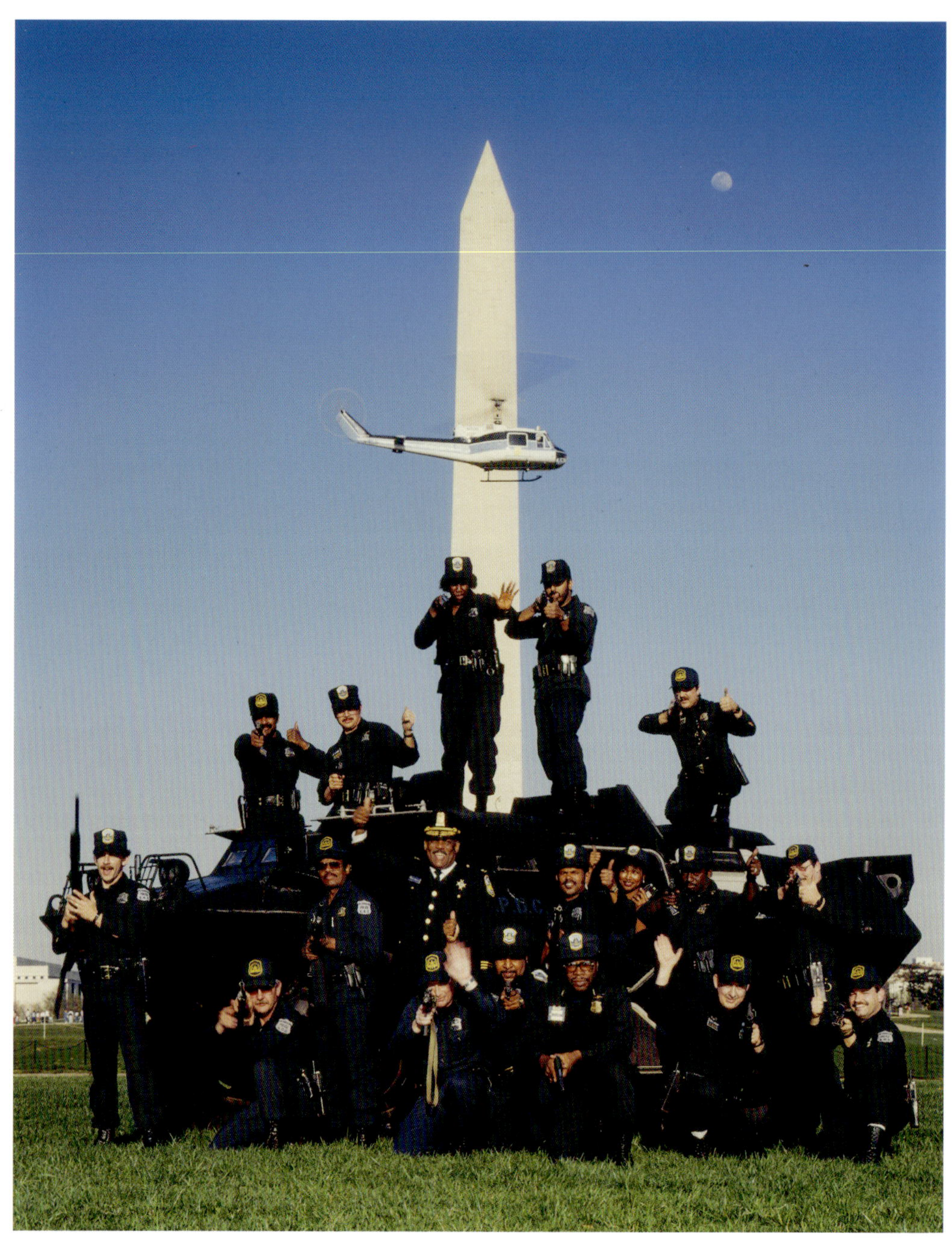

D.C. Swat Team, Washington, D.C., 1987

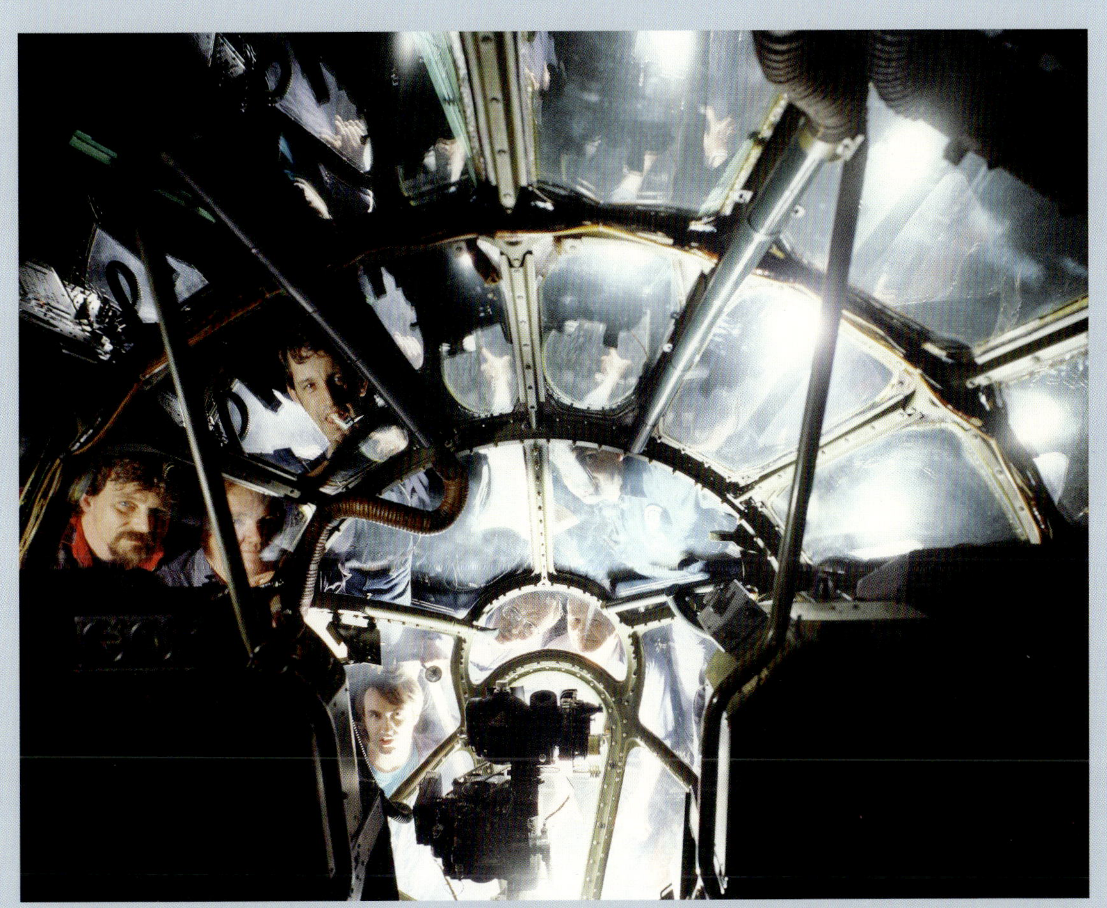

Aircraft Restoration Technicians for the Enola Gay, Suitland-Silver Hill, Maryland, 1987

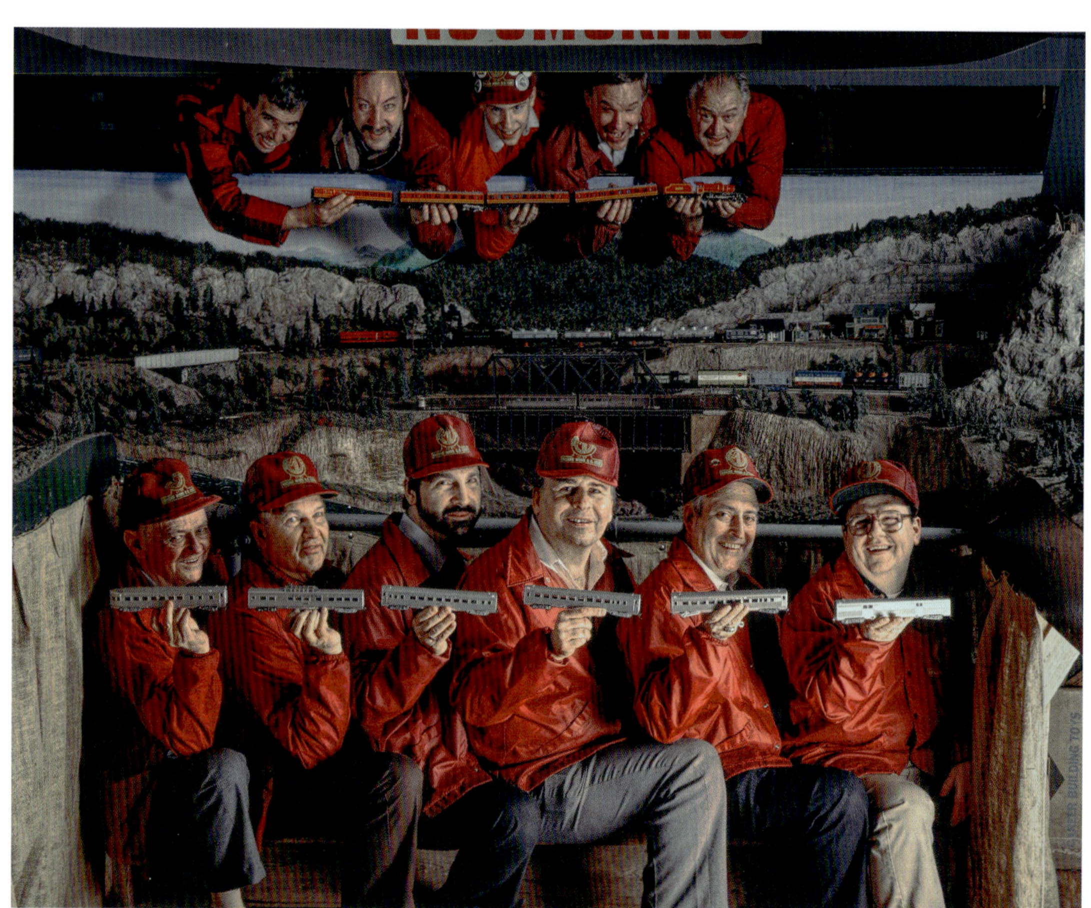

Nassau Lionel Operating Engineers, Merrick, New York, 1989

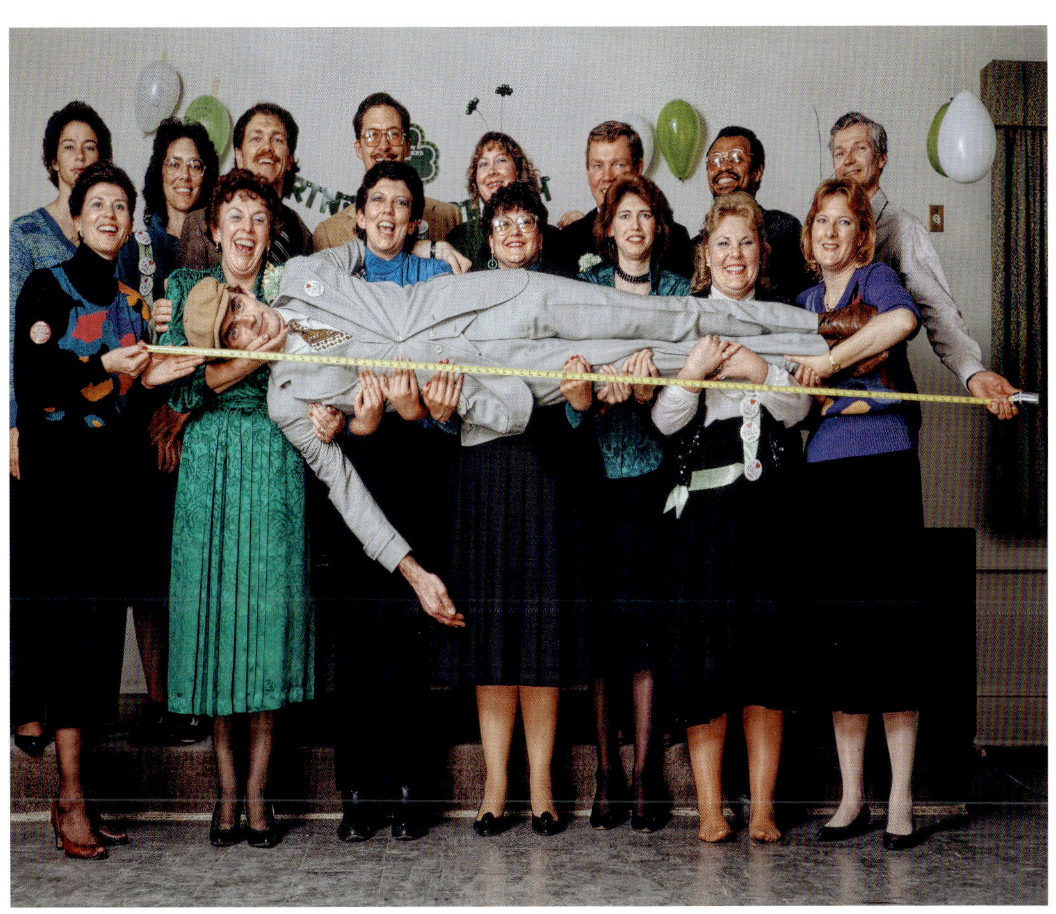

Tall Social Club of Washington, D.C., Arlington, Virginia, 1988

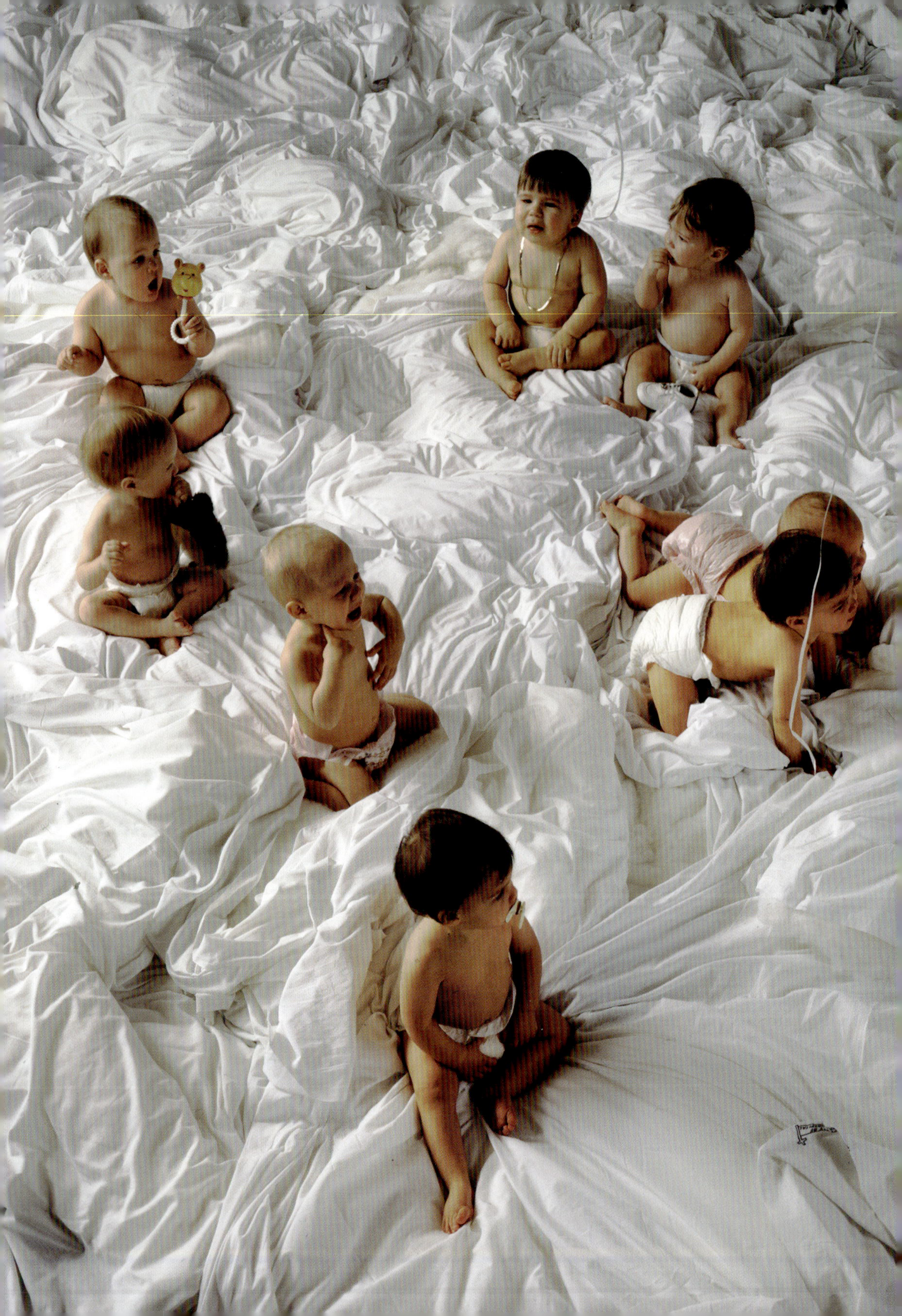

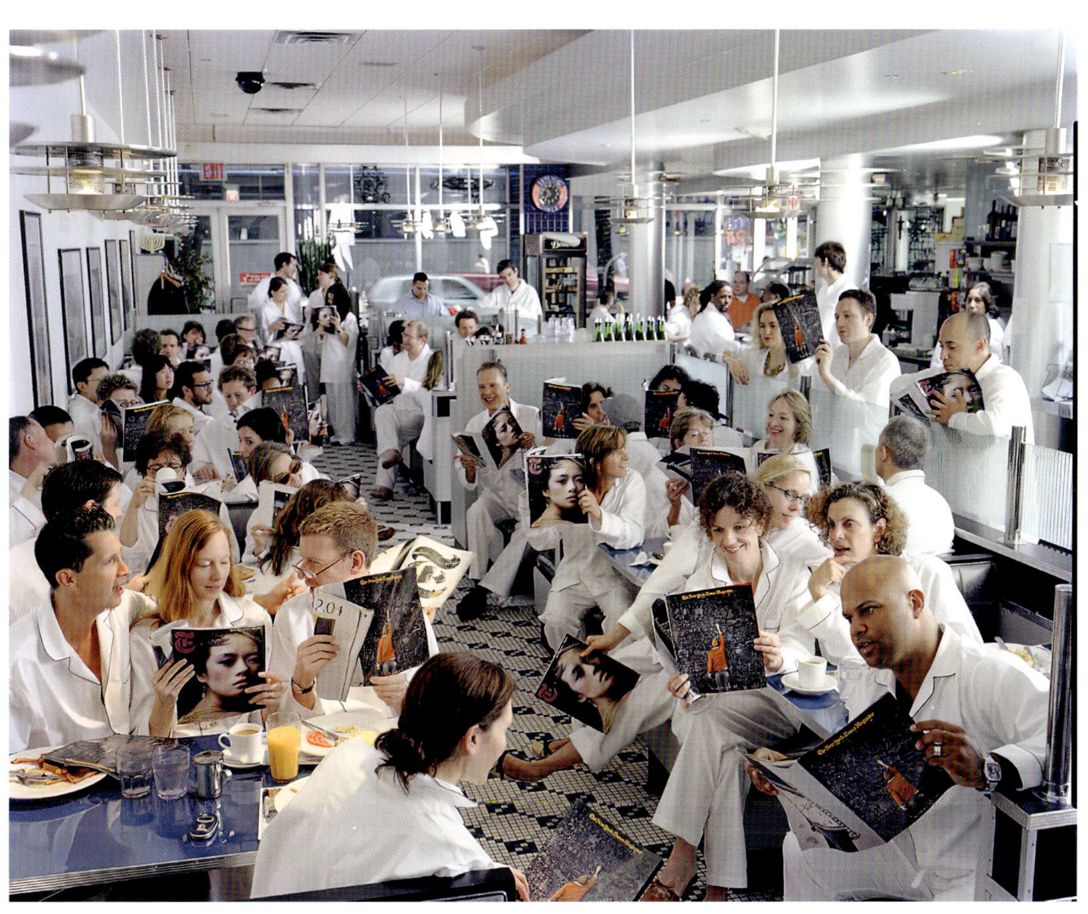

Editorial Staff of *The New York Times Magazine*, New York, New York, c. 2013

LEFT PAGE
New Year's Babies, Silver Spring, Maryland, 1989

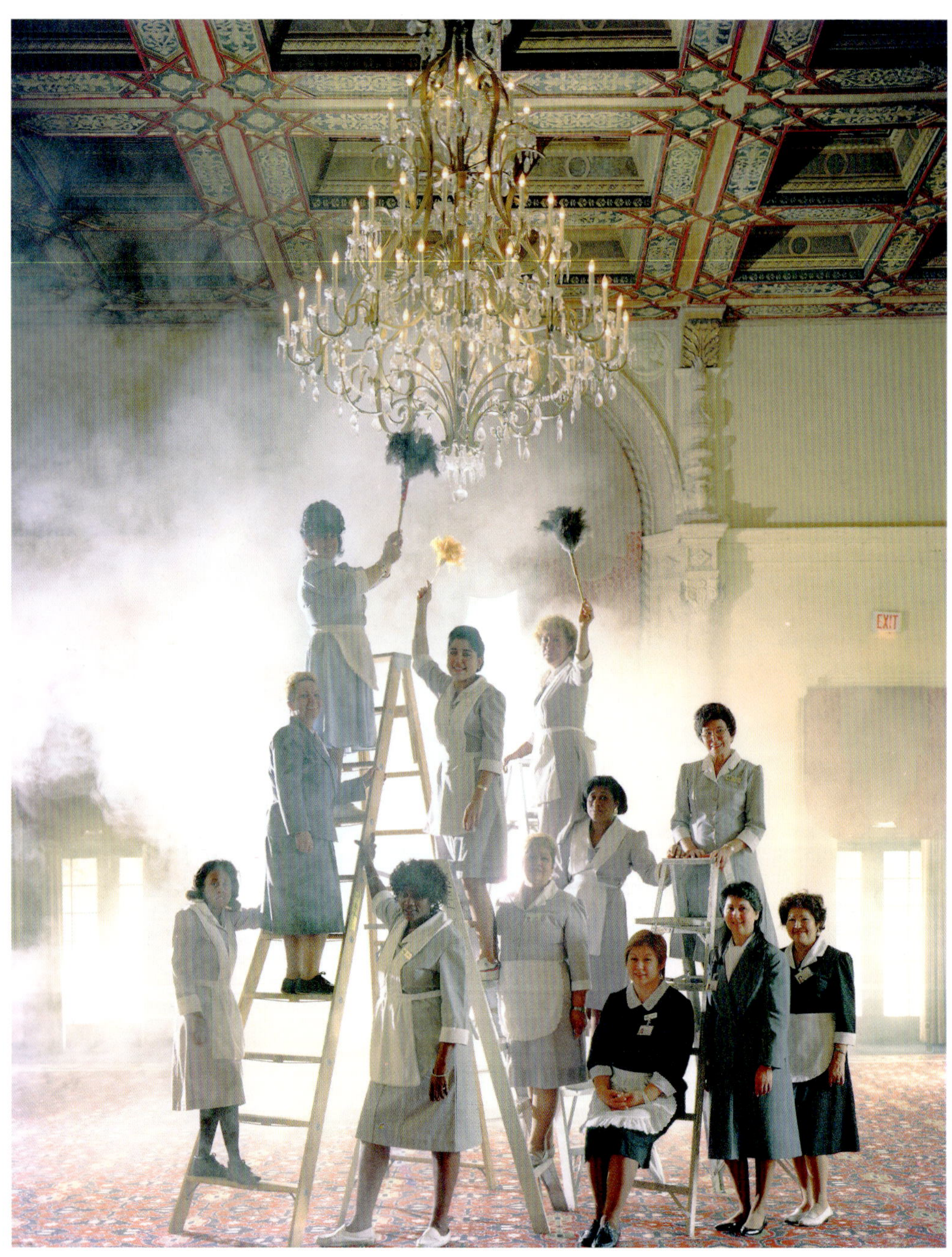

Chambermaids for The Biltmore Hotel, Coral Gables, Florida, c. 2000

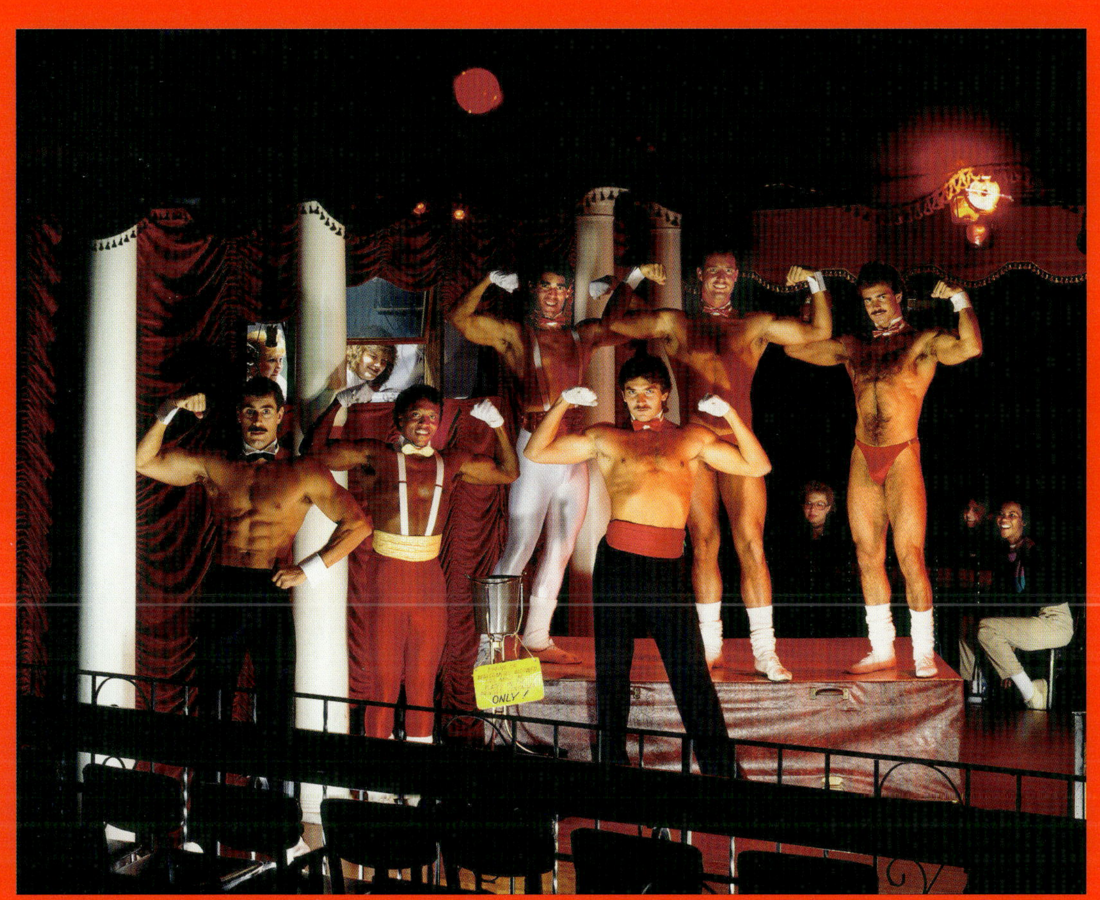

Performers at Hangar House, Camp Springs, Maryland, 1987

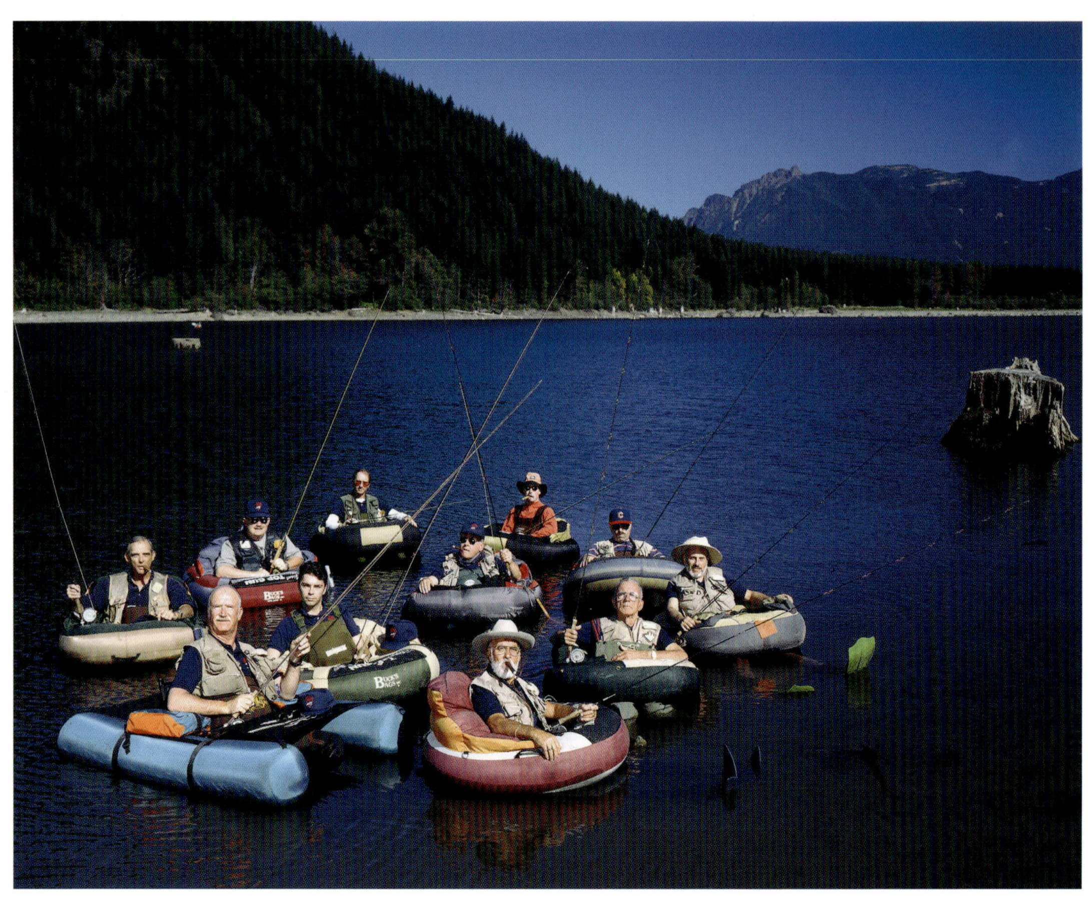

Rubber Boat Fishermen, Rattlesnake Lake, Washington, 1994
RIGHT PAGE
July 4 Pyrotechnicians, Washington, D.C., 1988

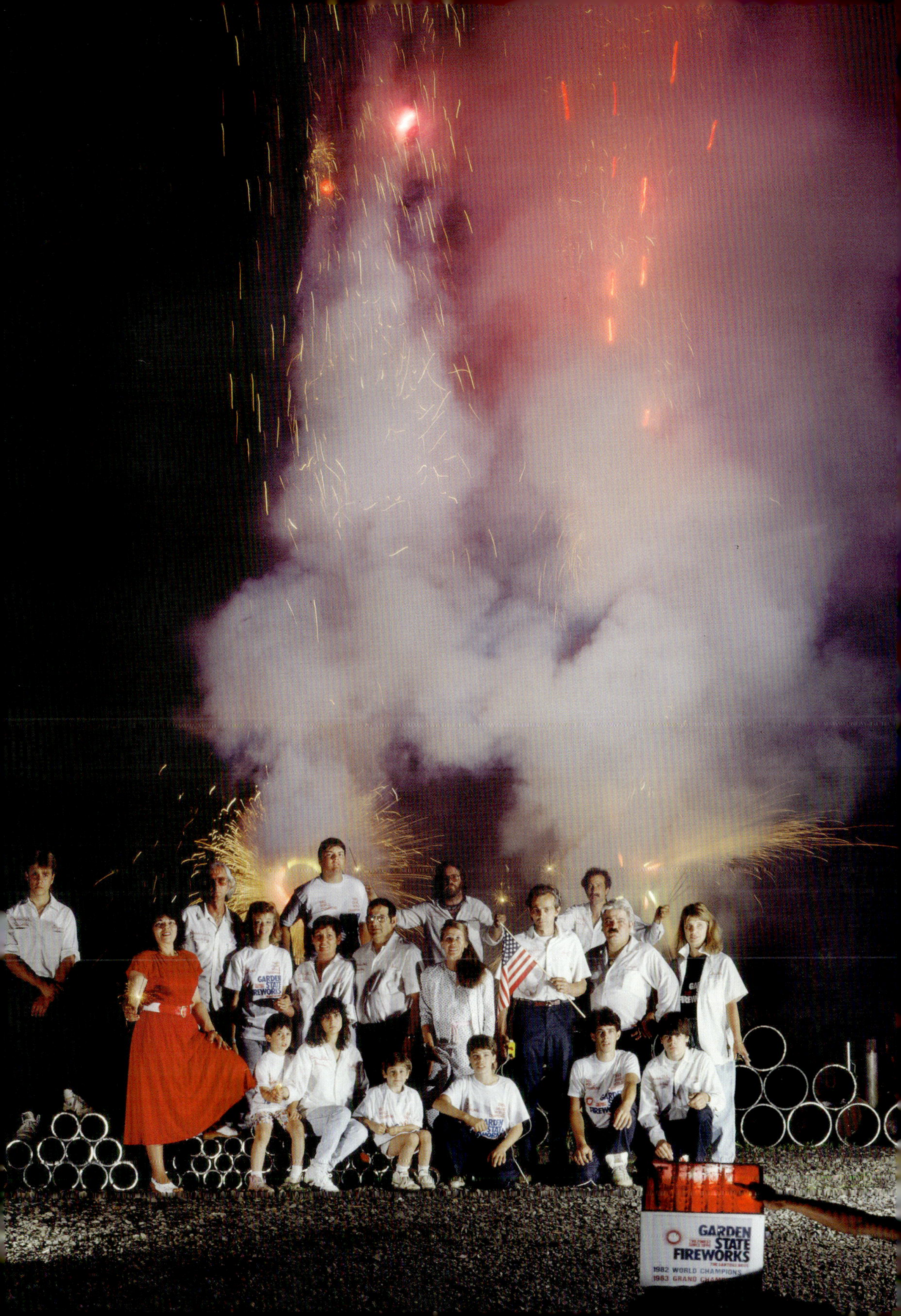

GARDEN
STATE
FIREWORKS
1982 WORLD CHAMPIONS
1983 GRAND CHAMPIONS

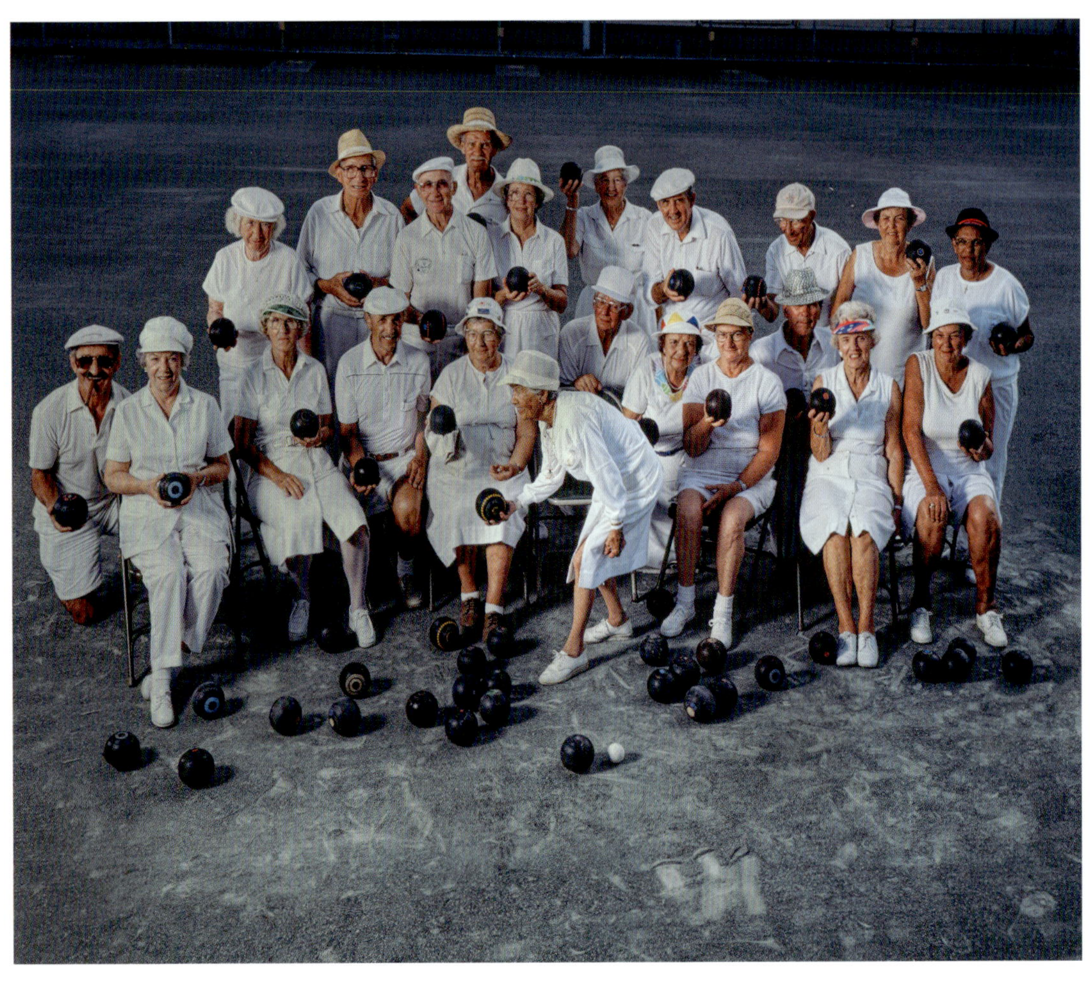

St. Petersburg Lawn Bowling Club, St. Petersburg, Florida, 1972-75
RIGHT PAGE
Capital Croquet Club, Washington, D.C., 1988

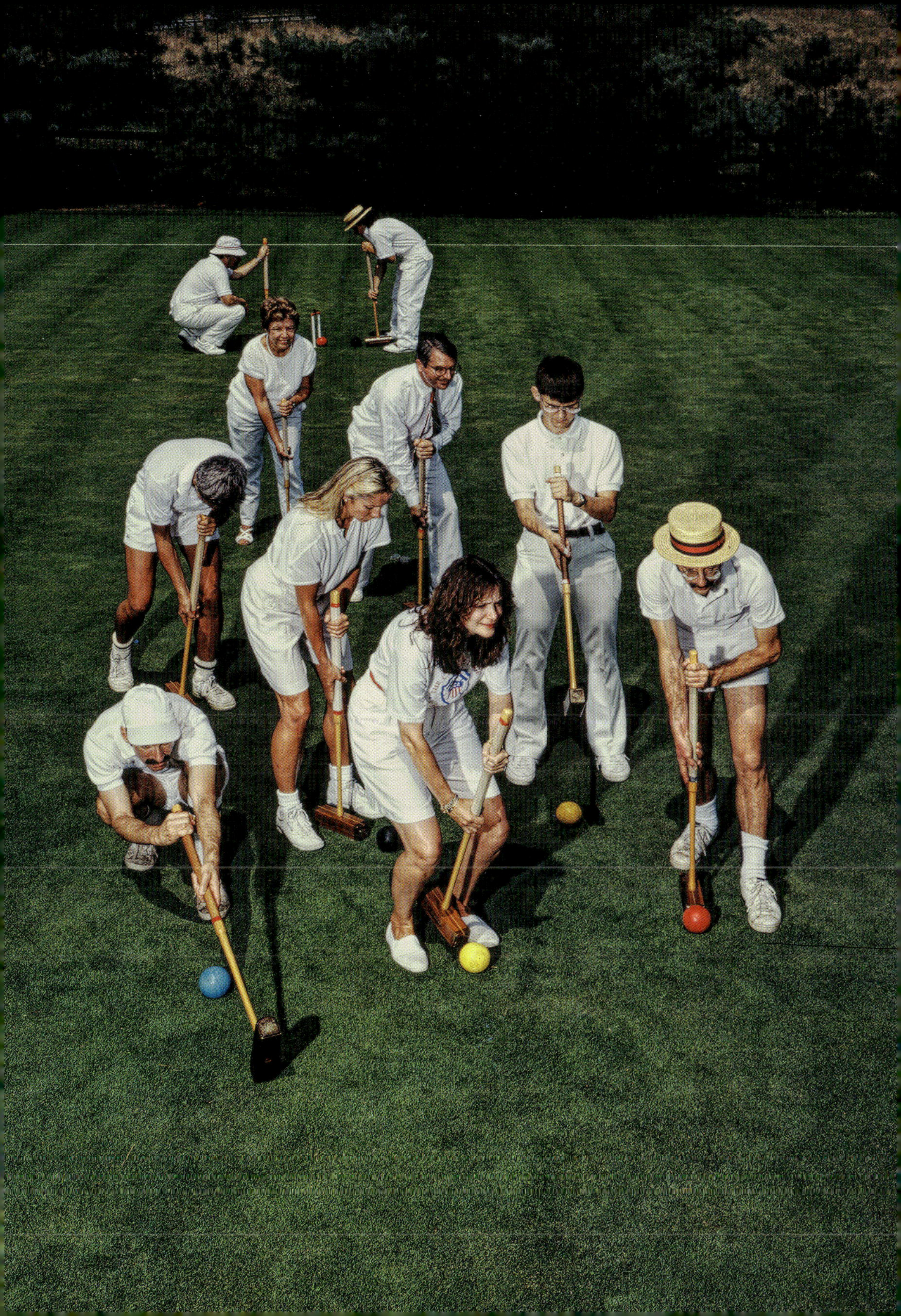

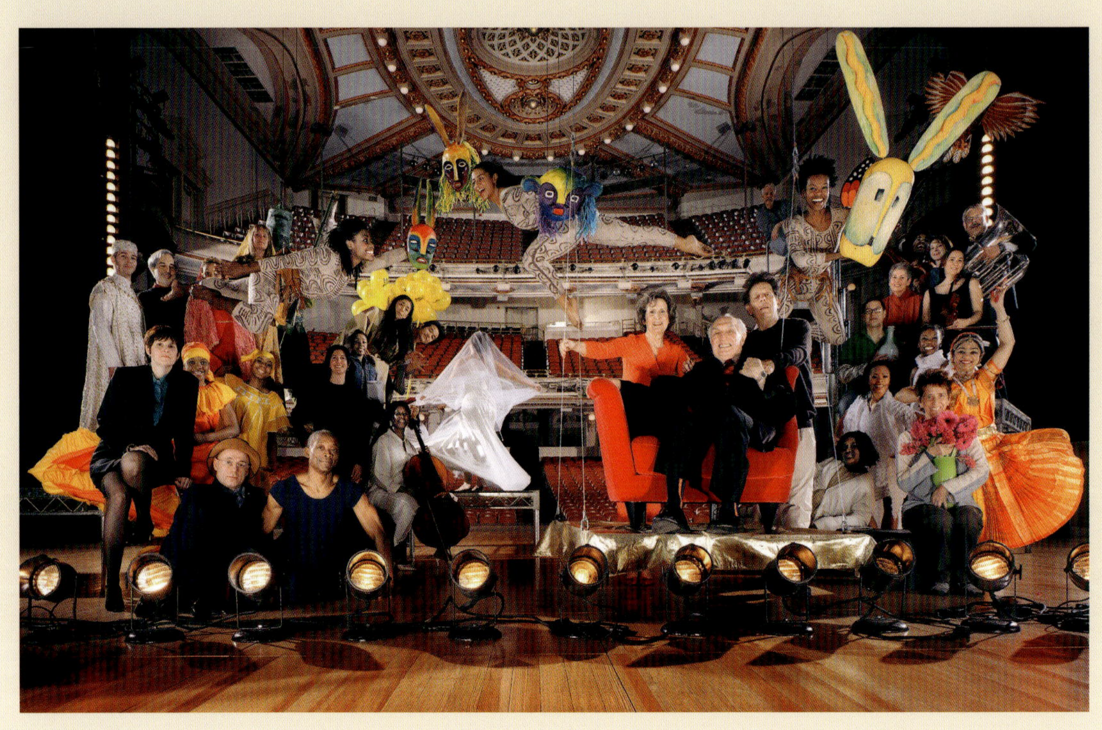

Brooklyn Academy of Music, Brooklyn, New York, 2011

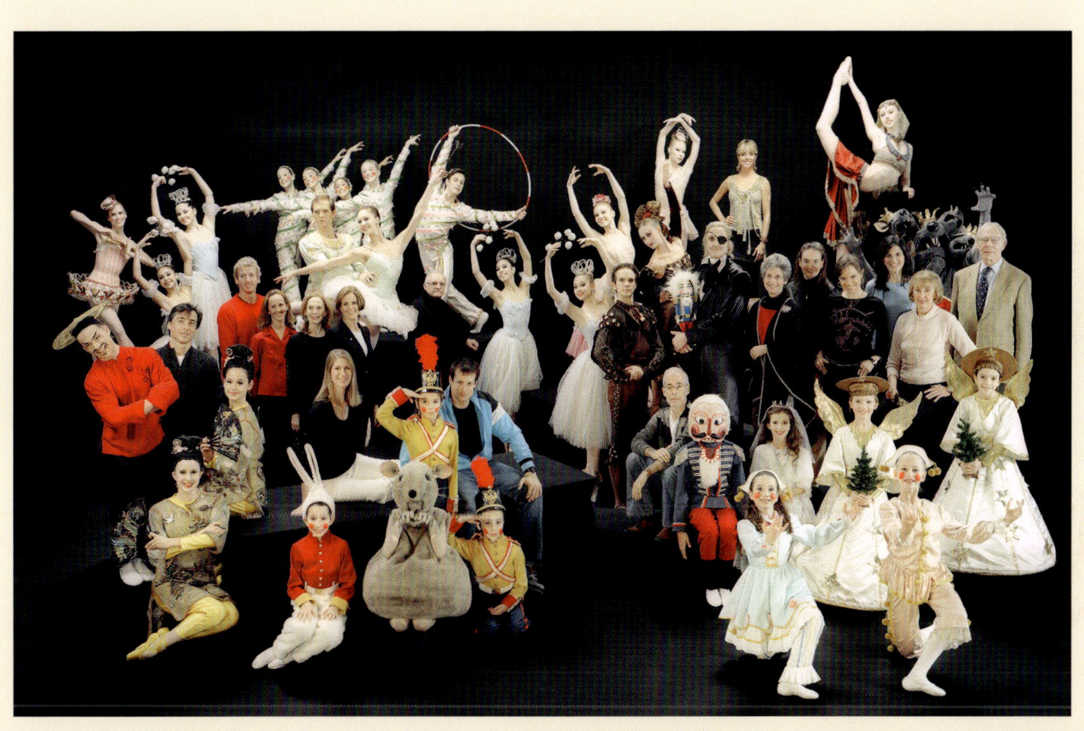

New York City Ballet, Alumni of the Nutcracker, New York, New York, c. 2010

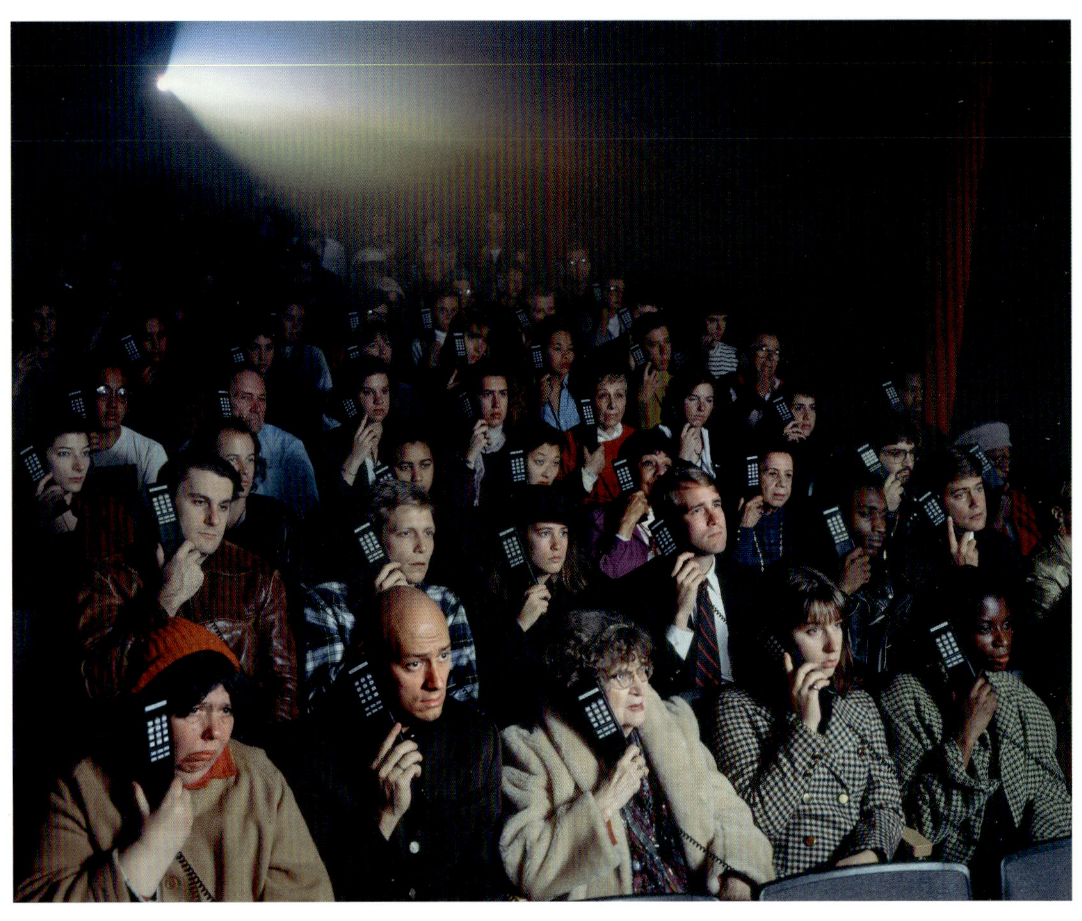

Cell Phones, New York, New York, c. 2000

Art School Life Drawing Class, New York, New York, 1978

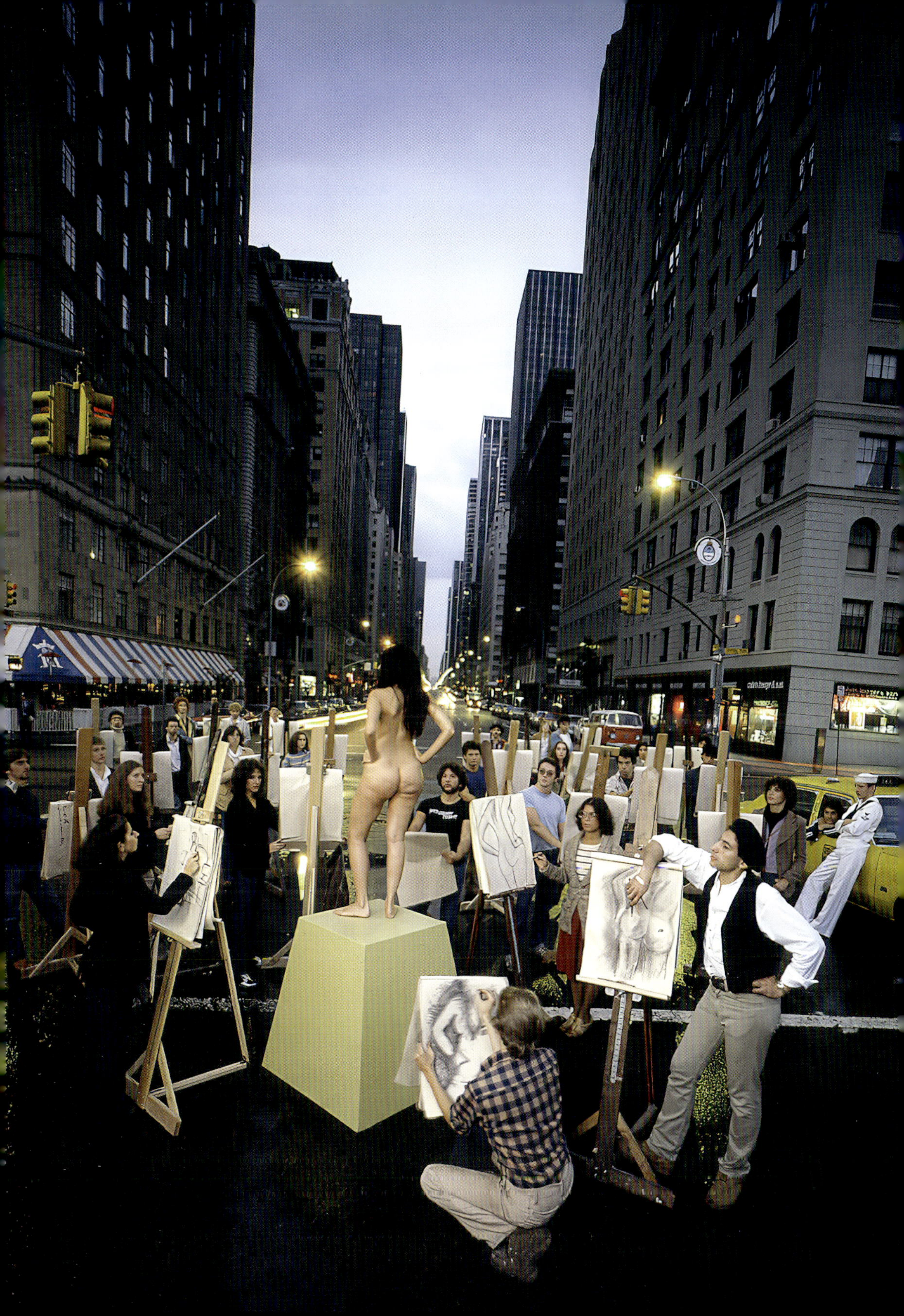

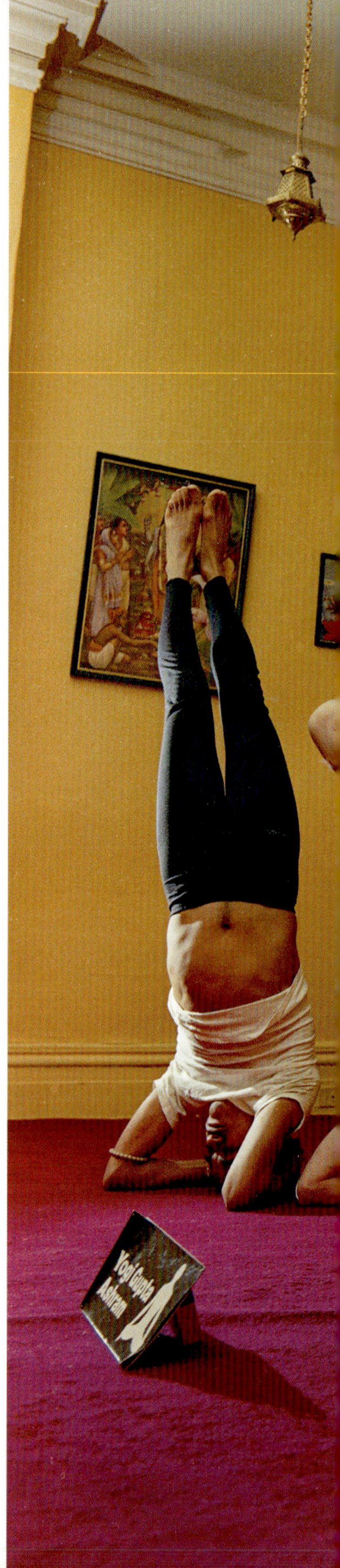

Yogis, Los Angeles, California, 1974

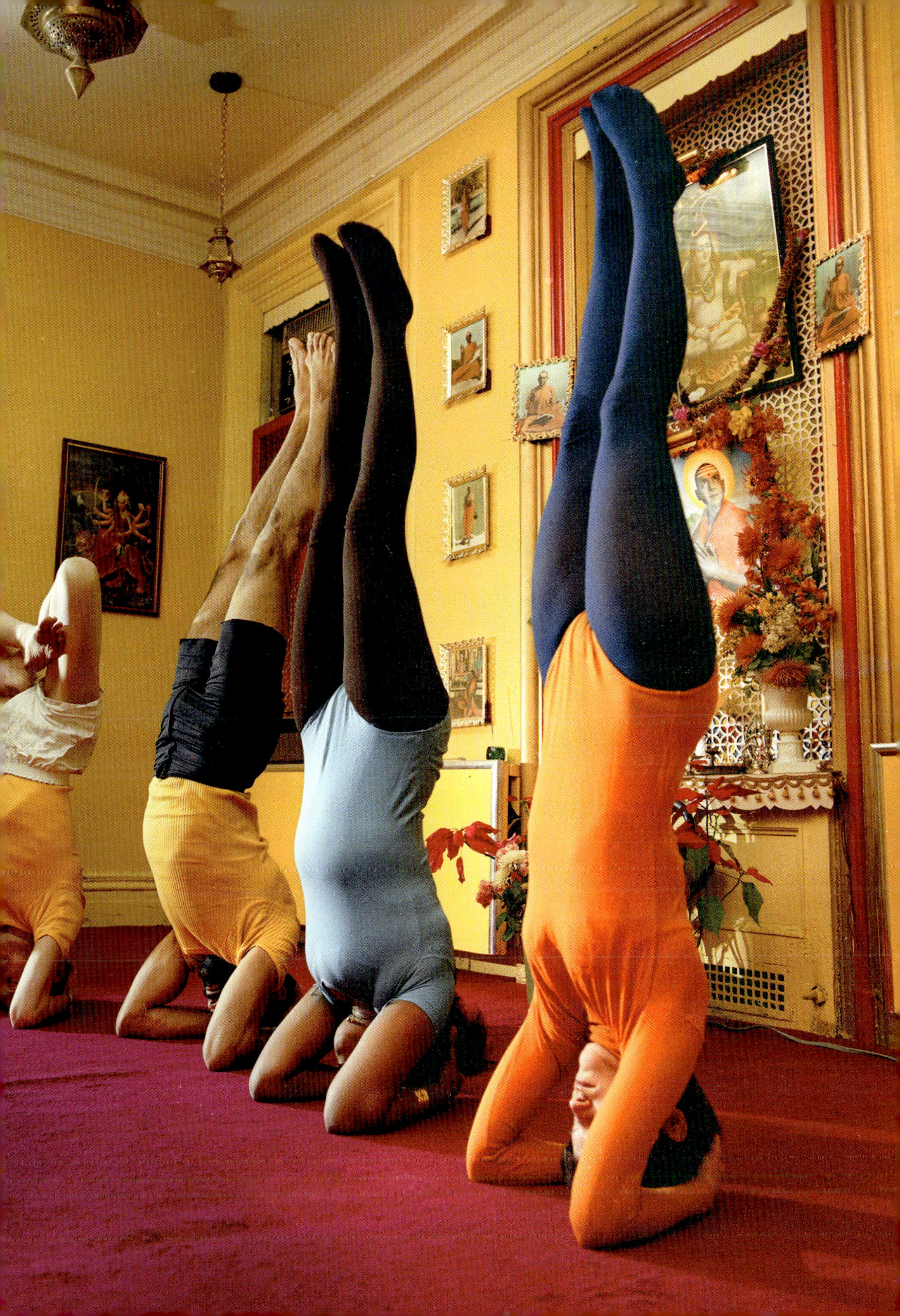

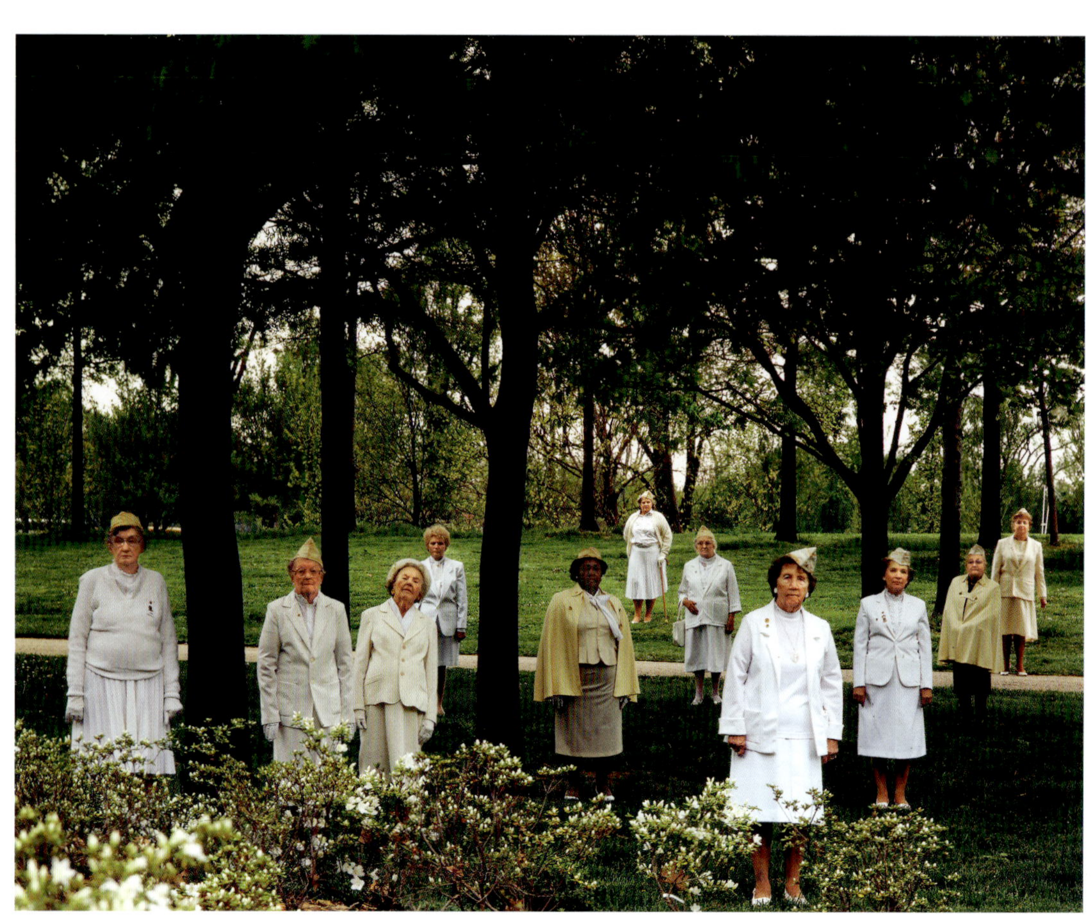

Gold Star Mothers, Washington, D.C., 1988

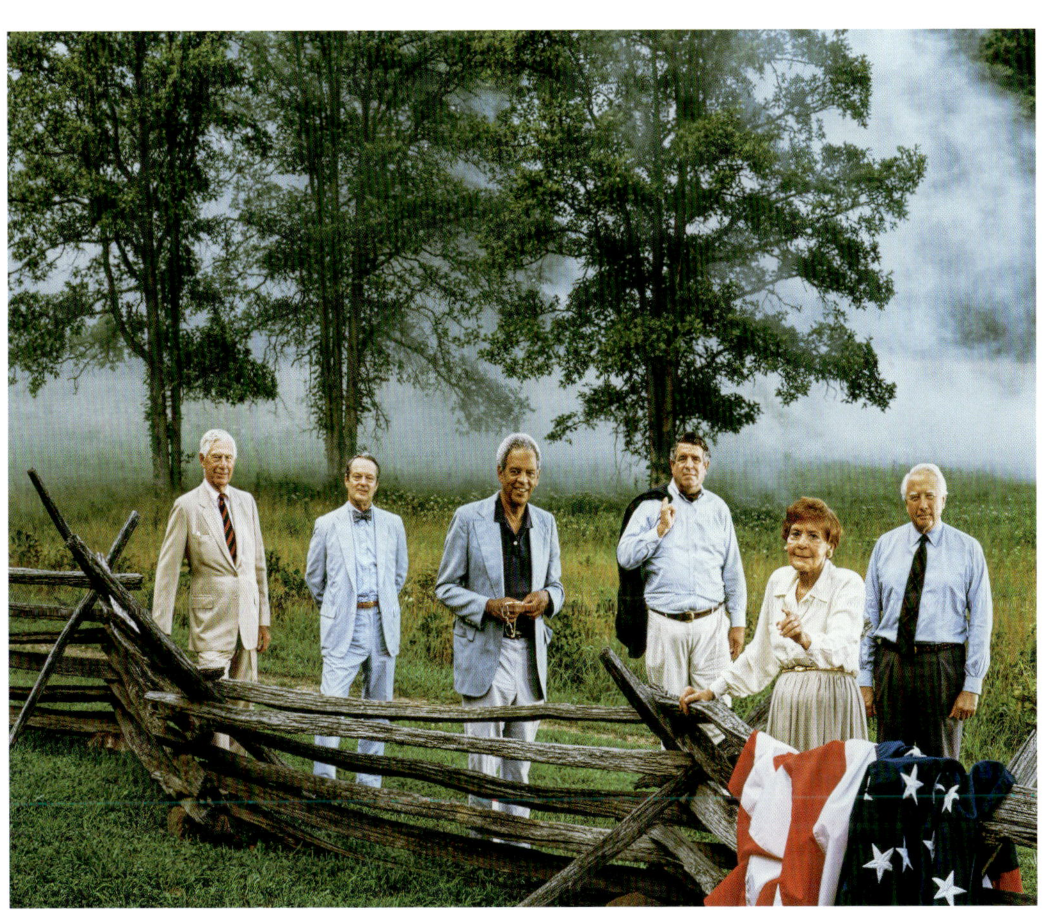

Advisory Panel for Protect Historic America, Manassas, Virginia, 1994

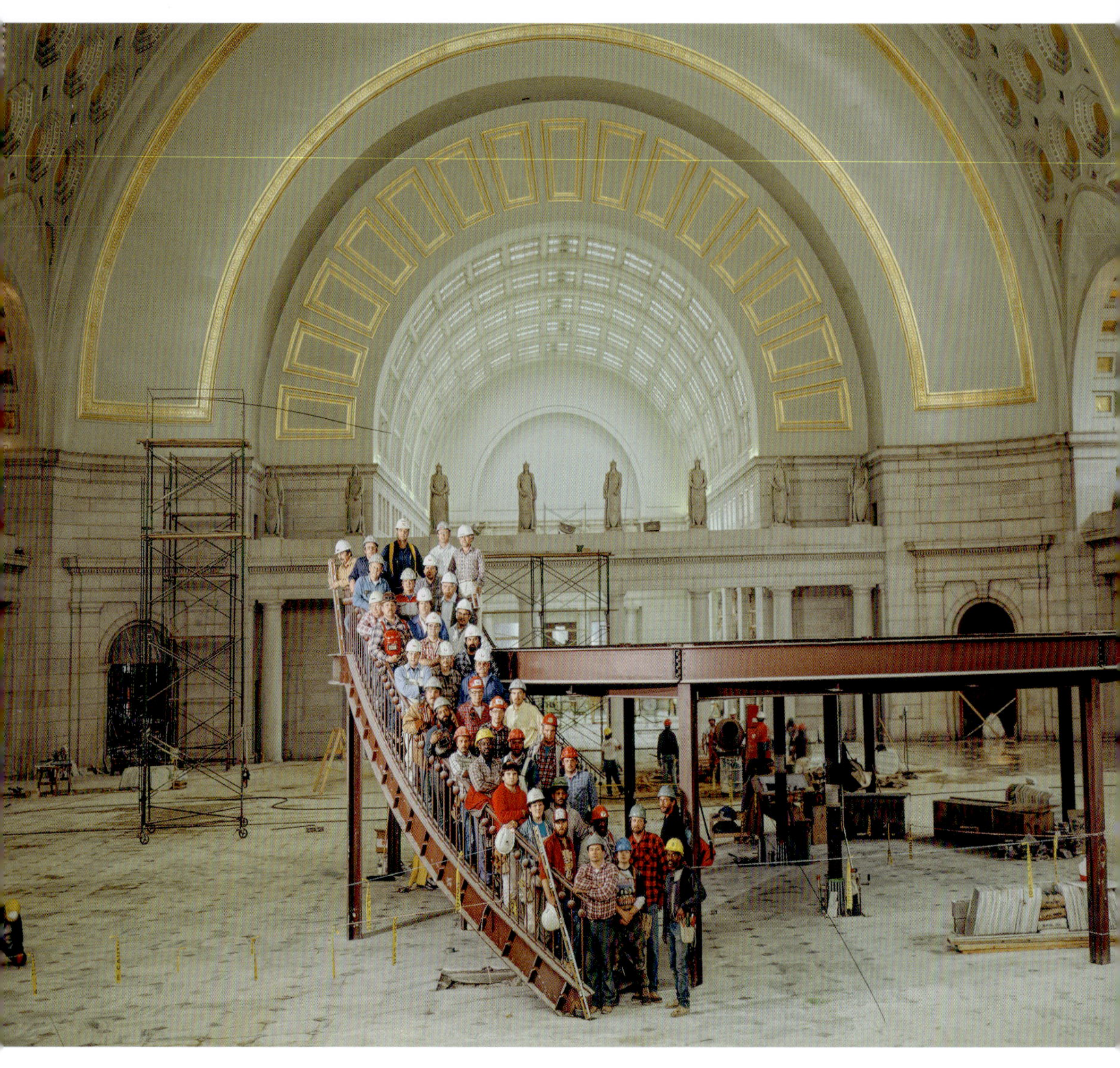

Union Station's Restoration Crew, Washington, D.C., 1988

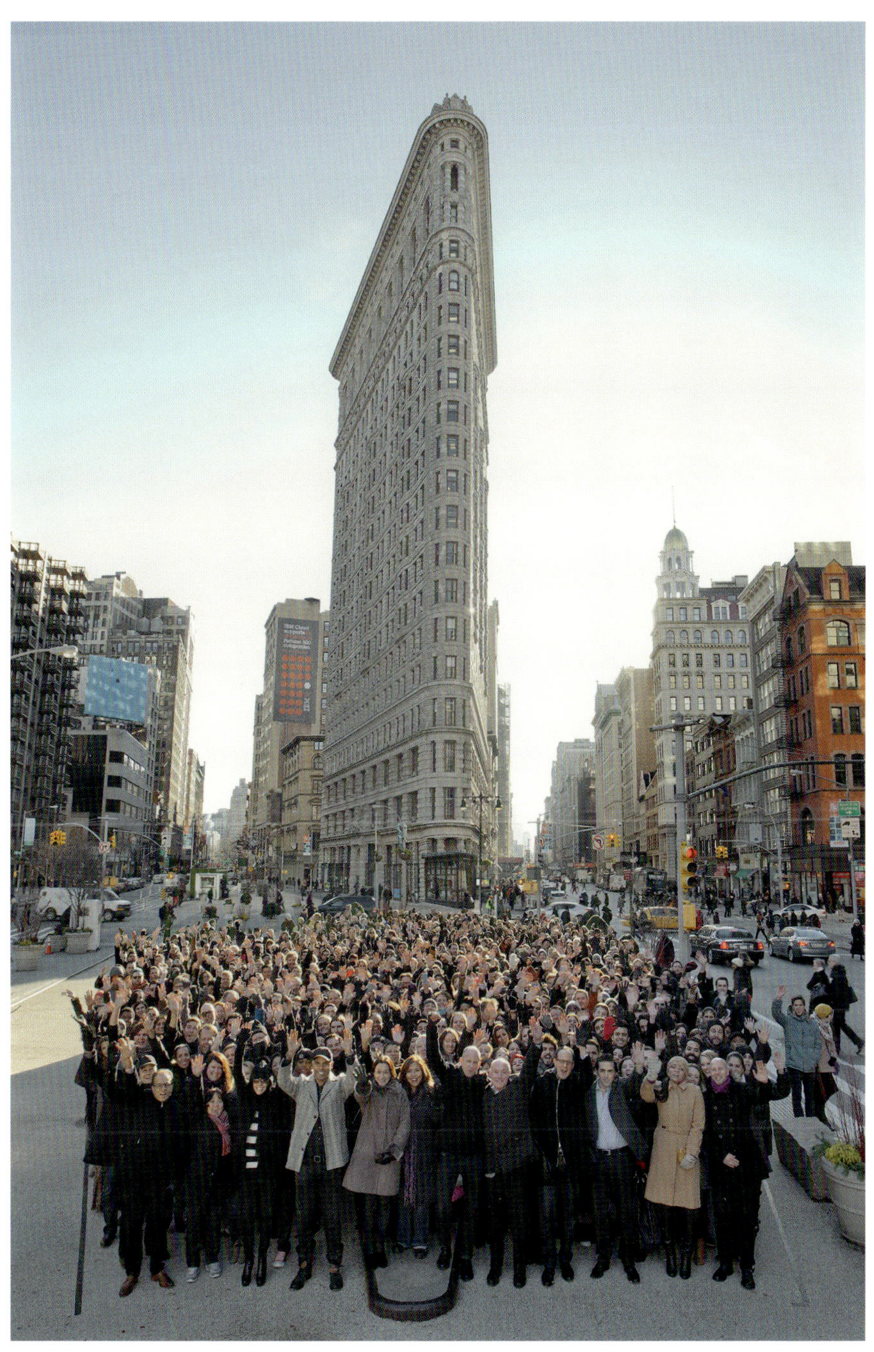

Grey Advertising Agency, New York, New York, 2013

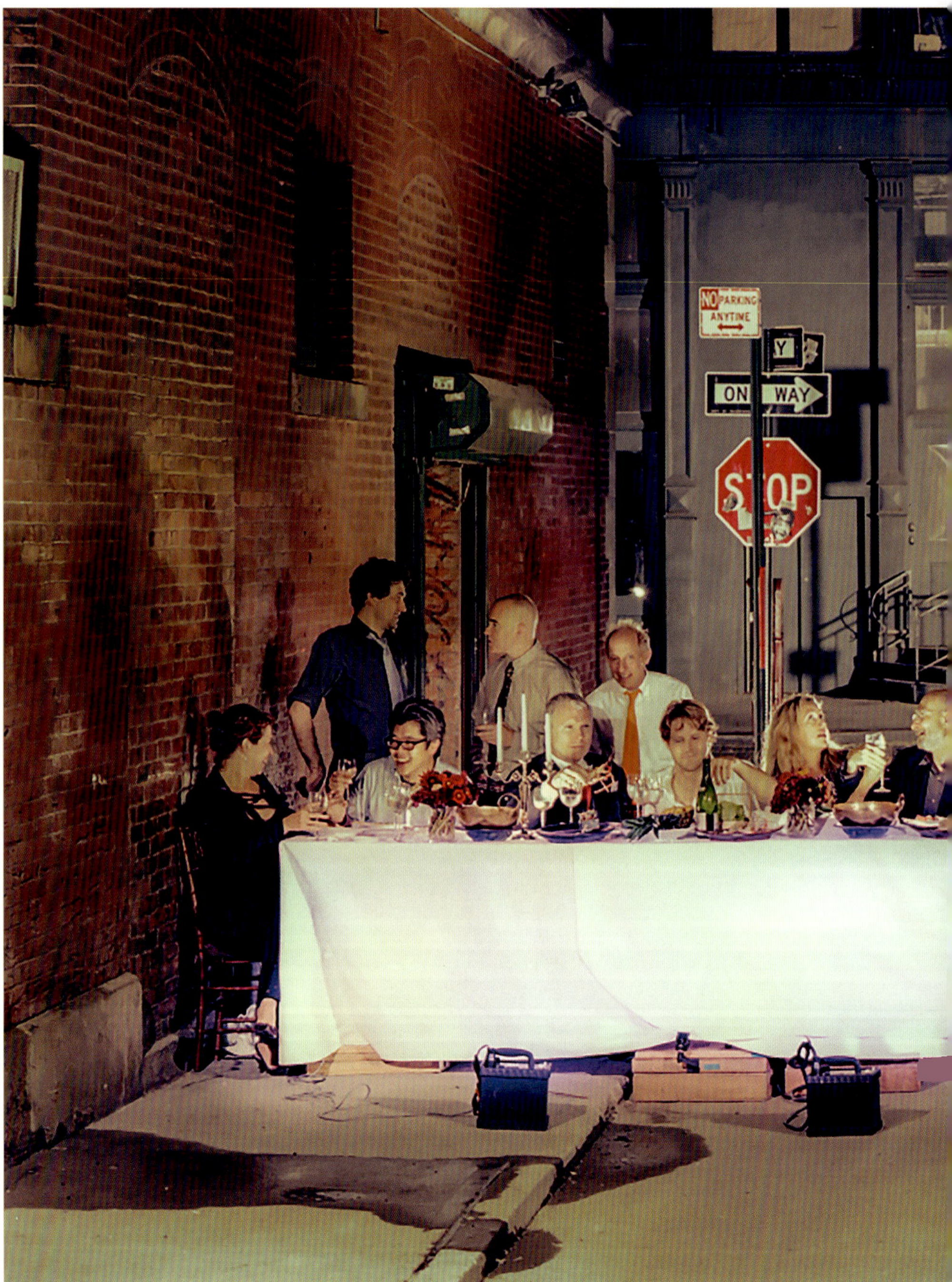

NO PARKING ANYTIME
ONE WAY
STOP

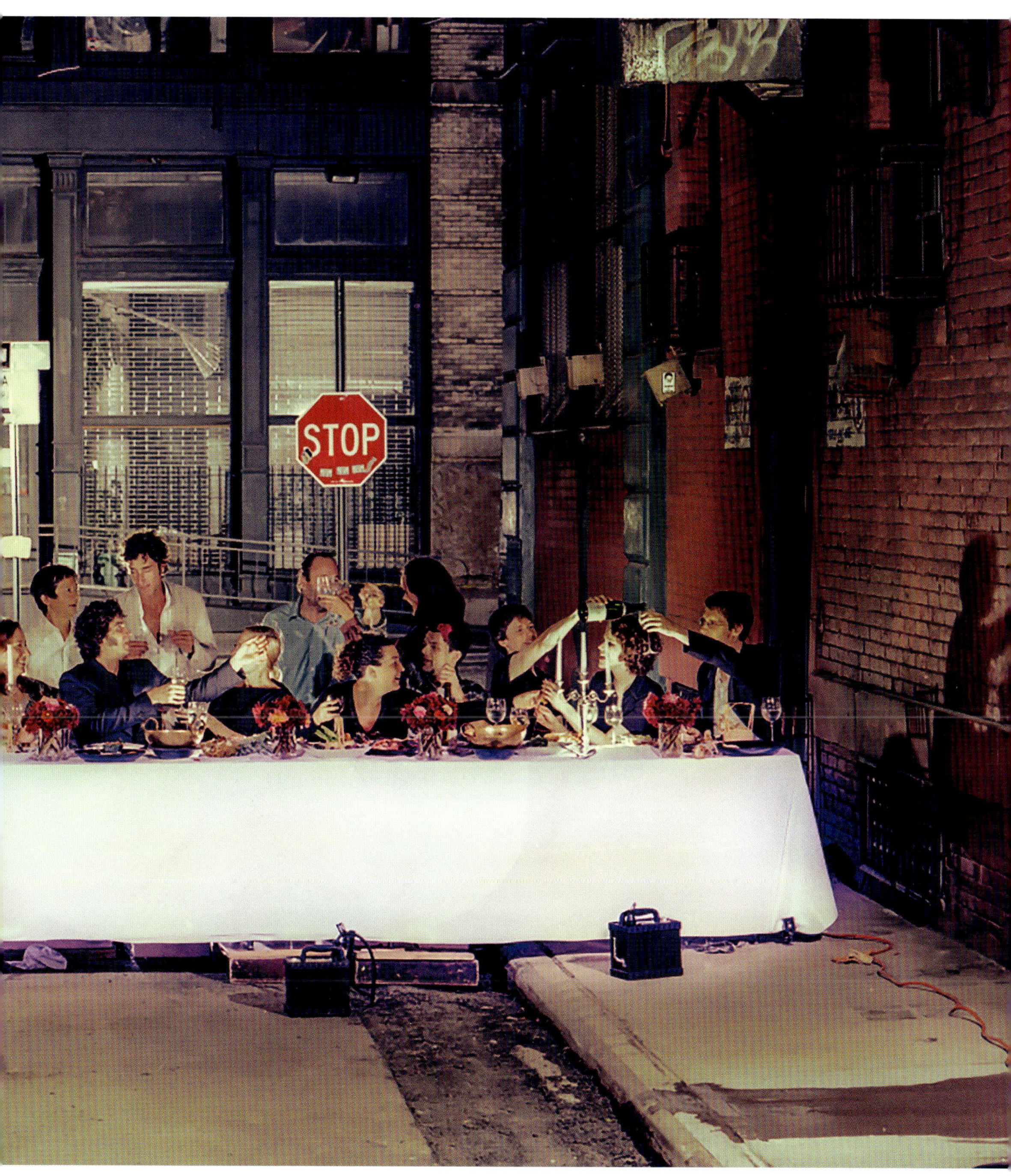

Downtown Independent Democrats, New York, New York, 2005

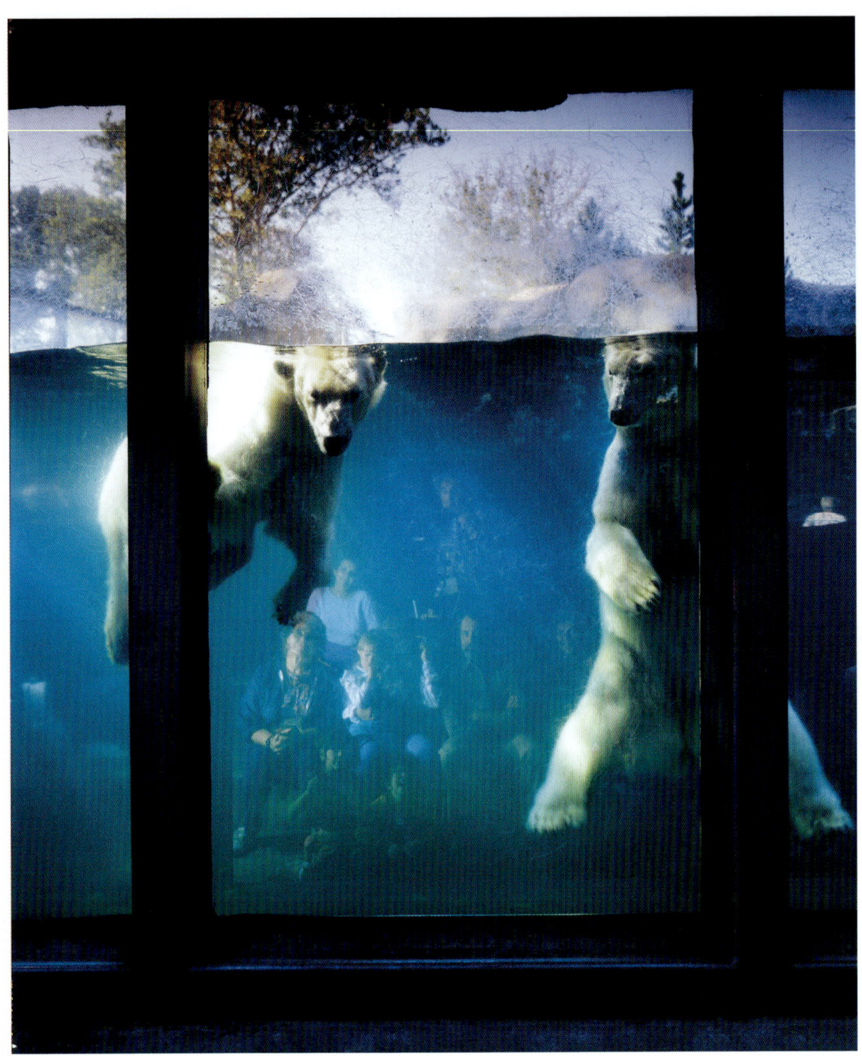

Polar Bears, Philadelphia, Pennsylvania, 1987

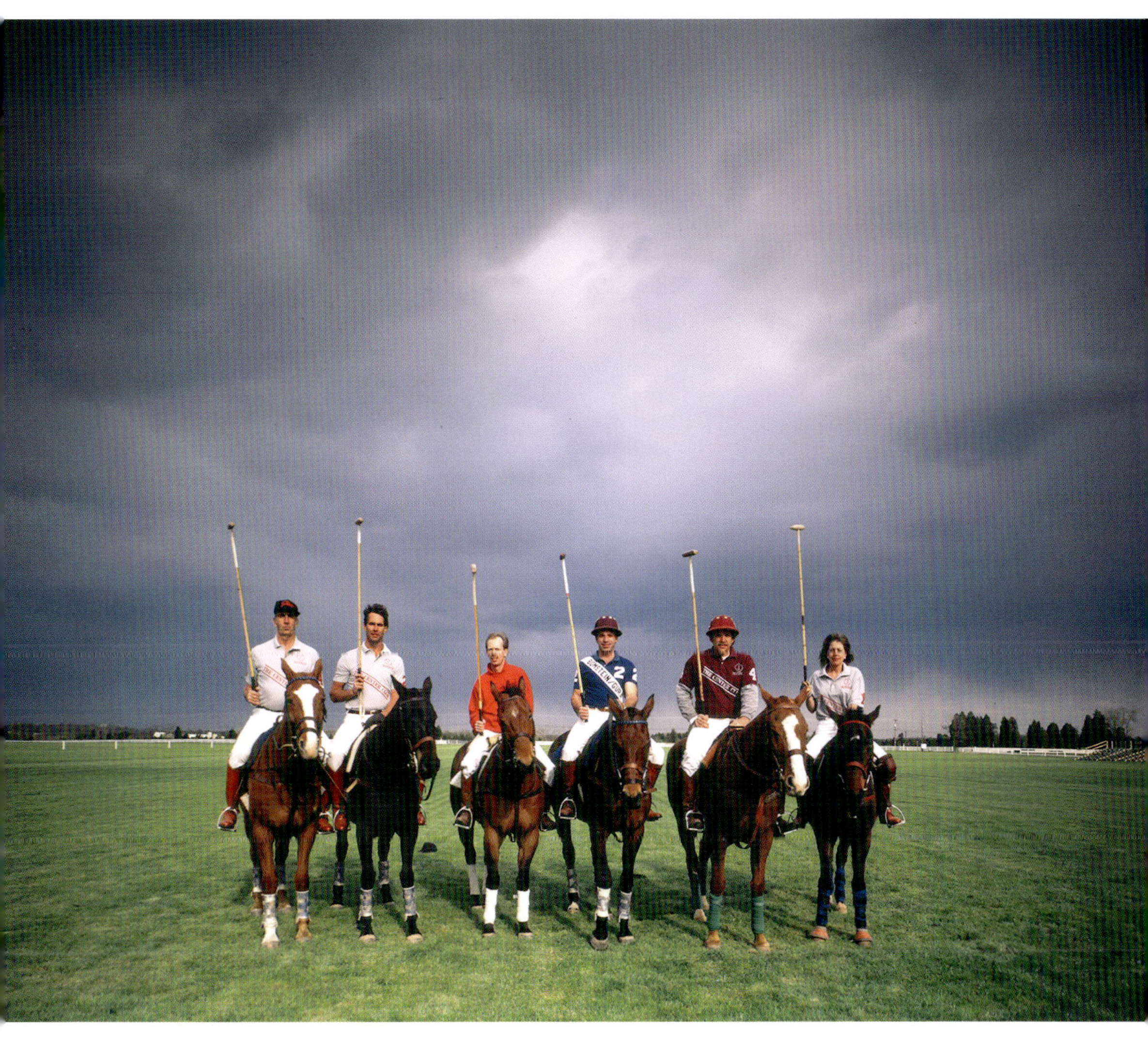

Members of the Potomac Polo Club Players, Poolesville, Maryland, 1988

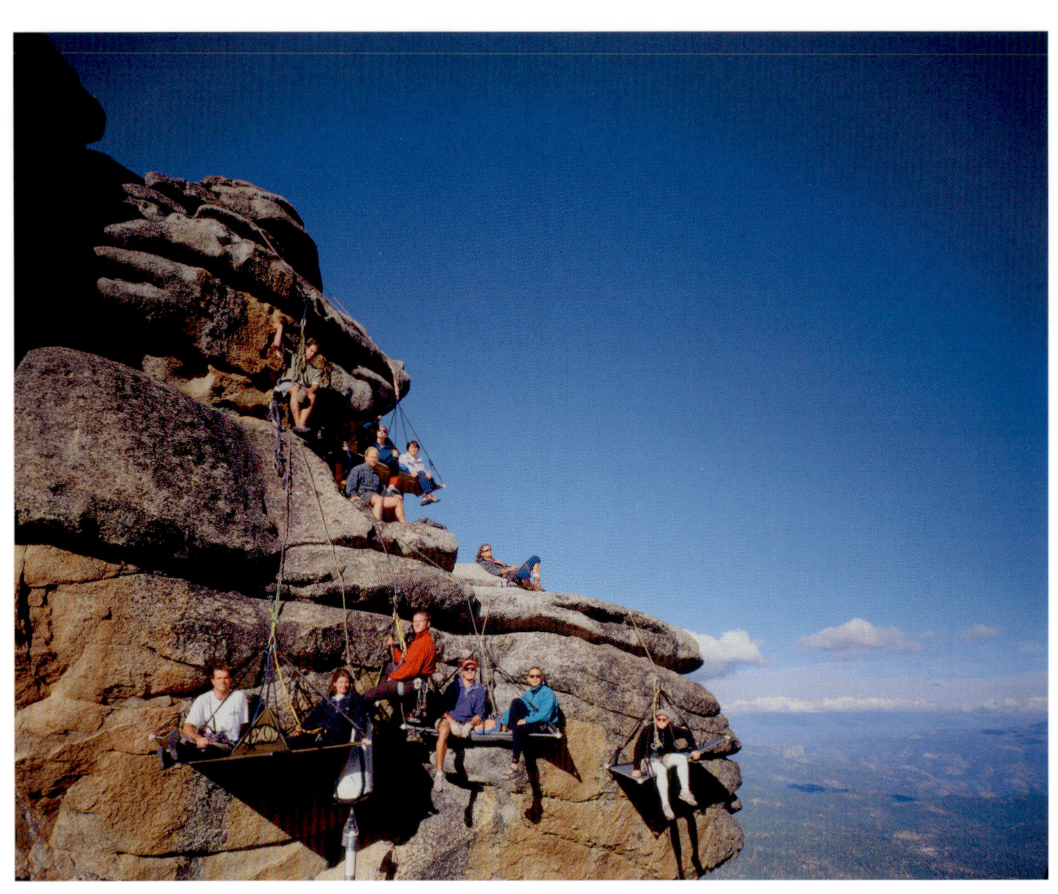

Rock Climbers, Oregon, 1994

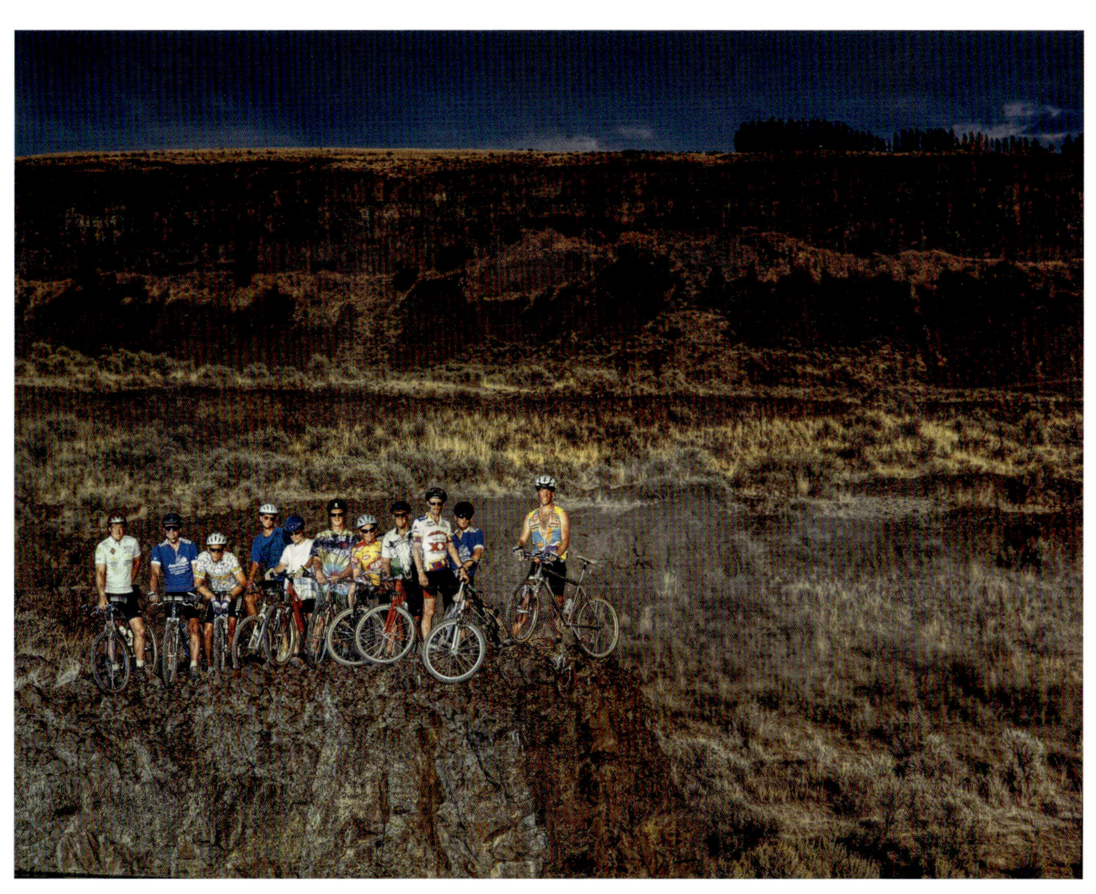

Mountain Bikers, Oregon, 1994

Liberian Orphans Chorus, Matthews, North Carolina, 2006

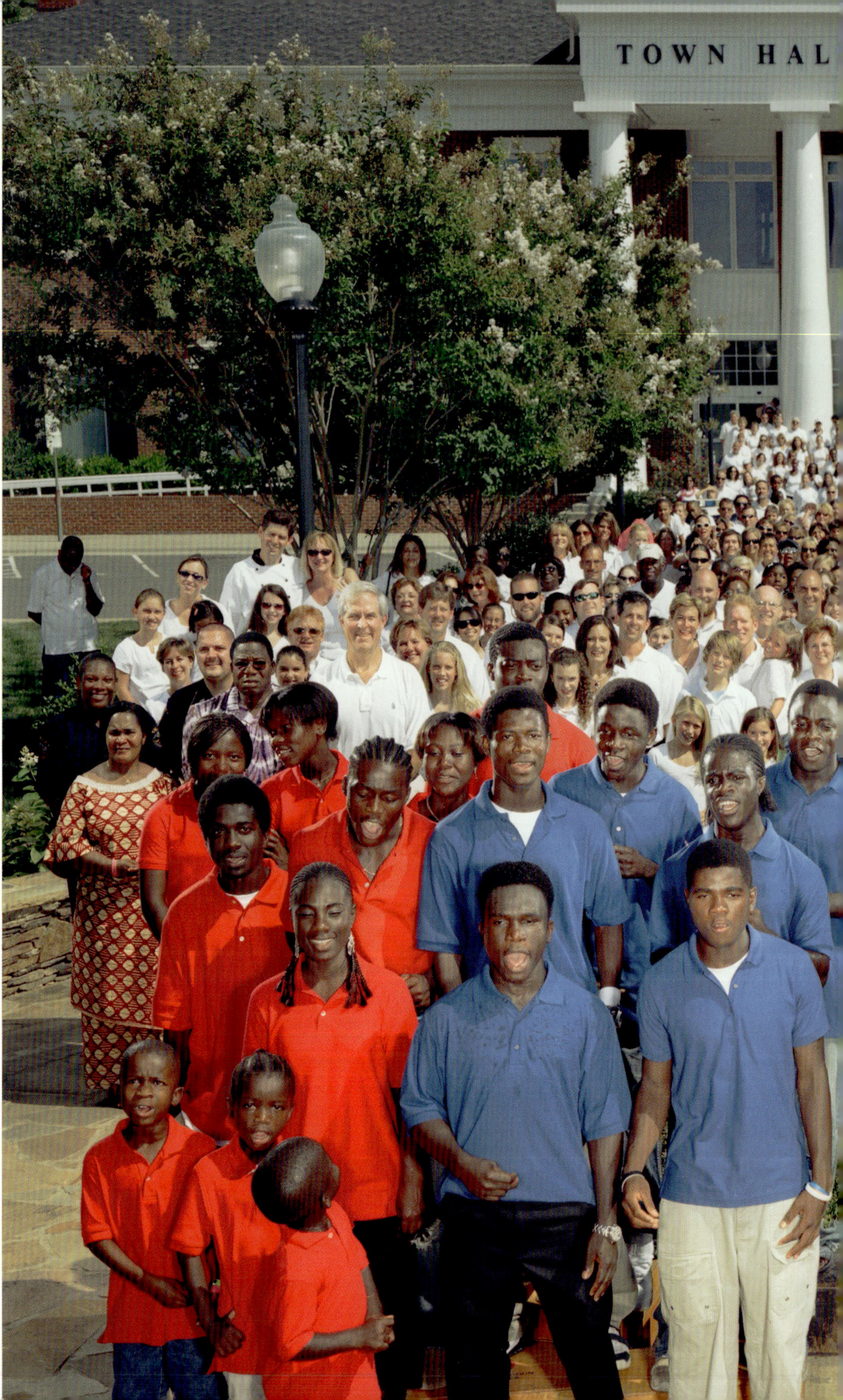
TOWN HAL

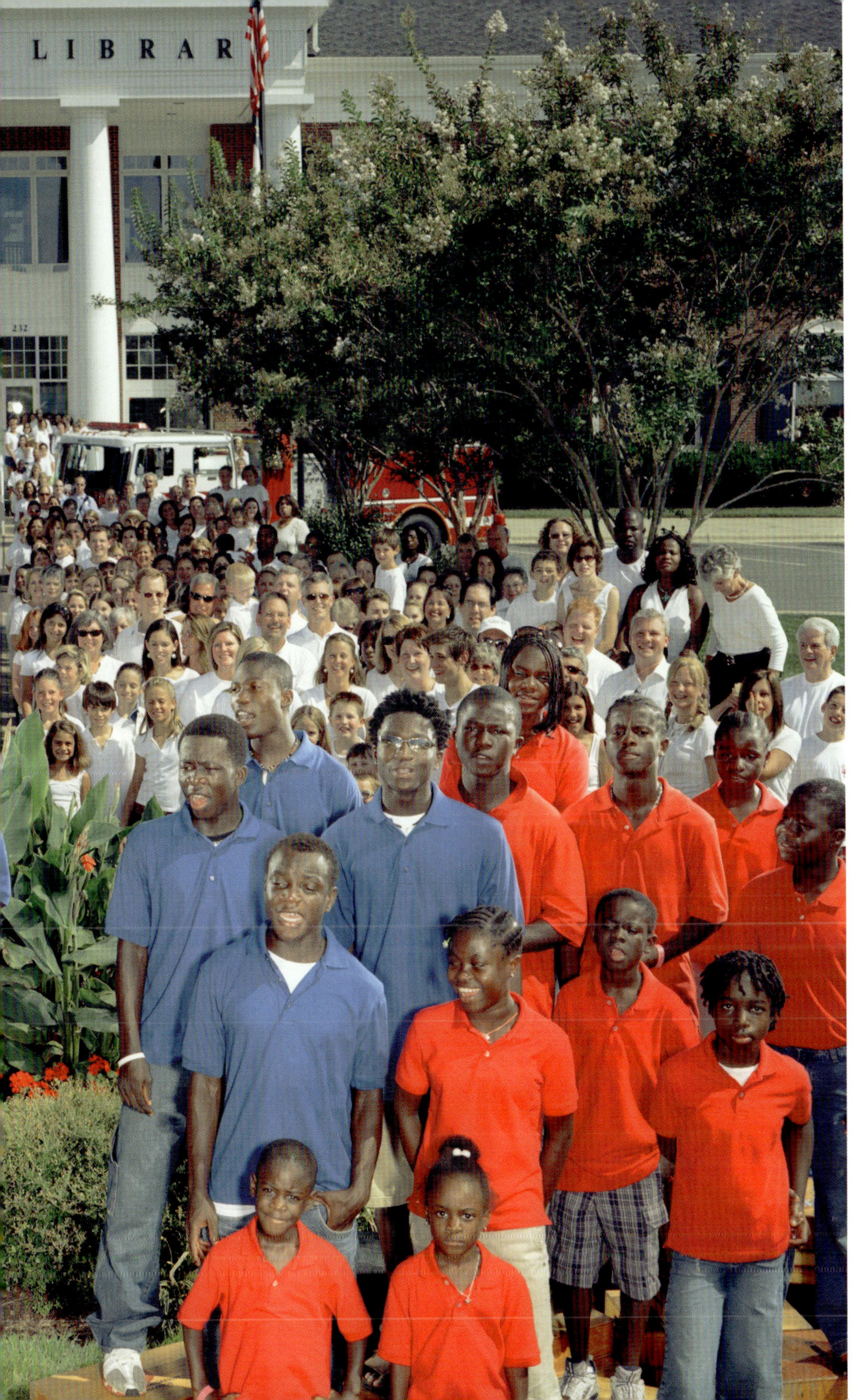

LIBRAR

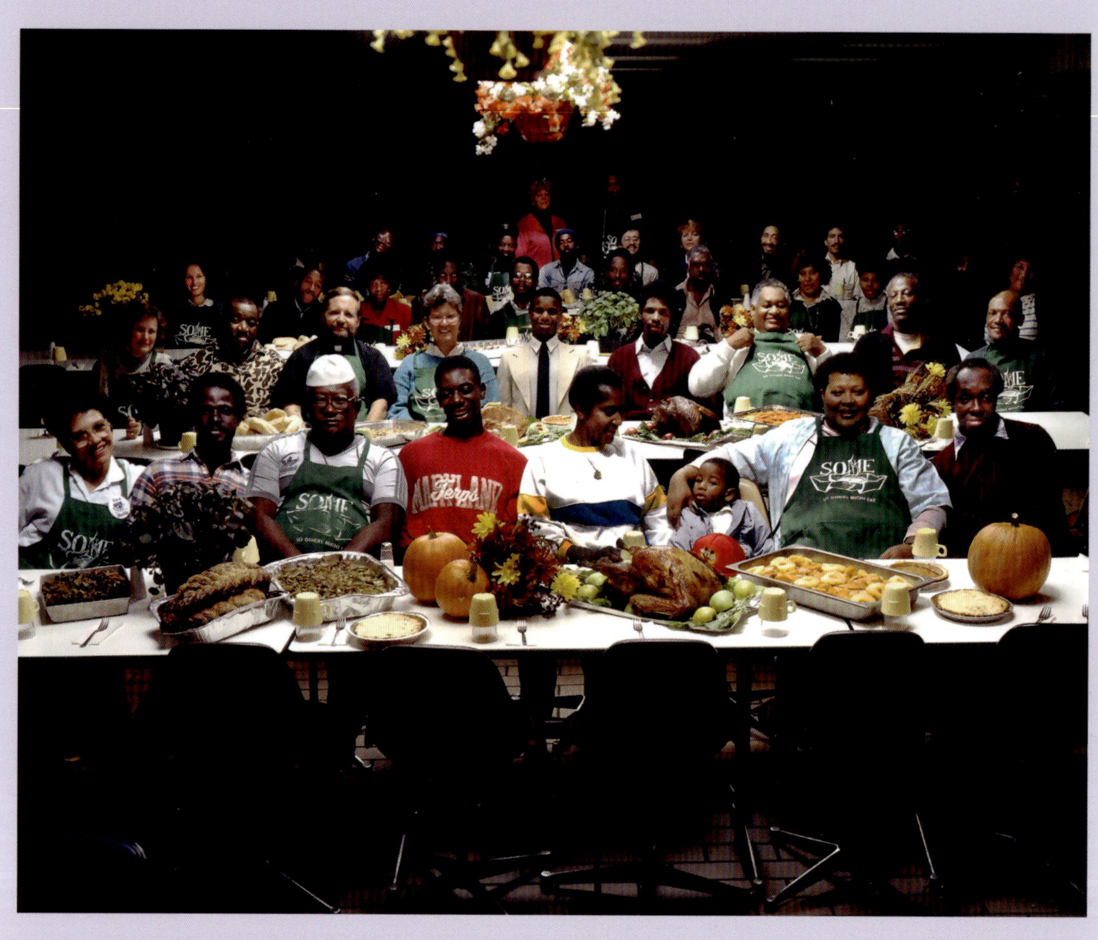

SOME Inc. (So Others Might Eat), Washington, D.C., 1988

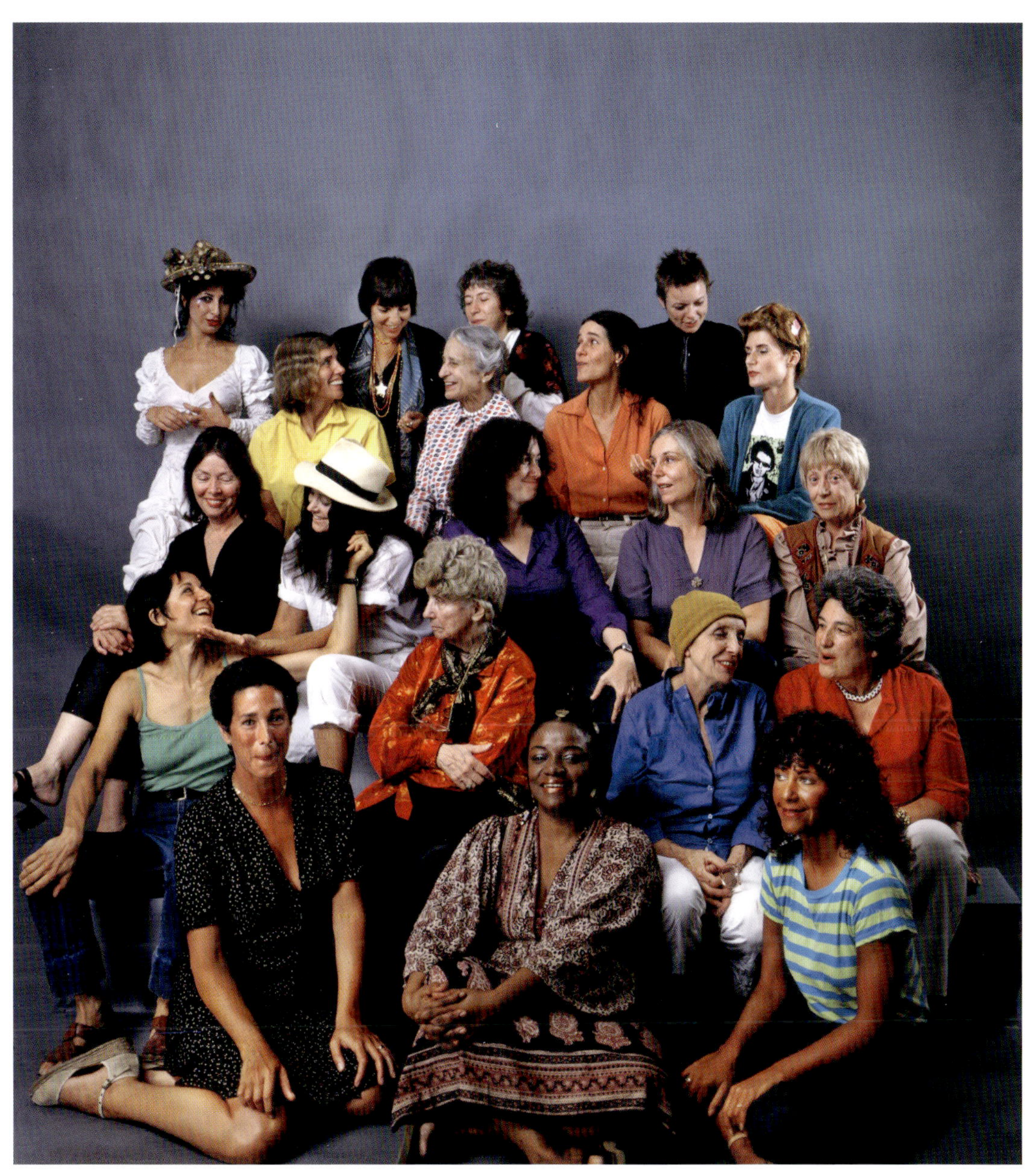

Women Artists, New York, New York, 1980

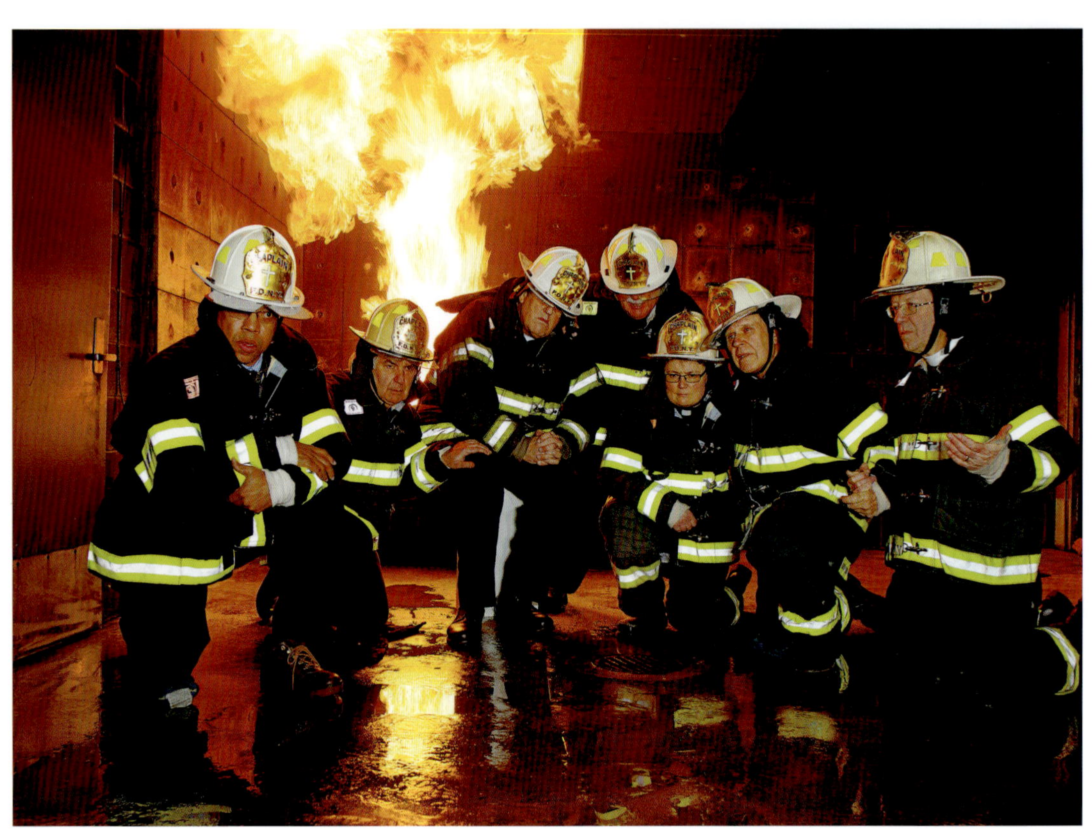

Chaplains of the Fire Department of New York, New York, New York, 2015

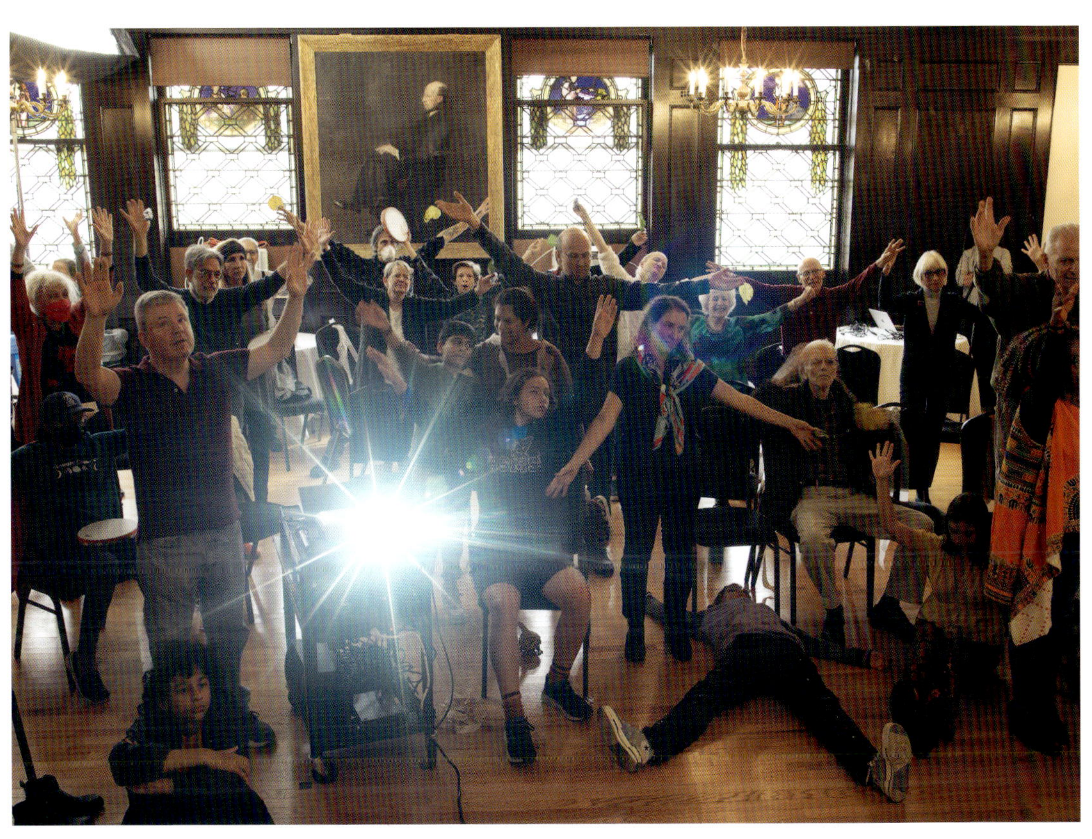

New York Society for Ethical Culture, New York, New York, 2023

OVERLEAF

Mahayana Buddhist Temple, New York, New York, 2017

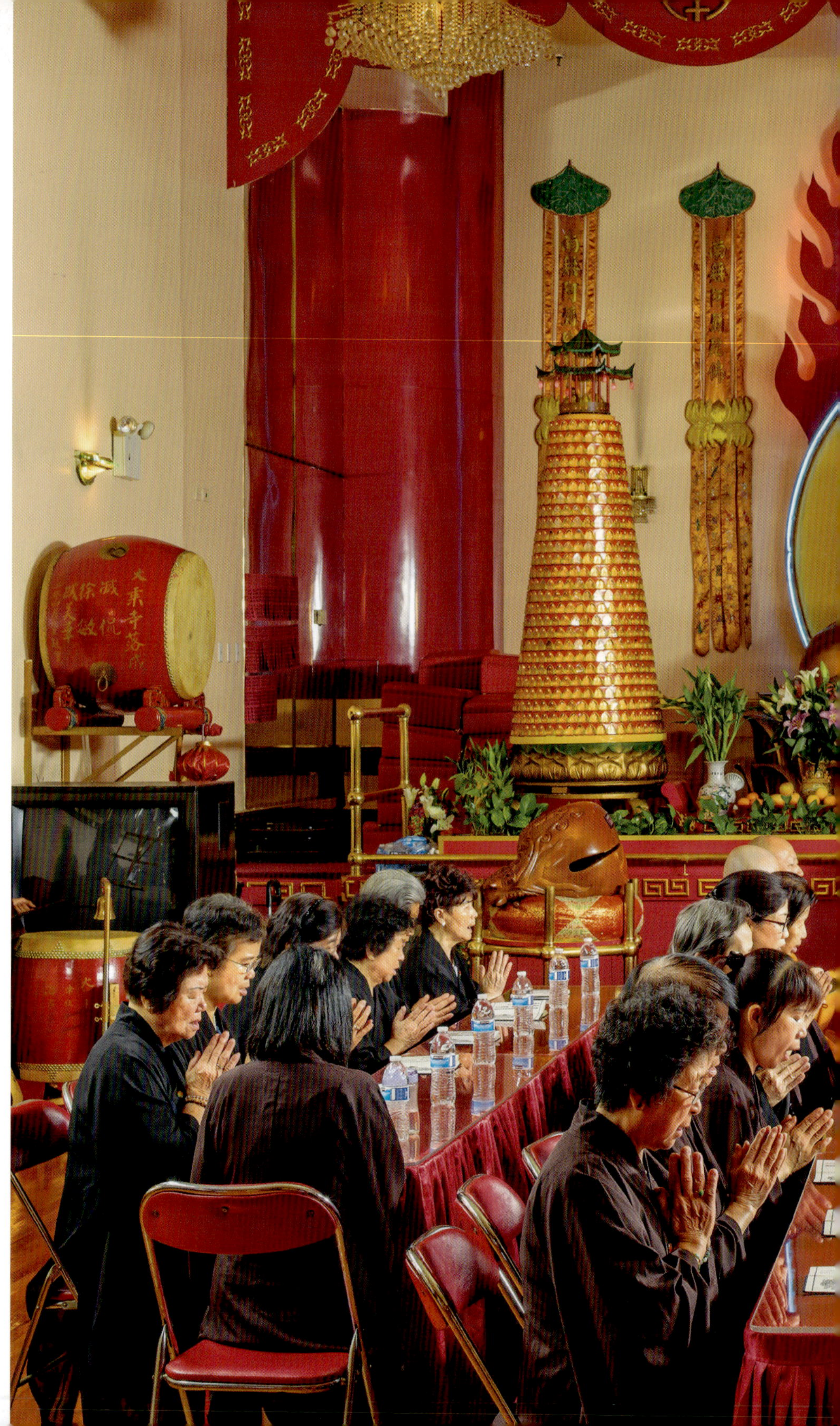

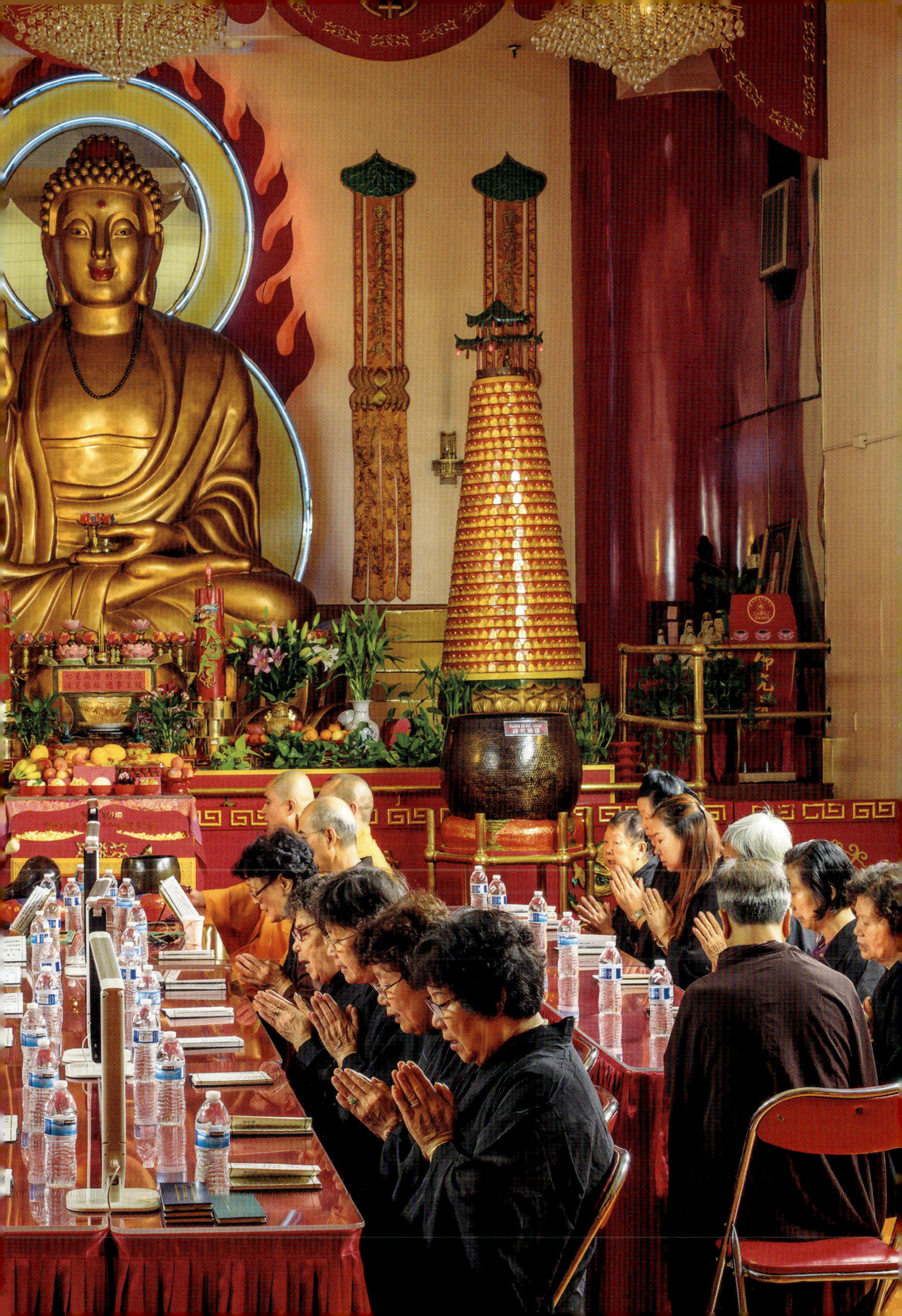

Extended Captions from the First Edition of *When Two or More Are Gathered Together*

STATEN ISLAND FERRY
New York, New York

Approximately 700 personnel operate and maintain the boats.

Transportation Administrator: Michael Lazar
Deputy Administrator/Commissioner: Vito J. Fossella, P.E.
Deputy Commissioner: Gerard Esposito

The Staten Island ferry system provides mass-transportation commuter service between Whitehall Street Terminal, Manhattan, and St. George Terminal, Staten Island. Six boats are operated during rush hours, while two boats normally undergo maintenance or are in dry dock for inspection or repairs. The boats run between St. George Terminal and Whitehall Terminal in approximately twenty-five minutes and handle nearly thirty thousand commuters daily.

Employees must pass civil-service requirements.

Pedestrian and vehicle fares help pay for the service, with the City of New York subsidizing any balance.

An annual boat trip is conducted for disabled persons and is sponsored by the Anchor Club, a philanthropic organization within the department. Personnel work without pay. Annually there is a dinner dance and a picnic sponsored by the Anchor Club.

Ferryboats have been traveling between Staten Island and Manhattan since Staten Island was first settled in the 1600s. The first notice of regular service, in 1745, was an advertisement in the *New York Weekly Post Boy*, which read: "Sylvania Seamens who keeps the upper ferry at the narrows, on Staten Island side, having good boats for that purpose, proposes, besides the proper attendance at the said ferry, constantly to keep a passage boat to go from thence to the City of New York, which will certainly set out every Tuesday and Friday and return the same day if possible, and at any other time, if passage or freight justify."

The City assumed ownership on October 25, 1905, after service deteriorated and a serious accident occurred. The ferry is under the jurisdiction of the New York City Department of Marine and Aviation, an agency of the Transportation Administration.

The Staten Island Ferry has become a popular choice of producers, directors, and advertisers for "on location" filming of motion pictures, television shows, and commercials, and of well-known magazines as a background for fashion layouts. The ferry has maintained an impressive safety record since 1905. During the past forty-five years approximately one billion passengers have traveled on the ferry. The boats have covered some 5 billion miles without a single fatality and have managed to arrive 95 percent on time.

NATURAL GLASS CORVETTE ASSOCIATION
Denville, New Jersey

100 members

President: David M. Feldmar
Vice-President: David Wiese
Treasurer: Gerry Peterson

Members meet on alternating Wednesday nights.

Natural Glass Corvette Association is dedicated to the promotion of good will in the community.

Members must own a Corvette.

The N.G.C.A. is a non-profit corporation supported by membership dues.

In addition to club meetings, the N.G.C.A. holds rallies which begin in Denville and cover up to a fifty-mile range. Non-members attending the rally follow the members, who determine the route direction. Shows are held to judge cars on the condition of their exteriors, interiors, and engine compartments. If the car is in its original condition, it is judged on authenticity. The nicest-looking car usually wins. Any Corvette owner may enter the competition.

The N.G.C.A. provides a chance for Corvette owners to socialize with other people who are interested in Corvettes. It is also a couples club. Caravans, picnics, and an annual Christmas party are activities shared by members.

N.G.C.A. was started in 1971 and is a division of the National Council of Corvette Clubs, whose total membership is about ten thousand. N.G.C.A. was a recent participant in the Morris County Mall Show.

COALITION OF LABOR UNION WOMEN (C.L.U.W.)
Detroit, Michigan

3,200 women

President: Olga Madar
Vice-President: Addie Wyatt
Recording Secretary: Joyce Miller
Corresponding Secretary: Patsy Fryman
Treasurer: Gloria Johnson

The group exists to organize the 30 million unorganized women workers under collective-bargaining agreements and make the unions more responsive to the needs of all women, including the 4 million women who are already members of unions.

The union meetings take place at the discretion of the local chapters throughout the country.

Any person who is a member or retiree of a national or international union or bona fide collective-bargaining organization may be a member of the Coalition of Labor Union Women.

The union is financially sustained by membership dues.

The group was formed in 1973 when seven women union leaders met to respond to a need within the union movement for a consolidated approach by union women to deal with their special concerns as women and union members in the labor force.

The activities of the Coalition of Labor Union Women center on enforcing affirmative action programs to correct inequities in hiring, salary, promotion, classification, benefits; training and educating women leaders in the union and the community to become active participants in the political and legislative processes of unions and the nation by seeking public office or government appointments at local, state, and national levels.

CHAPTER 76 OF THE DISABLED AMERICAN VETERANS (D.A.V.)
Whitestone, New York

1,500 members in local chapter; one half million, nationally

Commander: Don Sioss

Meets on the second and fourth Tuesday of each month.

The group's purpose is to help all amputees at whatever social, health, or employment level required.

The membership is nationally organized with local chapters throughout the country.

In order to join, one has to be an amputee veteran.

The D.A.V. is supported by private donations and membership dues.

The organization was formed in 1918 right after World War I when there was a need for political action for the social rehabilitation of amputees.

The activities of the group include examining legislative problems at the general meetings, psychological counseling, and employment notifications. Also, the group makes regular visits to vets in hospitals.

There is an annual Veteran's Day Dinner Dance. The group also gives out an annual award known as "Amputee of the Year" to the person who has done the most outstanding job in helping the group throughout the year. Famous members include financier Orin Lehman and actor Harold Russell.

THE HARROWGATE STRING BAND, INC.
PHILADELPHIA MUMMERS AND NEW YEAR'S
SHOOTERS ASSOCIATION
Hulmeville, Pennsylvania

80 members

President: Robert Rippman
Vice-President: James McKnight
Captain: Joseph Fries
Business Manager: Walter Ehrenfeuchter

The local group was organized in order to promote good music and to have fun. Its main interest is string-band music. All the string bands that make up the Mummers Association exist for "one purpose and for one purpose only"—to compete on New Year's Day in the Mummers Day parade.

In order to become a member, one fills out a membership application, which is reviewed by the executive board and finally passed by the music director, and the members in a secret ballot.

The band functions fifty times a year in concerts, variety shows, and parades. In addition, it holds four social nights with friends and families of members. At the end of the year the band spends three or four months working on the costumes with the help of friends and family. The fifty concerts and appearances are performed for pay, but the group makes several charity appearances as well.

The Harrowgate String Band has for three years finished in the top ten of twenty-two bands competing in the New Year's Day parade.

NEW YORK CITY FIRE DEPARTMENT (F.D.N.Y.)
New York, New York

11,448 firemen
811 civilians

Fire Commissioner and Chief of Department: John T. O'Hagan
First Deputy Fire Commissioner: Stephen J. Murphy

The organization is locally based within the New York City area.

The main purpose of F.D.N.Y. is the suppression of fire and the saving and maintaining of human life.

To become a member of the New York City Fire Department, one must pass the civil-service test, and then go through a training program with the Fire Department.

The organization is financially sustained by New York City.

F.D.N.Y. became an official fire company of the city of New York in 1865. Until that time there were several volunteer fire companies. Because of their fierce pride and competitiveness, street brawls often occurred in front of a fire. As fighting the fire was more important than fighting each other, New York decided to maintain its own official fire department. As the city's needs have grown F.D.N.Y. has computerized dispatching to handle the estimated 400,000 alarms each year. The Super Pumper is the only existent engine of its type in the world. It can draft water from any source, including rivers. If the nozzle of this engine were pointed straight up at a building, its spray would reach the sixty-fifth floor.

The department is considered to be among the most colorful in the world because of all the "fire buffs" involved in the organization. Mayor Fiorello LaGuardia was such a "fire buff" and would respond to fires with the department in the middle of the night.

HOLLAND TUNNEL
New York, New York

275 employees

Tunnel Manager: Lawrence J. Lewis
Assistant Manager: Philip Leahy
Chief Tolls Supervisor: Marie Jones
Port Authority Police Commander: Captain Emanuel Greene
Assistant General Foreman: James Rich
Nurse: Camille Dorin

The Holland Tunnel shortens the time required to traverse the Hudson River from Canal Street in Manhattan to Jersey City, New Jersey, and handles approximately sixty thousand vehicles daily. It is open twenty-four hours a day.

Employees must pass civil-service requirements.

The Port Authority of New York and New Jersey, which manages the tunnel, is a self-supporting, incorporated agency of the two states, functioning without burden to the taxpayers.

In 1906 legislation paved the way for a study for a bridge. In 1913 the commissions were authorized to consider a tunnel, because land in Manhattan needed for the bridge approaches was too costly. The commissions were given authority in 1919 to construct a tunnel between Canal Street in Manhattan and Jersey City. Clifford Holland, a young tunnel engineer, was chosen to build the tunnel. Construction began October 12, 1920. At five o'clock on the afternoon of November 12, 1927, American flags were unfurled at each entrance to the tunnel by a button pressed at the White House by President Calvin Coolidge. Thousands of guests gathered to hear speeches and were permitted to walk on the newly finished roadways. The first traffic passed through at 12:01 a.m., November 13. The tunnel was built by the New Jersey Interstate Bridge and Tunnel Commission and the New York Bridge and

Tunnel Commission.

Since 1930 the Holland Tunnel has been owned and operated by the Port Authority. Many engineering problems were solved during the construction of the tunnel. The ventilation problem in a tunnel of such great length was fundamental. Four ventilation buildings, two on each side of the Hudson River, house immense fans which provide a change of air every ninety seconds. Methods and principles developed during the construction of the Holland Tunnel form a basis for construction of underwater tunnels throughout the world.

Three tunnel engineers served as Chief Engineers on the project: Clifford Holland, Milton H. Freeman, and Ole Singstad. Only Mr. Singstad lived to see its completion.

Length of north tube 8,558 feet
Length of south tube 8,371 feet
Width of roadway 20 feet
Operating headroom 12 feet 6 inches
External diameter 93 feet 5 inches
Cost up to 1973 $69,300,000

J.F.K. INTERNATIONAL AIRPORT CONTROL TOWER
FEDERAL AVIATION ADMINISTRATION

Jamaica, New York

52 staff members, 39 controllers

The staff guarantees the safe and expeditious control of air traffic, maintains safe control in and out of the airport, and also considers noise-abatement procedures.

Staff members must meet civil-service requirements. Their schooling at an F.A.A. school in Oklahoma City for 16-18 weeks is paid for by the government. On-the-job training at different towers throughout the country follows. Maximum initial employment age is thirty, which is also the average age of a controller.

Air-traffic controllers are required to be able to think fast on their feet, to make snap decisions, and, most importantly, to know how to keep the airplanes separated on the four major runways. Controllers are responsible for all moving traffic both in the air and on the ground. All are qualified to do each other's job. There are three areas of duty: clearance delivery, which is telling the pilot which runway, route, etc., to use; ground control, which involves controlling all moving ground traffic; and local control, which entails clearing the aircraft for landing and takeoff on selected runways.

The $1 million, 150-foot-high steel control tower was completed in September 1952, and a renovation in 1971 made it one of the most modern towers in the world. More than $1 million worth of air-traffic control electronic equipment is housed in the tower. Special radar scanners allow controllers to observe all aircraft movements on the airport's nine miles of runways and twenty-two miles of taxiways, as well as airborne aircraft movements within a thirty-mile radius of the airport. The control tower also controls and monitors various other navigation aides, including the Instrument Landing Systems, VAS/ installations, VORTAC facility, airfield lighting, and a telecommunications network.

The tower services approximately one thousand aircraft each day, with one plane landing or taking off every 2½ minutes. The busiest times are between 2:00 p.m. and 10:00 p.m. Controllers work with the New York Common Instrument Flight Rules Room control facilities and the New York Air Route Control Center in Bohemia, New York.

The safety record is excellent.

SALVATION ARMY HEADQUARTERS BAND

New York, New York

33 members in the Eastern territory

Band Master: Derek Smith
Executive Officer: Roland Schram

During the band season, from October through May, there is a weekly rehearsal plus regular Friday-night performances at the Army's temple.

The band's main objective is to present music as an expression of religious faith, rather than music for music's sake.

To become a band member, it is first necessary to be a member of the Salvation Army and then to audition for the Band Board. The band is made up strictly of volunteers, as is the entire Salvation Army.

The Salvation Army Band began informally in England when brass bands were popular with the working classes and attracted attention. The band gradually became organized and today is of professional quality.

Besides the weekly temple performances, the band plays at other events, such as the National Music Educators' Conference in Atlantic City, New Jersey, and the Brass Conference for Scholarships held in New York City.

Derek Smith, the Band Master, is a coronet soloist and was well known in England, where he played for the Queen's Guard Band. Another former member, Philip Smith, now plays with the Chicago Symphony.

EMPIRE HOSE COMPANY #3

Merrick, Long Island, New York

45 volunteers

Captain: Keith Hartin
1st Lieutenant: Mike Gleason
2nd Lieutenant: George Moore

Regular company meetings take place on the first Tuesday of every month.

The purpose of the group is to put out fires whenever they occur in the area—24 hours a day, 365 days a year.

Membership is local—from the Long Island community.

In order to join the organization, a volunteer must be at least eighteen years of age and have no criminal record, supply six references, and pass a physical examination.

The company is sustained financially by collecting money from fund drives on a door-to-door basis.

Engine Company #3 is one of two new volunteer fire companies formed from a split of the original Merrick Hook and Ladder Company #1, which was begun in 1890. The other company formed at the time of the split was Friendship Engine and Hose Company #2. The split occurred because the original Merrick Hook and Ladder Company was only a truck company. (Trucks cannot supply water; the water came from yet another company farther north.) The two new companies are complete operations.

Other than fighting fires, the company has a drill team which participates in tournaments every Saturday all over the Island. The team, known as the Buckeyes, takes part in contests such as "Man & Machine against Time," which uses various firefighting apparatus to test the skill and dexterity of volunteers.

The company is proud to note that they have not lost a single member in the service of fighting fires.

THE WHEELMEN

Swarthmore, Pennsylvania

600 family memberships

Commander: Edwin Gerling
Vice-Commander: Robert Menker
Treasurer: Samuel Haney
Secretary: Charles Sanford

The group meets in many different states at antique bike tours, parades, and meets.

The object of the group is to encourage saving, restoring, riding, and displaying antique bicycles; to renew America's pride in its bicycling history; and to encourage the return of cycling to American life.

Wheelmen membership is open to anyone—whether or not an antique bicycle owner. All privileges are granted to all members, but members must have ridden a ten-mile tour in order to vote.

General activities include publication of a quarterly magazine, tours through rural countryside, antique car shows, college homecomings, and special holiday observances, obstacle course runs, tandem tourneys, and other contests. Ladies may join their gents in riding the high-wheelers and showing off the 1890's fashions. There are ladies' races and costume judging. The organization also holds an annual race of highwheelers on the Indianapolis Speedway.

Wheelmen revenue is derived from parade fees, dues, sustaining memberships, and public sale of its magazine.

The group was begun in 1967 as a national, non-profit, incorporated organization. It includes, in addition to the above listed officers, a board with a historian, editor, and associate editor, photographer, League of American Wheelmen representative, and captains of each state chapter.

Special awards include first prizes in the Philadelphia Mummers parade and in the Washington Cherry Blossom parade. In addition, Ed Berry, Jr., a fellow Wheelman, rode his Columbia highwheeler from San Francisco to Boston during the summer of 1971 to attract attention to the bicycle movement.

GAS CHAMBER
BASIC TRAINING COMPANY OF THE THIRD BASIC COMBAT TRAINING BRIGADE

Fort Dix, New Jersey

Approximately 150 men

Commanding General: Major General William A. Patch
Deputy Commanding General: Brigadier General Theodore Genes, Jr.

The mission in basic training is to provide the recruit with the fundamental skills every soldier needs before proceeding on to specialized training.

All recruits in basic training go through gas-chamber exercises after three weeks of training. The purpose of the gas exercises is to build confidence in the infantryman-in his ability to use the gas mask well, and to know what to do during a gas attack.

CAMP TAHOE

Loch Sheldrake, New York

Approximately 150 boys

Directors: Irving and Gussie Mason

The aim of Camp Tahoe is permanent weight loss through re-education in eating habits, physical activity, and development of new interests. The usual weight loss is 20 to 45 pounds. Life at Tahoe is a normal "all boy" environment, where a strong spirit of self-confidence, pride, and self-respect is developed in each boy.

The camp is exclusively for boys who are extremely overweight from overeating.

The camp is financially sustained by camp fees from the participants.

Campers' activities include swimming, Trimnastics, and Circuit training. In addition, campers exercise with "the boot"—a weighted canvas shoe used to trim down hips and thighs and strengthen leg muscles. Other activities include baseball, basketball, and other sports, plus treasure hunts, campfires, carnivals, and cookouts. Traditionally the camp holds "Banquet and Awards Night," at which the highest prize is given for "Camper of the Year."

Camp Tahoe was started by Gussie Mason, its present director, in response to her own past overweight problems. Mrs. Mason describes herself as a fat child and a fat woman until she learned how to keep the weight off. She, along with her husband, Irving, started the camp because they had great compassion for the overweight child.

At the camp the boys do the "Tahoe Trot" as they go from activity to activity. Trotting—rather than walking—helps tone up muscles and increases lung capacity.

THE STAR TREK CONVENTION
STAR TREK ASSOCIATES, A DIVISION OF
TELLURIAN ENTERPRISES, INC.

Brooklyn, New York

10,000 international members

Officers:
Thom and Dana Anderson
Claire Eddy
Stuart Grossman
Stuart Hellinger
Devra Langsam
Dave Simons
Barbara Wenk
Joan Winston
Ben Yalow
Joyce Yasner
Steven and Elyse Rosenstein

The Star Trek Convention meets each February on Washington's Birthday weekend.

The main objectives of the organization are to cause a film to be made and to bring back the *Star Trek* television series.

To become a member, one must purchase a membership in the yearly convention.

The organization is supported by membership fees.

The convention provides an opportunity for *Star Trek* fans to exchange memorabilia, such as buttons, books, and pictures. There is also a costume call at which they can appear as their favorite *Star Trek* character.

The *Star Trek* Convention was started by Elyse Rosenstein and Devra Langsam in the spring of 1971, because they did not want *Star Trek* to die in the hearts of its fans.

It was decided to retire the five-year mission after the 1976 convention was held.

FEMINIST STUDIO WORKSHOP COLLECTIVE OF THE WOMAN'S BUILDING

Los Angeles, California

Approximately 1,500 members

Core Faculty:
Sheila de Bretteville
Arlene Raven
Ruth Iskin
Suzanne Lacy
Helen Roth
Dina Metzger

The main purpose of the group is to provide public facilities and resources where a community of women of all ages, classes, cultures, ethnic origins, and races can develop the voices and forms through which women's culture becomes public and known.

The center is public and open seven days a week.

It is open to all women, local or national. To become a member, a woman should send a contribution to the organization.

The organization is financially supported through foundation grants and membership contributions.

The Woman's Building was started in 1973 in Los Angeles by a group of women artists who felt disenfranchised from the artistic community, and who felt the need to create a distinctly women's culture based on women's experiences.

The center is involved in classes, community organizing, concerts, conferences, conversation, celebrations, designing, exhibits, lectures, creating artwork, media presentations, meetings, performances, printing, readings, rental facilities, research, women's services, and therapy. It sponsors the Feminist Education Summer Workshop in Los Angeles and Chicago. This is a workshop in the methodology of feminist education for women teaching in colleges.

MARSHALL CHESS CLUB, INC.

New York, New York

400 members

President: Walter Goldwater
Vice-Presidents: Allen Kaufman, Andrew Soltis

The club meets at its headquarters on Tenth Street in New York City. The membership is mainly local.

The organization exists in order to promote the playing of chess as a recreation.

Requirement for membership is an application and the recommendation of two members.

The Marshall Chess Club is supported mainly by dues and by some gifts.

General types of activities include tournaments, exhibitions, and lectures.

The club was organized in New York in 1915 as a congenial gathering place for lovers of chess and a home for American Chess Champion Frank Marshall.

Famous members in the organization include Edward Lasker, who is now president-emeritus, Bobby Fischer, Reuben Fine, and most of the other great American chess players.

THE ASSOCIATED BLIND, INC.

New York, New York

Approximately 350 individuals

President: Joseph E. Travers
Vice-President: Joseph Kramer
Secretary-Treasurer: Bernard Perlman
Assistant Secretary: Irving M. Selis

The Associated Blind serves blind and visually handicapped people of all ages, races, and religions. Its objective is to improve economic, social, and cultural opportunities for blind and visually handicapped people. The Associated Blind, Inc., exists to fill the need for an organization of the blind, conducted and controlled directly by the blind.

The organization is supported by voluntary contributions.

The Associated Blind was formed in 1938 after more than four years of study, research, and evaluation of the problems of blind people. The study was conducted by thirteen men and women who were blind themselves.

Activities include social service—locating suitable housing facilities, visiting blind people in homes, hospitals, and institutions, counseling and interceding on behalf of welfare clients, teaching Braille, and the consultation and guidance of families of the newly blinded—and recreation, including arts and crafts, socials and parties.

The group is involved in the dissemination to the general public of "Our Ten Commandments for the Sighted" and "Take Care of Your Eyes." The group has also designed the American flag in Braille.

CAPITOL WRESTLING CORPORATION

Washington, D.C.

40 wrestlers

President: Vincent J. McMahon
Director: Robert J. Marella
Secretary-Treasurer: Phil Zacko

The main purpose of the organization is to book and promote professional wrestling events throughout the world.

Wrestlers come to the organization from all over the country. To be booked through Capitol Wrestling Corporation, one must be a professional wrestler. The average age of a wrestler is about thirty-one.

The group is financially sustained by the fees and commissions from booking and promoting professional wrestling activities.

The organization was started in 1961 in Washington, D.C.

In addition to its regular wrestling events, the organization does benefits for such institutions as schools and orphanages. Famous wrestlers who have been booked through Capitol Wrestling are Bruno Sammartino, Ivan Putski, Andre the Giant, Ivan Koloff, and Guerilla Monsoon. The most famous bout was in 1964, when Bruno Sammartino wrestled

Guerilla Monsoon for 1 hour and 22 minutes without a single fall. Bruno Sammartino, Capitol Wrestling's most famous box-office success, is known for his back breaker and bear hug.

WOMEN EMPLOYED (W.E.)

Chicago, Illinois

1,000 members

Executive Director: Day Creamer

The organization meets weekly.

Its main aims are the enforcement of equal-opportunity laws and equitable treatment for working women.

Membership is open to any woman office worker in the Chicago Loop area.

The group is financially sustained by membership dues.

The organization was started in 1973. At that time several women in the Loop conducted a study of salaries and positions of office workers and discovered that women earned $8,000 less per year than men and that only 14 percent of the women in the Loop worked in professions. W.E. was initiated to remedy this situation and launched during National Secretaries' Week in 1973.

Activities include targeting companies with discriminating practices, dealing with government agencies responsible for enforcing equal-opportunity laws, and helping working women change arbitrary and unfair practices in their offices.

W.E. has won $500,000 in back wages for several hundred women employees of a major insurance company, $13,000 in back wages for eight women at a Chicago bank, and a $200,000 equal-pay case for janitorial women at the same bank.

THE AMERICAN BEGONIA SOCIETY

Culver City, California

Over 4,000 members

President: Margaret Ziesenhenne
Vice-President: Charles A. Richardson
Second Vice-President: Walter Hansen
Third Vice-President: Peggy McGrath
Secretary: Margaret Ireton
Treasurer: Walter J. Barnett

A national convention is held annually and local branches hold monthly meetings.

The objective of the group is to promote interest in begonias and other shade-loving plants and to bring information to its members.

Persons who wish to learn more about begonias and meet others with the same interest may join.

The American Begonia Society is a non-profit, horticultural organization supported entirely by members' dues, and has members in several foreign countries.

The society issues a monthly magazine, *The Begonian*, which covers all phases of growing as well as branch news. It offers a correspondence course of twelve lessons on judging, with emphasis on growing, grooming, and showing. It supports a research department that provides information on culture and propagation, and the Clayton M. Kelly

Seed Fund, which dispenses seeds from many countries. A nomenclature department classifies and registers many types of begonias, and a library containing many books on begonias and other shade plants provides another service. During the National Convention, the last weekend in August or the first in September, there is a begonia and shade-plant show at which a number of awards are given. The awards are for outstanding service to the organization, outstanding plants, and for new varieties of plants.

The organization was founded in 1932 by Herbert P. Dyckman.

GRAND CANYON NATIONAL PARK
NATIONAL PARK SERVICE

Grand Canyon, Arizona

About 250 employees

Director, National Park Service: Gary Everhardt
Superintendent, Grand Canyon National Park: Merle E. Stitt

The organization is operative all year round.

Employees are chosen from all over the country by the Civil Service Commission.

The Grand Canyon National Park was established as a game preserve by President Theodore Roosevelt in 1906. In 1908 President Roosevelt changed it to a National Monument. President Wilson established it as a National Park through an Act of Congress on August 25, 1916. The area was set aside for the conservation of the natural resources of the Grand Canyon of the Colorado River.

The organization is financially sustained by federal appropriations.

The Grand Canyon is one of the Seven Natural Wonders of the World. Approximately 3 million visitors come to the park each year. The National Park Service Ranger Academy is located at the Grand Canyon. Other activities include public safety, visitor activities, maintenance and administration programs.

CEMETERY WORKERS AND GREENS ATTENDANTS UNION
LOCAL 365 S.E.I.U. A.F.L.-C.I.O.

Ridgewood, New York

Approximately 2,000 members

President: Sam Cimaglia
Vice-President: Sigmund Czak
Recording Secretary: Stephen Cimaglia
Secretary-Treasurer: John Thompson

The main objectives of this organization are to seek proper wages and benefits for cemetery workers and to promote their welfare.

One becomes a member of this union thirty days after being hired by a cemetery.

The local is financially sustained by monthly dues of $5 and initiation fees for new members of $50.

The organization was started in 1937 by workers in Greenwood Cemetery and then spread to sixty-three cemeteries located in New York City and in all five boroughs, Westchester, Nassau, and Suffolk Counties, and New Jersey.

One of the main extra activities of the union is a Scholarship Awards program for children of members. Each year two $1,200 scholarships are given. The program was started in 1968 and will continue for as long as the organization exists.

In November 1973 President Sam Cimaglia went on a fourteen-day hunger strike to get a contract with the Newark Diocese Cemeteries. He also served a twenty-day jail sentence for a June 1973 strike of New York metropolitan area cemeteries.

INTERNATIONAL TWINS ASSOCIATION
Muncie, Indiana

Approximately 1,200 members

Co-Presidents: Dale and Dean Vaughn
Co-Vice-Presidents: Torry and Terry Collinson
Co-Secretary and Co-Treasurer: Judy Whiteacre Stillwagon and Julie Whiteacre Kirk

The International Twins Convention is held annually over Labor Day weekend in various cities throughout the United States.

The group is organized by twins, for twins, as a non-profit organization, and its main purpose and objective is promotion of the spiritual, intellectual, and social welfare of twins throughout the world.

The only requirement for membership is to be a twin.

The group is supported by membership dues and funds collected during each convention.

During the International Convention, tours are held locally to promote the group. A business meeting is conducted and fellowship among twins from all parts of the country is shared. Also, an "All Twin Judging Contest" is held, with forty-six trophies awarded to twins in various categories, including King Twins and Queen Twins, oldest twins, youngest twins, most identical boy and girl twins, most identical woman and man twins, most unlike twins, and twins traveling the farthest distance to attend the convention.

In 1930, the Rev. Edward M. Clink, an Evangelistic song leader, and his twin sister, Elsie Clink Parker, aged forty-seven years, held a picnic in Warsaw, Indiana, with thirteen sets of twins attending. The event was so successful they decided to continue the tradition each year. Within four years the attendance had grown to over one thousand twin sets. In 1934 the first national convention was held in Fort Wayne, Indiana, and the Rev. Clink was elected the first president. In 1937 the National Twins Association became an international group and was incorporated.

The largest attendance recorded was in 1939, when some 2,500 sets of twins and approximately 25,000 spectators attended the convention.

INTERNATIONAL SOCIETY OF BIBLE COLLECTORS
El Cajon, California

150 members

President: Dr. Arnold D. Ehlert
Vice-President: Rev. Gerald C. Studer
Secretary: Gerald L. Gooden
Treasurer: Donald H. Roher

There are no meetings.

Organized in 1964 at Biola College and Talbot Theological Seminary in La Mirada, California, to form a fellowship for Bible collectors and to provide a journal of information concerning Bible translations.

The organization is supported by personal membership dues and library subscriptions. *The Bible Collector* is issued quarterly by the International Society of Bible Collectors and is the official organ of the society.

Membership is open to those who apply and pay dues.

WORLD BODY BUILDING GUILD (W.B.B.G.)
Brooklyn, New York

25,000 members

President: Dan Lurie

This international organization meets in different cities all over the world to hold muscle- and body-building shows and events. They also hold special body-building dinners.

The purpose of the group is to promote physical fitness throughout the world and to sponsor physical-fitness contests.

In order to join the organization, applicants are asked to write for an application.

Members pay $8 for membership and for a subscription to the organization magazine, *Muscle Training Illustrated*. The organization is also helped through Dan Lurie's financial contributions. The World Body Building Guild is a non-profit organization.

It was started twelve years ago by Dan Lurie, who has been in the physical-fitness business for thirty-five years.

The organization sponsors the following annual contests: Mr. World, Pro Mr. America, Miss Body Beautiful U.S.A., and Teenage Mr. America. It holds a Mr. International contest in Mexico and a Mr. Canada and Mr. North America contest in Canada. Other contests take place in Greece, Italy, Brazil, and England.

It also grants a Sexiest Man of the Year Award (Burt Reynolds last year; Robert Redford this year)—and a Sexiest Woman of the Century Award which was given to Mae West.

Famous past members are Steve Reeves, Joe Bonomo, Rich Park, Senator Jacob Javits, and Charles Atlas.

LLOYD ROD AND GUN CLUB
Highland, New York

125 members

President: George Rizzo
Vice-President: Joseph Cina
Secretary: John Fraino
Treasurer: James Casabowro

This local club meets on the second Tuesday of each month at the clubhouse.

According to the philosophy of the club, hunting is a form of conservation even though it sounds destructive. The real objective is to strive for sound conservation practice—to enjoy nature by taking something from it but not abusing it. The organization hopes to instill an appreciation of nature and shooting, and is involved in team and competitive shooting.

To become a member, a person must have a "clean record" and be sponsored by a member in good standing.

The Lloyd Rod and Gun Club is a non-profit organization and is supported by annual membership dues of $10 per member.

General activities include trap shoots and a dinner to raise funds for club and community activities.

The club was started in 1937 by a local conservation officer named Al Roberts and four or five friends.

The group has received a special award from the Boy Scouts. It owns about twenty acres and leases another seven hundred acres. At the end of the season the group holds an annual game dinner, where the members eat what has been shot that season. This includes moose, antelope, bear, deer, duck, pheasant, and partridge. The club is a bona fide member of the National Rifle Association (N.R.A.) and the Ulster County Sportsmen Federation, Inc.

STATUE OF LIBERTY

Liberty Island, New York

58 permanent and seasonal employees

Director, National Park Service: Gary Everhardt
Unit Manager: Luis E. Garcia-Curbelo
Acting Unit Manager: Dean R. Garrett
Chief of Area Services: Howard Cream

The Statue of Liberty was conceived as a memorial to the friendship between France and the United States. In subsequent years it has come to have a much broader significance. To the world it has become a symbol of the ideals upon which the United States is founded.

Employees are generally required to have a college degree in the natural sciences. Maintenance personnel must qualify in the various maintenance fields.

The Statue of Liberty, a division of the National Park Service, is funded by federal taxes.

The statue's history began when the French historian Edouard de Laboulaye proposed that a memorial be built to mark the alliance of France and the United States during the American Revolution. Frederick Auguste Bartholdi was its sculptor. He conceived it as a gigantic statue standing in New York Harbor, at the gateway to the New World, representing not only the friendship of the two nations but a common heritage—liberty.

In 1956 Congress changed the island's name from Bedloe's Island to Liberty Island, in recognition of the statue's significance symbolically and to establish the American Museum of Immigration on the island to honor those who chose these shores as their home.

In addition to general tourist activity, the statue maintains a museum. Organizations, such as the Ladies Auxiliary of the Veterans of Foreign Wars and the Committee to Free Captive Nations, hold annual celebrations at the statue.

NERVELESS NOCKS

Churchville, Pennsylvania

7 members

Director: Eugene S. Nock

The membership is now comprised of the Nock Family. To become a member, one must try out and be accepted by the Nock family. Acceptance is based on talent and availability.

The aim of the group is to provide "thrill" performances for its audiences.

The activities of the group include aerial acts and ground acts which involve balancing feats and pedestal equilibristics. The group features a triple exchange in mid-air in which all members of the troupe switch sway poles. They are the first and only act to perform simultaneously on four sway poles completely free of guy wires. The poles are 120 feet high.

The Nerveless Nocks came from the family that began Switzerland's "Circus Nock" in 1840—six generations ago. In 1954 the Nocks left Europe to join Ringling Brothers and Barnum & Bailey Circus and four years later began to book independent performances.

After the Nerveless Nocks performed outside the Desert Inn in Las Vegas, Nevada, in 1958, Ed Sullivan was moved to say, "They are the greatest circus thrill act I've ever seen.

GIRL WRESTLING ENTERPRISES

Columbia, South Carolina

25 members

President: Lillian Ellison

Girl Wrestling Enterprises trains and books professional women wrestlers. The main purpose is to teach wrestling as a profession.

To be eligible, a girl must weigh 130 pounds and be eighteen years old, at least 5 feet 3 inches tall, and in good health.

The group is financially supported by tuition fees.

Girl Wrestling Enterprises was started by Lillian Ellison because she felt she could produce good wrestlers. She feels that wrestling gives a girl a sense of security and is a good profession because it offers opportunities to travel.

Girl Wrestling Enterprises believes that women can be as good as or better than men at the sport of wrestling. The group also gives dwarf girls an opportunity to learn the sport and was the first to train dwarf girls to wrestle.

The organization encourages its members to help the underprivileged become professional athletes.

Lillian Ellison has held the Women's World Championship in wrestling since 1956.

XAVIER HIGH SCHOOL
UNITED STATES ARMY JUNIOR R.O.T.C.

New York, New York

380 cadets

Director: William T. Wood

This national group meets during regular class hours and is part of the curriculum of the school.

The program seeks to develop in each student self-reliance, leadership, responsiveness to constituted authority, attributes of good citizenship and patriotism, a knowledge of basic military skills, and an appreciation of the role of the United States Army.

If one is enrolled in the high school, is a United States citizen, is fourteen years old, and has a good academic record, good conduct and character, and meets physical requirements, he may be selected by the

Senior Army Instructor. The school must also approve the choice of its members.

The organization is financed by the Department of the Army and Xavier High School.

The Cadet Corps was founded by Rev. John Larkin in 1847. In 1915 it was enlarged from one to two battalions. In 1935 the performance of the Xavier Regiment at the annual spring review was of such caliber that the reviewing officer, Major General McCoy, recommended that the corps be incorporated into the Junior R.O.T.C. program. The Cadet Corps has been an R.O.T.C. corps since that date.

Activities include band, rifle team, drill team, military club, and participation in civil events of local importance. (For example, the cadets were the Mayor's Honor Guard and Color Guard at the opening of the New York City observance of the Bicentennial.) Annual events include participation in the Columbus Day parade and the Saint Patrick's Day parade. The cadets also host a mid-winter military review and a spring review.

Xavier Junior R.O.T.C. has received honor-unit-with-distinction awards each year.

MESQUITE RODEO CORPORATION
Mesquite, Texas

President: Jim Shoulders
Managing Director: Neal Gay

Rodeos are held every Friday and Saturday from April through September.

The corporation provides Dallas metropolitan area residents with the opportunity to see professional Texas rodeos.

Rodeo participants must obtain a permit from the Professional Rodeo Cowboys' Association and then compete to win $1,000. All contestants must be associated with or be members of P.R.C.A.

The group is supported by cash receipts from the performances.

Rodeo events include bareback bronco riding, ladies' barrel race, saddle bronco riding, bull riding, and calf roping. The Mesquite Championship Rodeo is the nation's longest-running professional rodeo, and over 200,000 people attend during its five-month season. Prizes exceeding $70,000 are awarded annually. Bull riding is the favorite event and manager Neal Gay buys some two hundred bulls annually, keeping those that look like good prospective bucking and fighting bulls.

The Mesquite Rodeo was organized in 1957 by Neal Gay and Jim Shoulders.

On the third Sunday of each month, the Mesquite Riding Club holds a Playday for all Dallas area riders. The Mesquite Quarter-Horse Show is held in June and the Mesquite All-American Youth Rodeo is held each July for children 10-18 years old and draws more than three hundred contestants from some fifteen states. The Mesquite Junior Rodeo is held in September. Over the past three years rodeo riding schools have been conducted at the Mesquite arena, and champion cowboys such as Larry Mahan and Monty Henson have been instructors.

Private rodeos are staged for convention groups throughout the year. A benefit rodeo is conducted in conjunction with a local radio station to help a needy family or an individual who has met with bad luck.

Some famous members of the Mesquite Rodeo Corporation are Monty Henson, Don Gay, Pete Gay, and Jim Shoulders.

BURNS INTERNATIONAL SECURITY SERVICES, INC.
Briarcliff Manor, New York

42,000 employees

Chairman of the Executive Committee and Director: D. Bruce Burns
Chairman of the Board and Chief Executive Officer and Director: Frederic E. Crist
President and Director: Edward W. Hyde
First Vice-President and Director: William J. Burns
Senior Vice-President and Director: George E. B. King
Vice-President, Treasurer, Comptroller and Director: William E. Porter

Burns Security provides effective security for individual needs in the United States, Canada, Great Britain, the Caribbean, and South America.

The company requires pre-employment, on-the-job, and refresher training programs to maintain the professional competence of the guard force. Programs are conducted by instructors who have had security, military, or police experience.

Burns Security offers its 21,400 clients the latest in security techniques. Their services include uniformed guards, electronic security services, crowd-control specialists, personal guides, hostesses, ushers, doormen, ticket takers at conventions and sporting events, professional management planning, and creation of security programs.

Guards are trained in security measures which may arise on the job—fire prevention, theft and sabotage detection, traffic control and pass authorization, personal-safety techniques including first aid—and are given advice in proper client courtesy. Burns Security consultants offer special assistance in designing fire prevention and security programs for nuclear facilities to meet requirements of the Atomic Energy Commission.

Burns installs and monitors electronic systems and has engineers active in research on new security devices and systems.

Burns investigative services handle any legitimate investigation, with cases ranging from the investigation of contest winners, to locating missing persons and witnesses, to the most complicated criminal and industrial espionage.

Undercover investigators are used as part of the management control services to aid clients in detecting inventory losses, thefts, or leaks of vital information. These special investigators are assigned to an actual job and work alongside the company employees during normal working hours so that no suspicion is aroused in the people they have been assigned to investigate.

Burns does not operate for rewards, nor does it handle divorce or matrimonial investigations, labor management problems, spying on competitive firms, or any activities involving questionable ethics or investigation of public officials.

The organization was founded in 1909 by William J. Burns, former head of the Federal Bureau of Investigation. Burns has been the official detective agency for the American Bankers Association for the past sixty years, and for almost forty-four years, the official detective agency for the American Hotel and Motel Association, providing over 43 million hours of guard service annually.

MISS U.S.A. PAGEANT MISS UNIVERSE, INC.
New York, New York

51 contestants—all fifty states plus the District of Columbia

President: Harold L. Glasser

Vice-President and Executive Director: Robert E. Parkinson

The pageant is held each May and is telecast nationally.

In order to enter the Miss U.S.A. contest, a girl must win the local contests in her area and then the state title—Miss Illinois, Miss California, etc.

The girl who is selected as Miss U.S.A. becomes a goodwill ambassadress for the United States.

The first Miss U.S.A. contest was held in 1952.

The pageant is financially sustained by cash considerations from pageant sites, and by fees from the international telecast. Miss Universe, Inc., is a subsidiary of the Kayser-Roth Corporation, a division of Gulf and Western.

The winner of Miss U.S.A. competes in the Miss Universe pageant, which is the largest television show in the world, viewed in over fifty countries by more than 500 million people.

SGT. HARVEY L. MILLER POST 1434
VETERANS OF FOREIGN WARS (V.F.W.)
Baldwin, New York

86 members

Commander: George Ridder
Senior Vice-Commander: John Wahlers
Junior Vice-Commander: Vincent Delia

Members meet on the first Monday of each month.

This national organization honors the dead by helping the living; they provide hospital care, educational and pension benefits for all veterans who served overseas.

To be eligible for membership in the V.F.W., one must be an honorably discharged veteran with overseas combat area service. Membership is then approved by the local post.

The group is supported by annual membership dues.

The post's primary activity is visiting Northport Hospital for Veterans. It also sends packages to soldiers during wartime, sponsors Little League baseball teams, gives Father's Day gifts to senior citizens, and annually raises the flag in a ceremony on the Fourth of July.

The Sgt. Harvey L. Miller Post is named after the son of a prominent Baldwin banker who was killed in action in World War I. The organization was started after World War I and in 1927 received its original charter and was authorized by an Act of Congress to be the V.F.W.

The post has received awards for 100 percent membership from National Headquarters and for sponsoring a Little League baseball team and a junior rifle team. There is also a women's auxiliary post attached to the Sgt. Harvey L. Miller V.F.W. Post.

WOMEN'S INTRAMURAL SOFTBALL TEAM OF WARNER COMMU-
NICATIONS, INC.
New York, New York

Approximately 4,000 employees

Chairman and Chief Executive Officer: Steven J. Ross
Executive Vice-President: J. Emmett
Executive Vice-President: Emanuel Gerard
Executive Vice-President: David Horowitz

Executive Vice-President: Caesar Kimmel

The Women's Softball Team was started as an extracurricular activity for women members of the company. It plays other publishing company teams in a special company league.

Team activities take place in the spring and summer of each year.

The company started in the funeral business under the name of Riverside Funeral Chapels and expanded by going into the parking-lot business under the Kinney Corporation. Once in the funeral and parking-lot business, it further diversified into office-building cleaning and maintenance, publishing, and construction services. It then acquired the Ashley-Famous Talent Agency and, in 1969, Warner Brothers. Today it is also involved in cable and public TV, the recorded music industry, and music publishing.

K & P DISTRIBUTORS, INC.
SABRETT FOOD PRODUCTS CORPORATION
New York, New York

50,000 employees

President: Rocco Pagnotta

Employees are members of Provision Salesmen and Distributors Union Local 627, A.F.L.-C.I.O.

The Sabrett Food Products division manufactures rolls, frankfurters, hamburgers, and sausages for wholesale distribution. They service over two thousand vendors daily within the five boroughs of New York and are sustained from these profits.

The vending of frankfurters was started in 1920 when the public needed a quick snack at a reasonable price. In addition to manufacturing the food sold in vending carts, Sabrett Food Products has a division called Carts Unlimited Corp., which sells the vending carts. Mobile vending is one of the top money-making low-investment enterprises in the country. It provides refreshment to people in areas such as playgrounds, parks, beaches, and fairgrounds, where a full-time restaurant is not feasible.

NATIONAL CHEERLEADERS ASSOCIATION
Dallas, Texas

3,500 members

Director of Southern Methodist University Clinic: Eugene S. Ward
President of National Cheerleaders Association: Lawrence Herkimer

The cheerleading clinic takes place yearly during the first three weeks of August.

The main objective is to promote and teach cheerleading and school spirit.

Anyone applying to the clinic must be in secondary school or college.

Tuition supports the clinic.

Tumbling, pom-pom, and cheerleading routines are taught.

Lawrence Herkimer was head cheerleader while a student at Southern Methodist University and upon graduating in 1949 started the National Cheerleaders Association in Dallas. The Southern Methodist University Clinic is one of the first and largest run by the National Cheerleaders Association.

Awards given are the Spirit Stick Award for the cheerleading squad with the best spirit, the Spark Plug Award for the school with the greatest spirit, plus red, blue, and yellow ribbon awards for individual achievement.

RINGLING BROTHERS AND BARNUM & BAILEY CIRCUS
Washington, D.C.

Approximately 500 performers
Approximately 600 animals

Co-Producers: Irvin Feld, Kenneth Feld

The organization is international and tours in over eighty cities, eleven months of the year.

The purpose of Ringling Brothers and Barnum & Bailey Circus is to provide family entertainment for children of all ages.

The circus has open application. Acceptance is based on aptitude and hard work. Scouting for established acts is also done.

The group is financially sustained primarily by ticket sales.

There are animal acts of all kinds and famous animal trainers working with tigers, lions, polar bears, horses, and elephants. There are teeterboard acts, perch acts, trapeze acts, clowns and showgirls, aerial acts, bareback riders, and production numbers.

The circus gave its first performance in New York City in 1871. In 1919 it officially became known as Ringling Brothers and Barnum & Bailey Circus. It was purchased in 1968 by Irvin Feld. He revamped the circus and created a second unit so that the circus could reach more cities and larger audiences. He brought it out of the big top into the hard top, which is the type of arena used throughout American cities today.

The production spectacle parade includes fifty-two children from the audience who share in the circus performance and become part of the show.

WILHELMINA MODELS, INC.
New York, New York

Approximately 325 models

President: G. Wilhelmina Cooper
Chairman of the Board: V. Bruce Cooper
Secretary-Comptroller: Frances Rothchild

The main purpose of the organization is to supply top-quality models to the advertising and fashion worlds.

The absolute minimum height required for a Wilhelmina model is 5 feet 6½ inches. The beginning age is between sixteen and twenty-one. Open interviews are conducted Monday through Thursday between 9:30 and 10:00 a.m. The Wilhelmina model agency does not necessarily encourage models to come from or go to modeling schools.

The agency is financially sustained by client service charges and models' commissions.

Wilhelmina models' activities include advertising and high-fashion magazine work, catalogue modeling, runway modeling, and TV commercials.

CARTIER, INC.
New York, New York

Approximately 120 employees

President: Alfred Montezinos

Store hours from 10:00 a.m. to 6:00 p.m., Monday through Saturday.

A prestigious retailer, Cartier's sells rare gems, gold and silver jewelry, traditional china, crystal, and sterling silver. The store is renowned for its outstanding quality and special personal services.

Special jewelry exhibits are held on the average of three times a year.

Cartier's was founded in the nineteenth century by Louis François Cartier, who created outstanding jewelry for the courts of Louis XV and Louis XVI. In 1847 his grandson and namesake started a small factory in Paris, and soon the Cartier name spread throughout the courts of Europe. The New York firm was established in 1908 and in 1917 moved to its present quarters at Fifth Avenue and Fifty-second Street.

Throughout its history Cartier's has designed jewels for royalty, including the "Nuptial Imperial Crown of Russia" worn by Catherine Ilon her wedding day, the "Blue Venus," the "Hope Diamond," and the 69.42-carat, flawless, pearl-shaped diamond sold to Richard Burton in 1969.

SALT LAKE MORMON TABERNACLE CHOIR
Salt Lake City, Utah

375 singers

President: Oakley S. Evans
Choir Director: Gerald D. Ottley
Commentator: J. Spencer Kinard
Chief Organist: Alexander Schreiner

The choir rehearses each Thursday evening and broadcasts each Sunday morning from the Mormon Tabernacle on national radio.

Members of the Tabernacle Choir and its staff live by the principles of righteousness expressed in Doctrine and Covenants 103:36: "The Lord has promised that 'All victory and glory is brought to pass unto you through your diligence, faithfulness and prayers of faith.'" Members are required to be in good standing in the Church of Jesus Christ of Latter-Day Saints and to pass an audition. They are selected on the basis of character and musical ability. All services are rendered with no compensation other than the joy received in service. Choir members are from all walks of life and range from bankers, chemists, doctors, and engineers, to watchmakers, hog farmers, and service-station attendants. Nearly 30 percent of the members are homemakers.

In addition to its weekly Sunday broadcast, the choir sings at semiannual conferences of the church and usually makes one major tour a year. These tours have taken them to Europe, Mexico City, the New York World's Fair, the inaugurations of Presidents Lyndon B. Johnson and Richard MM. Nixon, the Expo '67 World's Fair at Montreal, and the Expo '74 World's Fair at Spokane, Washington.

The Tabernacle Choir was founded in 1847 by Brigham Young after he guided his followers across the country to Salt Lake City. A shelter called the Bowery was erected where Temple Square is now situated. In 1849 the choir got its first director, John Parry, and by 1857 it was housed in an adobe building complete with its first pipe organ, which was shipped from Australia. Sixteen years after the Mormons reached the Salt Lake Valley, the church began construction on a new auditorium, first used in 1867 and known today as the Mormon Tabernacle. News of the choir's excellence soon spread and the choir was invited to sing in other cities. First traveling by horse and wagon and later by railroad, the choir sang at the Columbian Exposition in Chicago in 1893, at the American Land and Irrigation Exposition in 1911, and at the White House at the invitation of President and Mrs. Taft.

Their weekly radio broadcast began in 1929 and is the oldest continuous radio program on nationwide networks. The program is carried by some 68 television and 355 radio stations in the United States and Canada and by more than 800 radio and television stations worldwide. The choir performed for the first intercontinental telecast via Telstar satellite, broadcast from Mt. Rushmore, and has been featured in two Cinerama productions as well as in several other motion pictures. It has produced over 35 record albums and tapes and has recorded with great orchestras including the Philadelphia Orchestra conducted by Eugene Ormandy and the New York Philharmonic under the direction of Leonard Bernstein.

Among its many awards are two gold records, a Grammy Award for "Battle Hymn of the Republic," and a Peabody Award for a television program, "Let Freedom Ring. "

THE NEW YORK PUBLIC LIBRARY ASTOR, LENOX, AND TILDEN FOUNDATIONS

New York, New York

Over 2,400 employees

Chairman of the Board, President and Chief Executive Officer: Richard W. Couper
Director and Chief Operating Officer: John Mackenzie Cory
Director of the Research Libraries: James W. Henderson
Director of the Branch Libraries: Edwin S. Holmgren

The main purpose of the library is to provide circulating and research facilities to citizens of New York City and New York State by means of libraries in the boroughs of Manhattan, the Bronx, and Staten Island.

Anyone who lives, works, or goes to school in New York State is entitled to a free borrower's card. The Friends of the Library is a new organization which enlists the financial support of contributors. In return, contributors receive special benefits from the library services.

The majority of services in the branch libraries are financed through New York City funding. The New York Public Library also relies on charitable contributions for support of its research divisions. The special collections are supported partly through restricted-purpose endowment funds.

The New York Public Library is one of the largest and most-used library systems in the world, serving over 14 million persons a year with books and periodicals in some eighty languages. The library has two kinds of facilities: research and circulation. The research libraries' materials do not circulate. The eighty branch libraries throughout Manhattan, the Bronx, and Staten Island are largely circulating collections whose materials may be borrowed for home use.

The library also offers a wide range of programs that extend its adult-education activities through films, lectures, discussions, performances, and exhibitions. In addition, there are book discussion groups, dramatic readings, concerts, art and law lectures, and poetry readings. For children there are story hours, film programs, and pre-school programs. The New York Public Library organizes a regular series of exhibitions of its holdings, both of the research libraries' special collections and of the regular collections of the research and branch libraries. Other activities include fundraising benefits, performing-arts

displays, and reference service.

The New York Public Library was founded in 1895, when the privately endowed Astor and Lenox libraries were consolidated with the Tilden Trust. Ground was broken for the central building in 1897, which was opened to the public in 1911. Among the many divisions at this central building are: Periodicals, Art and Architecture, Jewish, Oriental, special collections of Rare Books and Manuscripts, and a picture collection with a core of 2 million printed pictures. The Public Catalogue contains more than 10 million cards and also houses book catalogues from the Library of Congress and the British Museum.

The Schomberg Collection of Black Literature, History, and Art is a reference and research library devoted to black life and history. The Library and Museum of the Performing Arts houses the Dance Collection, the Music Division, the Theatre Collection, and the Rodgers and Hammerstein Archives of Recorded Sound covers the entire history of recordings, including all varieties of music and the spoken word. Books and magazines in Braille, on records, and on tape circulate by post-free mail from the Library for the Blind and Physically Handicapped.

BINGO CLUB OF THE ST. PETERSBURG SHUFFLEBOARD AND DUPLICATE BRIDGE CLUB

St. Petersburg, Florida

2,961 members

President: "Lou" Tuma
First Vice-President: Gustave Baldwin
Second Vice-President: Herbert Reed
Third Vice-President: Dorothy Murry
Fourth Vice-President: David Jameson
Fifth Vice-President: Susan Ballowe
Financial Secretary: Esther Burkett
Recording Secretary: Vernon Howland
Treasurer: Edgar Earisman

The group's purpose is to provide recreational facilities and companionship to members.

The Board of Governors meets on the second Tuesday of each month. The General Meeting and election are held on the third Tuesday in February.

Membership is open to all over eighteen years of age. It includes many local residents, as well as some from every state. Ninety-nine percent are retired. The Board of Governors may require a prospective member to be vouched for by two members.

The club is financed by annual dues of $12.50 per member and guest tickets of 50 cents per day.

The club was begun around 1925 to provide recreational facilities for visitors to St. Petersburg.

The activities of the organization include shuffleboard—there are 107 courts, which are used for seven statewide and national tournaments each year, in addition to the Yellow and Black Shuffleboard Tournament—an ice cream social, community singing, duplicate contract bridge, bingo, dancing, cribbage, canasta, and pinochle. The St. Petersburg Shuffleboard Club is recognized as the world center of shuffleboard; the National Shuffleboard Hall of Fame exhibit moved here in 1972. The club is located on St. Petersburg city property and is under the jurisdiction of the Department of Parks and Recreation. There has been no cost to the city since 1931. The club is a non-profit organization.

NEW YORK CITY TRANSIT AUTHORITY

Brooklyn, New York

37,500 employees

Chairperson: David L. Yunich
Senior Executive Officer: John DeRoos
Executive Officer of Rapid Transit: Steven Kauffman
Executive Officer of Surface: Marcus Gibson
Executive Officer Controller: Andrew T. O'Rourke

The authority's main objective is to provide efficient transportation at the lowest possible cost. The New York City Transit Authority provides daily service for 3½ million subway riders and 2½ million bus riders.

The New York City Transit Authority was started in 1953 as an outgrowth of the Board of Transportation and was reorganized in 1968 under the jurisdiction of the Metropolitan Transit Authority.

Special fares are granted to senior citizens, the handicapped, and students, and on Saturday night, Sundays, and holidays to the general public. Other services offered are the Culture Buses, Shopper's Special, and the Night Coach special buses.

Subways cover 230 miles of track, and there are 460 stations. Buses run over 949 miles on 202 separate routes.

NATIONAL ASSOCIATION TO AID FAT AMERICANS, INC. (N.A.A.F.A.)

Westbury, New York

1,000 members

President: William J. Fabrey
Vice-President: Eileen M. Lefebure
Recording Secretary: Lisbeth Fisher
Treasurer: Joyce Fabrey

The national convention is held each year in the spring or fall. Local chapters conduct regional meetings throughout the year.

The group promotes tolerance and understanding in society toward the larger-than-average citizen and works to increase the self-esteem of fat people.

Anyone is eligible to join regardless of weight, race, religion, sex, or age. The only requirement for membership is citizenship in the United States or Canada and a completed membership application.

The group is sustained financially by dues and donations.

N.A.A.F.A. members participate in a pen-pal project with other N.A.A.F.A. friends. A bi-monthly newsletter is published and a book service with discounts on books of interest to members is provided. There are a variety of public-relations activities; a clothing thrift shop (large sizes) is maintained; and a library of research materials is available. N.A.A.F.A.-Date, a dating program similar to computer dating, was created for heavier-than-average people, and for those who prefer their dates to be amply-endowed, as well as for those who have no weight preference. A fashion show using large-size models is held during the annual convention. N.A.A.F.A. combats discrimination against fat people in hiring and college-admissions procedures, in clothing, and in the world of advertising, life insurance, and organized medicine.

Started in 1969 by a group of nine co-founders as a non-profit organization dedicated to promoting tolerance and understanding of fat people and their problems, N.A.A.F.A. has members throughout the United States and Canada.

N.A.A.F.A. believes fat people sometimes have trouble being treated like human beings. They are exploited by commercial interests, receive unsympathetic treatment from doctors, and are the brunt of countless jokes. N.A.A.F.A. is dedicated to the concept that fat can be beautiful. Through friendship and fellowship, members are able to improve their outlook on life and help one another overcome the problems shared by fat people living in a thin-oriented society.

N.A.A.F.A. has been cited by several public agencies for their overweight teenager brochure and has been praised by several doctors for their approach to restoring self-esteem to fat people. They are recognized by clothing industries, advertising agencies, the medical profession, and the media for their unique efforts on behalf of fat people.

LADY DOROTHY CIRCLE #1460
THE COMPANIONS OF THE FOREST OF AMERICA

Jamaica, New York

Approximately 7 members

Chief Companion: Edith Heffernan
Secretary: Dorothy Corrigan

The society meets twice a month.

Membership is national, with local circles. The group is a beneficial organization and must be joined before the age of fifty-five in order to attain full benefits.

The group is financially sustained by membership dues.

The Companions of the Forest of America was originally founded to study California's forests. It has since evolved into a society devoted to the economic and social welfare of its members. The organization's founder, Annie E. Poe, bequeathed her house in Tarrytown, New York, to elderly members.

Among the activities of the companions is charity work in hospitals and institutions.

The members are expected to care for themselves from the ages of fifty-five through sixty-five. After that, they are entitled to live in the Poe House or the organization will pay for a hospital.

STATEN ISLAND COUNCIL CAMPFIRE GIRLS, INC.

Staten Island, New York

Approximately 800 members

President: Helen Gunderson
First Vice-President: Jean Morin
Second Vice-President: Charles Ochs
Treasurer: Arthur Gunderson
Secretary: Louise Helburn

The Campfire groups meet every day in various locations throughout the country.

The Campfire Girls is a program to serve young people, from age six through high school by means of a recreational/educational program.

The local council is funded by the Greater New York Fund, the Staten Island Community Chest and Council, plus fund-raising efforts of the local board and council membership.

The organization sponsors group meetings, camping, swim programs, outdoor high-risk programs, community-service development of the individual through group activities. It has, in addition, a Grand Council Fire, day camps, seven day-camping service programs, weekend camping programs, council-wide ceremonials, and fly-ups.

Recruitment drives for both young people and adults are held at least three times per year throughout the council area.

The council charter was issued in 1929 on Staten Island in order to bring quality girl programs to the youth of Staten Island.

Various national awards are given on an annual basis as is the council's own award. This is called the "Outstanding Volunteer of the Year Award." Special awards are also given to members for participation in various programs—swimming, camping, summer programs, etc.

S.S. SKATE
Groton, Connecticut

14 officers, 108 enlisted men

Commanding Officer: Richard Asafaylo

S.S. *Skate* is a nuclear-attack submarine whose purpose is to hunt and track other submarines.

Recent activities of the S.S. *Skate* are classified.

S.S. *Skate* was laid down on July 21, 1955, by General Dynamics Corporation in Groton, Connecticut, and was launched in May 1957. After a shakedown cruise of nearly a year, she set off for the Arctic, where she navigated over 2,400 miles under the ice and became the second ship to reach the North Pole. In the winter of 1959, S.S. *Skate* again headed for the Arctic during a period of extreme cold and maximum ice thickness. There she steamed under pack ice, surfacing ten times until she reached the North Pole, where she surfaced again to commit the ashes of the famed explorer Sir George Hubert Wilkins to the Arctic. In 1961, S.S. *Skate* returned to General Dynamics Corporation for a regular overhaul and to have her nuclear reactor recharged for the first time.

In July 1962, S.S. *Skate* again headed for the Arctic for a rendezvous under the ice with the *Seadragon*, based in Pearl Harbor. After successfully completing their meeting under the ice, the two submarines operated together for over a week. Over the next ten years *Skate* conducted various Atlantic Fleet and NATO exercises involved in the development of new undersea tactics and equipment. She operated under Arctic ice again on three separate occasions. In 1965, S.S. *Skate* became the first submarine to finish a major conversion program through the installation of the Subsafe package. This safety measure was instituted after the loss of the *Thresher* in 1963.

S.S. *Skate* was awarded the Bronze Star in 1958 upon returning from the North Pole for demonstrating "for the first time the ability of submarines to operate in and under the Arctic ice in the dead of winter."

CINEMA ST. MARKS CORPORATION
New York, New York

Approximately 6 staff members

Officers: Information unavailable

The Cinema St. Marks was organized to show good films at inexpensive prices.

The organization is financially sustained through the theater's admission price.

The cinema was begun in 1971 as a business venture.

The general activities of the Cinema St. Marks include film exhibition, live children's shows in the fall, and special midnight performances. The Cinema St. Marks is also the first dollar theater in Manhattan.

John Cassavetes and Gena Rowlands have spoken at the theater.

THE TROC THEATER
Philadelphia, Pennsylvania

Approximately 6 staff members

Owner: Al Baker
Manager: Bob Stephens

The main objective of the Troc is to provide good burlesque entertainment.

The organization is financially sustained by admission tickets.

The Troc Theater was started over one hundred years ago as an opera house. It was originally known as the Trocadero in the late nineteenth century and then switched to burlesque in the 1920's.

In addition to the regular activities of burlesque shows, the Troc sponsors "Amateur Night" once every six months. Anyone is eligible to enter the one-night striptease contest for a cash prize of $100 to the winner and $20 each to all the participants. Another event being planned is a Mr. Nude Contest on an amateur level, with female judges.

Tempest Storm, Blaze Starr, and Georgia Southern have all played at the Troc, in addition to comedian Billy "Cheese & Crackers" Hagen.

The Troc is the oldest operating burlesque theater in the country.

QUEENS BOROUGH LODGE NO. 878 B.P.O. ELKS
Elmhurst, New York

2,787 members

Exalted Ruler: Raymond F. Neubauer
Esteemed Leading Knight: Joseph Mansi
Esteemed Loyal Knight: Joseph R. Fabrizi
Esteemed Lecturing Knight: Charles Baran
Secretary: Joseph Bradt
Treasurer: George Kleinmeier, P.E.R.

The Queens chapter of the national "Grand Lodge" meets one Tuesday each month.

The organization demonstrates charity within the lodge and on a state and national level by awarding scholarships and making donations to Cerebral Palsy and other worthy charities.

To become a member, a person must be twenty-one years of age and male. He must be recommended by another member or secretary and must state the number of years he has been a believer in God. An interview by the Investigating Committee precedes final balloting and initiation.

The group is supported by annual dues and fees and also by money from the Bazaar Fund.

The Grand Lodge, Benevolent and Protective Order of Elks, works closely with the state Elks associations and subordinate lodges. There are some 130 lodges throughout New York State and 2,191 lodges throughout America, with approximately 1,558,772 members. A District Deputy Grand Exalted Ruler chosen at the National Convention governs the state lodges.

The Elks was founded in 1868 in New York City by a group of actors known as the "folly Corks," who met for social and convivial purposes. They then became the Benevolent and Protective Order of Elks, whose primary object was to practice charity, encourage patriotism and brotherly love, and conduct fraternal activities.

The Elks organize youth-activities programs for boys and girls of all ages and special projects for underprivileged, handicapped children. The Elks National Foundation is dedicated to granting Youth Leadership and Most Valuable Student awards and scholarships totaling over $4 million. They conduct Flag Day services and Mother's Day services. The Elks National Veterans visit hospitals to entertain veterans and hold Christmas parties for children. They sponsor hospitals, camping facilities, rehabilitation centers, blood and eye banks, as well as other worthy projects. The Charity Ball Bazaar is held annually over two weekends and raises funds for hospitals and child-care institutions.

A Sea Power Conference was held in 1975 at the Queens Borough Lodge. Attended by civic veterans and members of political and military organizations, the conference dealt with sea power of all nations. Americanism is a vital aspect of B.P.O. Elks, who are "watchfully devoted to the protection of our freedoms guaranteed under the Constitution." They vigorously support and defend law-enforcement officials who strive to maintain law and order. The Elks National Home in Bedford, Virginia, is a haven for retired members.

BACHRACH STUDIOS
New York, New York

200 employees

President: Bradford Bachrach
Vice-President and Treasurer: Fabian Bachrach

Bachrach Studios is famous for its serious portrait and wedding photography.

It is financially supported by the selling of these photographs.

Although Bachrach has studios in Boston, Philadelphia, Atlanta, and Chicago, the New York studios are the most important in terms of the variety and prominence of their clientele. Photographic subjects come from all over America and overseas. No special photographic techniques are used—just good, straightforward, balanced lighting, careful posing, good exposures, careful arrangements, and good composition.

Bachrach's was founded in 1868 in Baltimore, Maryland, by David Bachrach, who photographed the wagons, platform, and speakers at Gettysburg during Lincoln's famous Gettysburg Address. Bachrach Studios have since photographed all the American Presidents since Andrew Johnson. They attempt to get likely candidates to pose for portraits before becoming President, knowing it is easier to get the picture beforehand. As the official photographers of the Junior League and the Tuxedo Ball, Bachrach has photographed numerous debutantes, including Julie and Tricia Nixon.

Thousands of photographers have benefited from their training with Bachrach Studios.

The one hundredth anniversary of the founding of Bachrach Studios was observed in 1968 with celebrations in Boston, New York, Philadelphia, Washington, Chicago, and Atlanta.

SERENA STUDIOS, INC.
New York, New York

Over 1,800 students

President: Serena
Vice-President, Secretary, and Treasurer: Alan Wilson

The main objectives of this national dance studio are to promote Oriental dance as concert art, and to instruct non-professional dancers in the physical and mental benefits derived from Oriental dancing. The dancing concept is in keeping with the ancient Greek reverence for the body and its natural beauty. The qualities of poise, grace, femininity, stamina, and performing skill are emphasized.

Students may enroll at any time, and there are no initiation fees, ceremonies, or obligations. Men are excluded from class participation because of the nature of activities but are not excluded from "honorary" participation in social and artistic events.

Serena Studios is supported financially by student tuition.

Activities of the group include public and college performances, as well as appearances on radio and television. During the year classes are held and lectures and seminars are conducted.

Serena Studios was founded in 1967. The dancing method was developed over a ten-year period.

Awards are presented annually to deserving members. Countless hours are donated to charitable groups.

GARY OWENS SOCIETY OF GIRNERS (G.O.S.O.G.)
Hollywood, California

Number of members: no actual count
Executive President: Gary Owens
President: Frances Sayers
St. Louis President: Tom Straw
Kansas City, Missouri, President: Jack Elliot

The group attempts to make the world a less serious place in which to live by girning (contorting one's face and looking silly).

The Hollywood chapter tries to meet once a year. Other chapters meet when they feel like having a good time, and usually in connection with other events. The group has been dormant because the country has been in a state of depression and it is harder to girn when the world is not going well.

Anyone who girns is eligible for membership by sending a photo of him or herself girning to the Hollywood chapter.

There are no dues.

The group began when Gary Owens organized a girning contest on local television. People submitted photos and the winner, seventy-three-year-old Frances Sayers, swallowed her nose.

There are many famous girners, among them: Jack Thayer, president of NBC Radio, Arte Johnson, Lily Tomlin, Goldie Hawn, Phyllis Diller, Carleton (the drunken doorman of the Rhoda show), Lorenzo Music (producer of the Bob Newhart show), Howard Cosell, Glen Campbell, Roger Miller, the 5th Dimension, and Bob Hope. Practically everybody in show business has girned at one time or another in Hollywood with Gary Owens, the president.

It takes a great deal of courage to girn because one doesn't look his best while girning. Olivia Newton-John is an exception. She is so beautiful that even while girning she looks nice.

Mrs. Sayers received nationwide publicity when she appeared on the Tonight show.

CONTINENTAL BATHS
New York, New York

Approximately 1,200 members

Owner: Steve Ostrow
Manager: Charles Tisdale

The purpose of the baths is to provide a full-service organization to fill a person's health and social needs.

Membership is open to the general public.

The organization is sustained financially by membership fees and regular admission prices.

The activities include steambaths, sauna, swimming, sun bathing, entertainment, and disco facilities.

Bette Midler, Melba Moore, and the group known as Isis have all performed and had their start at the baths. The movie *Saturday Night at the Baths* features the baths.

JULIAN BILLIARD ACADEMY
New York, New York

Approximately 8 staff members

Owner: Ronny Hickers
Day Manager: Tom Chin

The academy is in business to provide a place for people from all walks of life to play billiards and pool.

It is sustained financially by fees for use of the facilities.

George Mikula, Jr., and Willie Mosconi have both played exhibition pool at Julian Billiard Academy. The organization is also the oldest billiard establishment in New York City.

THE MAGIC CASTLE
Hollywood, California

Approximately 3,000 members

President of Academy of Magical Arts: Bill Larsen
President of the Magic Castle: Milt Larsen
Board of Directors: Cary Grant, Dick Zimmerman, Bill Larsen, Peter Pit, Mark Wilson, Ron Wilson, Dai Vernon

The Magic Castle is the clubhouse of the Academy of Magical Arts, Inc., a non-profit organization dedicated to the advancement of magic in America.

Membership falls into two categories: Regular members must be amateur or professional magicians whose qualification in magic must be proved before a board of examiners before they are accepted into the club. Associate memberships are available to those who qualify as magic enthusiasts—people who enjoy watching the masters perform their art. The initiation fee is $300 and the yearly dues are $40. Each new member must be sponsored by two members in good standing. No one is admitted to the Castle unless he is with a member or has a guest card signed by a member.

The Magic Castle is the creation and brainchild of writer, magician, and do-it-yourself contractor, Milt Larsen. Some time ago, he bought the old Lane mansion in Hollywood in addition to the entire interior of a similar mansion on Los Angeles's millionaires' row of the nineties. After removing the priceless mantels, parquet floors, paneling, and stained glass, he proceeded to restore the castle and create the club as it is presently known.

The castle consists of several rooms where either dining or magical activities take place. The latest addition to the castle is the Houdini Séance Room for private parties of twelve only. After an extraordinary dinner, the guests are told that the thirteenth chair has been reserved for the medium, who, after appearing at the stroke of midnight, conducts the rest of the evening's activities.

The Academy of Magical Arts was originally formed in 1953 by William Larsen, Sr., a noted criminal lawyer turned magician.

THE LAST MAN'S CLUB, HEMPSTEAD POST 390 AMERICAN LEGION
Hempstead, New York

23 members (originally 66)

President: Frank Wettstein
Treasurer: Frank Eickoff
Secretary: Sydney Williams

The club meets once a year to share their common experiences.

The purpose of the club is to stay together for as long a time as there are surviving members, and to see who will actually be the final member of the club. When the club was started, a member, since departed, donated a twenty-five-year-old bottle of Three-Star Hennessy brandy brought back from the battlefront of World War I. This bottle is to become the property of the last-surviving club member. That last survivor, of course, may be a teetotaler or too weak to lift the bottle and pour himself a drink.

The club was started twenty years ago by World War I veterans. When the first member died, the membership rolls were closed and no other members were accepted.

Membership dues are the only means of support.

A catered dinner is held at each annual get-together and is followed by a short formal meeting. After the meeting is adjourned, the members swap anecdotes and then quietly leave.

THE TWO PENNY CIRCUS
Goddard College, Vermont

Approximately 25 members

Director: Donald Osman

The Two Penny Circus is an intimate theatrical touring troupe with an emphasis on clowns. The Two Penny Circus believes that everyone has their own personal clown within them and, through improvisation, workshops, and performances, hopes to help individuals discover their clown.

The group is interested in individuals with varying theatrical backgrounds.

The circus gives independent performances for financial support. It also received touring aid assistance from the Vermont Council on the Arts. It is a non-profit corporation.

The Two Penny Circus gives independent performances at schools, parks, camps, social agencies, fairs, theaters, and private engagements throughout the Northeast. In addition, it hopes to consolidate its theatrical energy in a collective work situation including clown workshops, rehearsals, performances, physical training, set design and construction, silk-screening, photography, public relations, teaching, and theatrical training.

Donald Osman is the founder of the circus, whose existence grew out of a clown show directed by Osman for his senior thesis work at Goddard College. The troupe today, however, is the result of a very natural growth and coming together of individuals with varying theatrical backgrounds. The Two Penny Circus has been in existence as a touring theater since January 1973.

Special events of the circus include two performances for the Hudson River Sloop Restoration committee, with Pete Seeger and Judy Collins lending support to clean up the Hudson River. The circus also participated as one of eight out-of-state groups at the annual Lincoln Center Community Street Theater Festival in New York City.

LIPKO COMEDY CHIMPS

Zanesville, Ohio

10 members

Owner/Trainer: Colonel Jerry Lipko
Assistant Trainer: Gary Lee Smith

The Lipko Comedy Chimps appear at all types of functions, including shows at shopping malls, circus speedways, schools and colleges, hospitals, state and county fairs, and sales meetings. They provide entertainment and distribute educational material on chimpanzees.

The comedy act has been booked for the past five years by Variety Attractions, Inc., and has appeared on numerous television programs, including the Mike Douglas Show, the Jimmy Dean Show, and the Red Skelton Show.

The Lipko Comedy Chimps was a childhood dream of Colonel Lipko. He began with one chimp and over the past eighteen years has owned as many as fifteen animals. Presently there are eight chimps in the act:

Skippy, 15 years old
Roses, 11 years old
Clyde, 5 years old
George, 4 years old
Barney, 3 years old
Sami, 3 years old
Hazel, 2½ years old
Eric, 2 years old

Lipko Comedy Chimps is licensed by the U.S. Department of Agriculture as a Class C exhibitor and carries a permit to possess and transport chimpanzees across state lines.

SARASOTA COUNTY ANGLERS CLUB

Sarasota, Florida

200 active members

President: William J. Mindlin
Vice-President: Harold Shell
Secretary: Lucille Shell
Treasurer: Frank Glenn

The local group meets monthly at the Sarasota Bank and Trust Building.

The club sponsors and operates the largest tarpon tournament in the United States and promotes all kinds of sportsman fishing.

One becomes a member through sponsorship by another member or by application to the club. Applications must be approved by the membership committee and voted on by the members. Membership is not required for the tarpon tournament.

Members, business establishments, and the Sarasota County Chamber of Commerce support the group.

The Anglers Club conducts seminars at schools, pensioner homes, and clubs and teaches through demonstrations how to fish, where to fish, and what gear to use. At regular club meetings speakers appear and movies are shown to help members achieve better fishing techniques. Reports on good fishing grounds are also presented. There are yearly fishing contests, including the tarpon tournament, which draws approximately a thousand people. A club magazine is printed and is free to members.

The club was started forty-five years ago by a group of wealthy and influential people who came down to Sarasota in the winter primarily for the well-known sport of tarpon fishing. Such people as the Palmers, who operate the Palmer National Bank, and the Shelbys, who head the Shelby Foundation, started the Tarpon Club. It later became known by its present name, the Sarasota County Anglers Club.

Awards are given in the form of engraved trophies, plaques, and cash prizes. The highest award is a trophy and cash prize of $300-$500 to the person who catches the largest tarpon. The largest tarpon on the club's record was caught by Lester Davis in 1949; it weighed 184½ pounds. The Sarasota County Anglers Club has among its members bank presidents, army generals, and heads of large organizations.

PRODUCT MANAGERS
A.T.&T. LONG LINES

Somerset, New Jersey

25 product managers

34,924 employees

President, A. T. & T. Long Lines: Richard R. Hough

Long Lines is the interstate and international operating unit of A.T.&T. A.T.&T. is actually made up of twenty-three Bell System-associated companies and Long Lines. The primary concern of Long Lines is the day-to-day management of the vast national resource that is the nationwide telecommunications network.

The organization is sustained financially by fees to customers for usage of telecommunications service.

A.T.&T. Long Lines was begun in 1900 as a response to the increase in long-distance telephoning. The chief responsibilities are to develop and operate the long-distance network. In addition to regular long-distance message telephone service, Long Lines provides private line circuits for the transmission of data, television, radio, teletypewriter, and telephoto services.

The Telephone Centennial was celebrated in 1976.

LITHUANIAN SCOUTS ASSOCIATION, INC.

Rancho Palos Verdes, California

Approximately 200 scouts

Regional Director: Vytautas Vidugiris
Director of Boy Scouts: Remiijus Vizgirdas
Director of Girl Scouts: Lea Vilimas

The organization meets twice a month.

The main purpose of the group is to instill in children of Lithuanian heritage the principles of international scouting, which are to be good citizens and to help one's fellow man and to practice belief in God, as well as to teach the heritage of Lithuania.

The association is financially supported by dues.

The group prefers that member children speak Lithuanian or have a Lithuanian background.

The organization was started in 1908, when the first patrol of men and women was formed in Lithuania according to the model of Lord Baden-Powell's scouting organization in England. In 1933 the Lithuanian Scouts were accepted by the International Scouting Committee.

The general types of activity include field trips, international jamborees, camping, and commemorative types of events.

The highest award that the Lithuanian Scouts present is the Award of the Iron Wolf. This is given to a member for outstanding lifetime service to the organization. It is based on the symbol for the largest city in Lithuania, called Vilna. The Iron Wolf symbolizes fame, power, and strength.

The Lithuanian Scouts Association thinks of itself as a group of scouts in exile, because scouting is not permitted in Lithuania under the current regime. Therefore, the group tries to keep alive the principles of Lithuanian culture and scouting in America.

SOCIETY FOR PHOTOGRAPHIC EDUCATION (S.P.E.)

New York, New York

Approximately 1,000 members

Chairman: Peter C. Bunnell
Vice-Chairman: Jim Alinder
Secretary: Richard Stevens
Treasurer: Wayne Lazorik

S.P.E. is a national organization. It meets annually in convention and has regional affiliate meetings.

The purpose of the group is to promote quality education in photography.

Membership is open to all through application.

The society is financially maintained by membership dues and various foundation grants.

S.P.E. was formed in 1963 as an effort to support and respond to the needs of photographic educators.

The main and most important activity of the society is the publication of its quarterly journal, *Exposure*. Other activities include general meetings, workshops, demonstrations, lectures, and seminars. The group also provides information with regard to curriculum and institutional facilities, and assists members in matters relating to academic appointments and academic freedom.

ELECTROLUX A CONSOLIDATED FOODS COMPANY

Stamford, Connecticut

Approximately 20,000 sales representatives on a national level

President: Charles McKee
Executive Vice-President: Stephen Sheridan

The main objective of Electrolux is to achieve the largest sales in vacuum cleaners possible.

To become part of Electrolux, one must apply to the local branch office.

The company is sustained financially by the sale of vacuum cleaners.

The organization was begun in 1924. It was the first vacuum-cleaner manufacturer to sell directly to the consumer.

The general activities of Electrolux center on the manufacturing and selling of its vacuum cleaners. In order to better achieve this, the company has a highly charged incentive program in which luxury cars and trips to Europe are offered to salesmen. There are also trophy cups awarded for a variety of sales contests.

Electrolux celebrated its Golden Jubilee year in 1974.

For Olivia and Anita

Acknowledgements
Special thanks to Roger Straus III, friend, inspiration, and publisher of the original *When Two or More Are Gathered Together*; Kevin Moore, editor of the new version and author of an essay that gets to the heart of the political moment as well as the photographs; Anita Burkhart, studio manager and producer; Jeff Hirsch at FotoCare for his constant support of my work and projects; and the incredible assistants, editors, and publishers who have helped me create these pictures throughout the years.

Photo Credits
New York Recycles! p. 78; *The Washington Post Magazine*, pp. 83, 84, 86, 89, 93, 95, 96, 97, 98-99, 100, 104, 105, 106, 107, 109, 110, 113, 115, 117, 124, 126, 131, 136; *Town & Country Magazine*, pp. 85, 88, 102; *A Day in the Life of America*, pp. 90-91; EAB Bank, pp. 92, 108; *Outside Magazine*, pp. 103, 114, 132, 133; *Z Magazine*, p. 111; *Connoisseur Magazine*, p. 112; *The New York Times*, pp. 118, 128-29; *New York Magazine*, p. 119; *Details*, p. 120; *Life Magazine*, p. 121; Grey Advertising Agency, p. 127; Linde Corporation, p. 130; *O, The Oprah Magazine*, p. 134-35; *ARTnews*, p. 137.

NEAL SLAVIN
When Two or More are Gathered Together

Edited by Kevin Moore

© Damiani 2024
© Photographs, Neal Slavin
© Text, the Authors

Published by Damiani Books srl
in collaboration with Fulton Street Editions

info@damianibooks.com
www.damianibooks.com

Printed in June 2024, Italy

ISBN 978-88-6208-8829-9

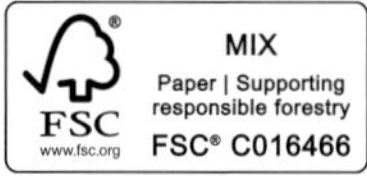

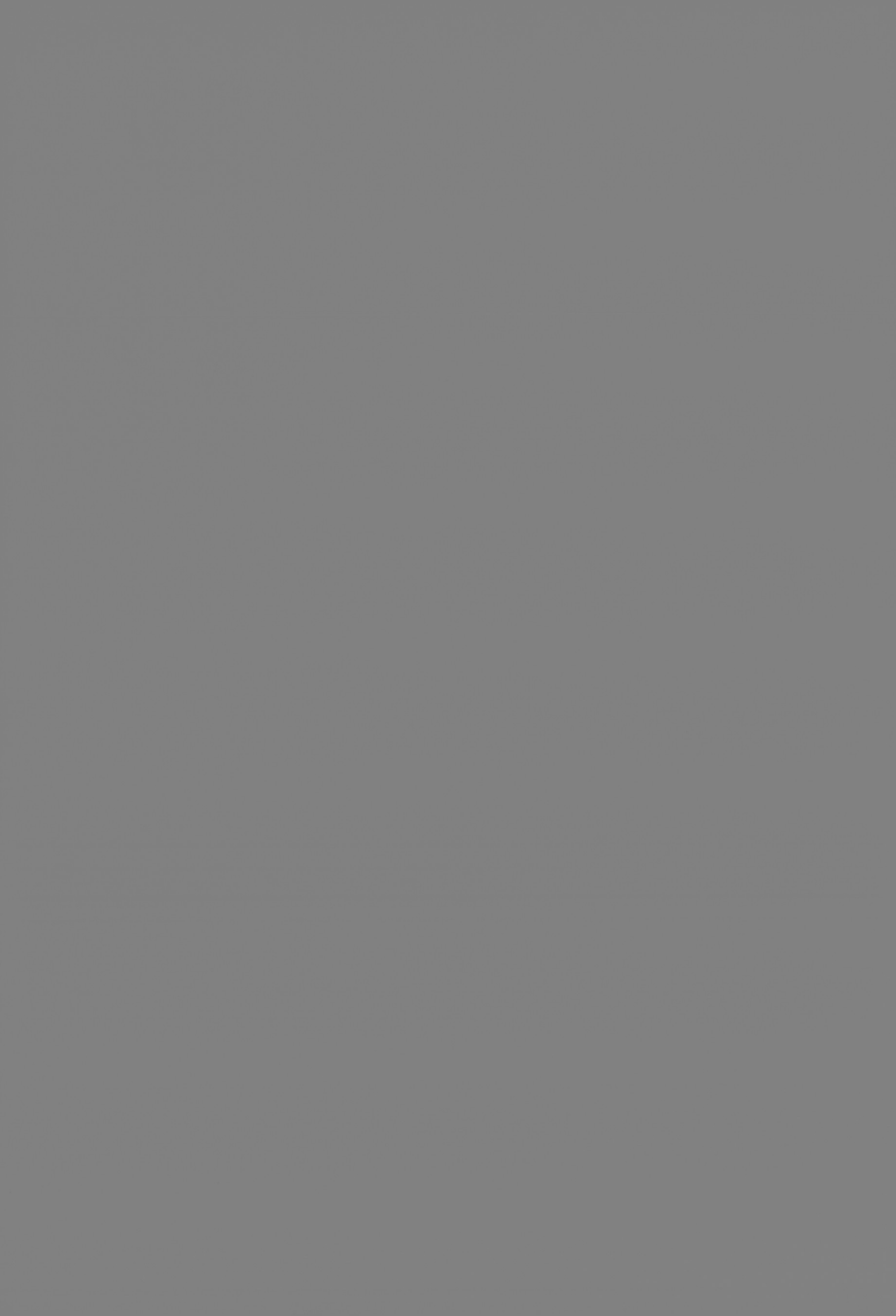